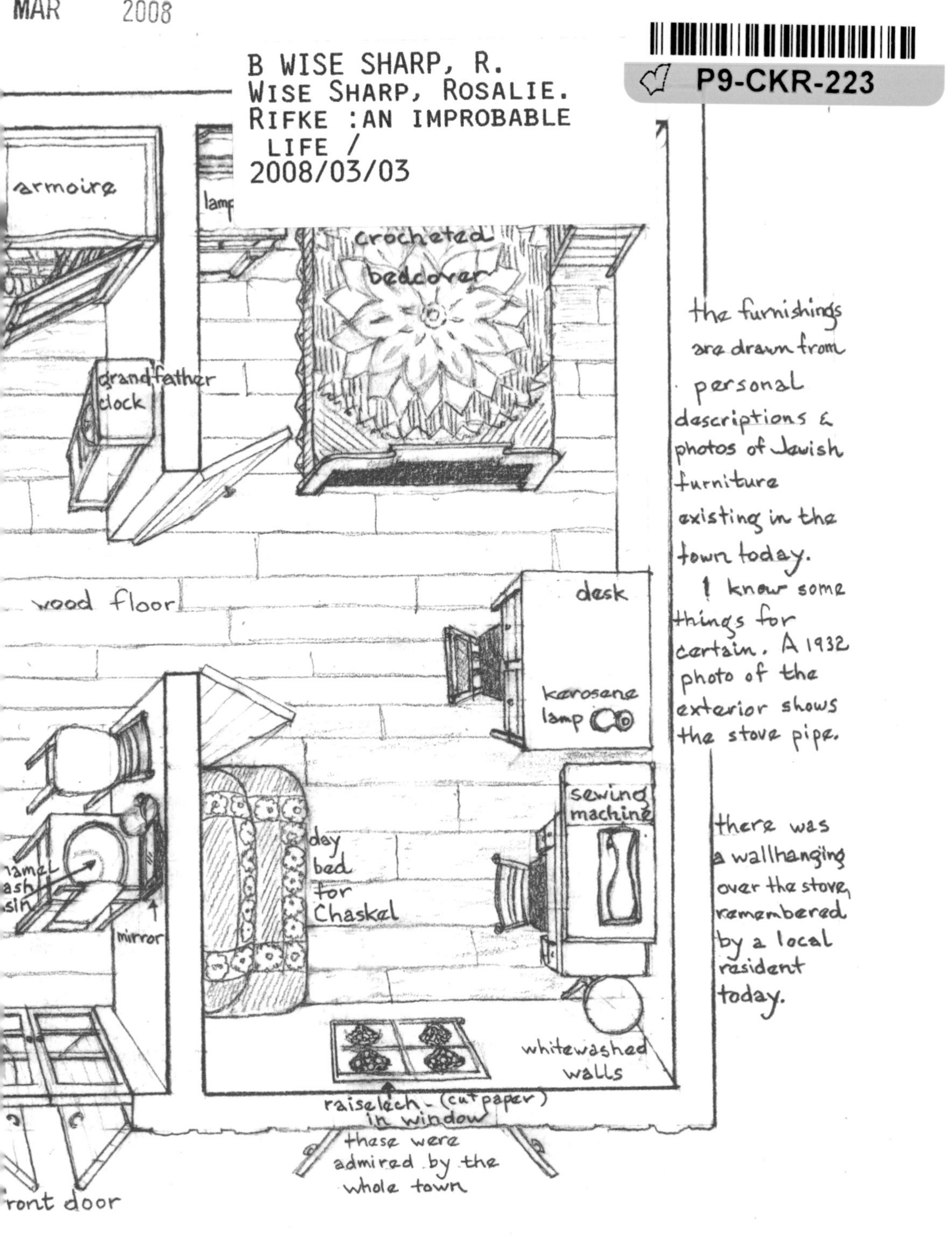
armoire
lamp
crocheted bedcover
grandfather clock
wood floor
desk
kerosene lamp
sewing machine
day bed for Chaskel
mirror
whitewashed walls
raiselech - (cut paper) in window
these were admired by the whole town
the furnishings are drawn from personal descriptions & photos of Jewish furniture existing in the town today.
I know some things for certain. A 1932 photo of the exterior shows the stove pipe.
there was a wallhanging over the stove, remembered by a local resident today.

no. 1, Zlote Street, Ozarow, 1932

and two blocks from the synagogue

rifke

ROSALIE WISE SHARP

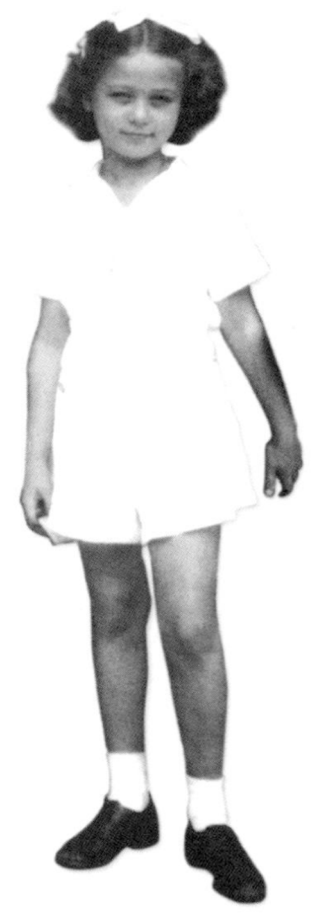

ECW PRESS

Published by ECW Press
2120 Queen Street East, Suite 200, Toronto, Ontario, Canada M4E 1E2

All royalties from *Rifke* will be donated to the Jewish Public Library of Toronto — Latner Centre for Jewish Knowledge and Heritage.

Library and Archives Canada Cataloguing in Publication

Wise Sharp, Rosalie
Rifke : an improbable life /
Rosalie Wise Sharp.

ISBN 978-1-55022-775-8 (bound)
ISBN 978-1-55022-777-2 (pbk.)
1. Wise Sharp, Rosalie — Childhood and youth. 2. Jews — Ontario — Toronto Biography.
3. Toronto (Ont.) — Biography. I. Title.
FC3097.9.J5W58 2007 971.3'5410049240092 C2006-906906-9

Cover and text design, and production: Tania Craan
Third Printing: Thomson-Shore

This book is set in Berkeley

With the publication of *Rifke* ECW Press acknowledges the generous financial support of the Canada Council, the Ontario Arts Council, and Government of Canada through the Book Publishing Industry Development Program (BPIDP) for our publishing activities.

DISTRIBUTION

Canada: Jaguar Book Group, 100 Armstrong Ave., Georgetown, ON L7G 5S4
United States: Independent Publishers Group, 814 North Franklin Street, Chicago, Illinois, U.S.A. 60610

Printed and bound in the United States

For Isadore

our children

and our children's children

Whoever cannot know his grandparents, nor the faces, places, sounds and smells of where they lived is memory's orphan.

ROGER CUKIERMAN

Author's Note

In my line of Jews, I am the last link to the vanished world of the Eastern European shtetl. If each member of a generation lived to 100, there would be a 2,000-year chain spanning 20 generations, and each of those lives would have been lived in the same way. And then the chain would break — exactly between my generation and that of my parents. For thousands of years, my forbears had kept the Jewish religion remarkably intact, their daily lives circumscribed by the joys of the same holy days decreed in the Old Testament. But that was to change with me. In a single generation, our habits and ways of thinking were traded for new habits and new ways of thinking.

I was born in Toronto into a traditional Jewish home, where much was as it had been in the Polish shtetl of Ozarow, from which my parents had emigrated in 1930. The food in our home was the same, the language was Yiddish, holy days were observed, and all gentiles were viewed as anti-Semitic.

Mine was a privileged beginning, with the added feature of growing up in a "foreign" land. Today I take joy in remembering that shtetl household, but at the time it was a source of embarrassment. We were the only Jews in the neighbourhood. I was looked on as a curiosity and, back then, I didn't want to be different.

But now it seems important to record the somewhat weird ways of my growing-up years, because there is not a single Jew left in Ozarow, and I'm the last generation of the shtetl breed.

Yiddish Pronunciation Guide

kh as the *ch* in *ach*, never like *ch* in *chicken* (e.g., *Kh*askel, my mother's brother, pronounced like Haskel but with a guttural *H*)

ay as in *aye*

ey as in *eh*

TABLE OF CONTENTS

Gevorn Iz Nit Geborn

BECAME SO ISN'T BORN TO

Dateline: July 8, 1998

It's Tuesday and we're on our way around the world in eight days.

Another business trip.

I buckle my seat belt and my resident butterflies flutter as I feel the surge and rattle of the Challenger 604 as it rockets into the air, the Downsview skyline falling away beneath us.

Issy is sitting across from me; it's just the two of us and the crew. Our eyes lock as we exchange a small smile. Then the smile morphs into a grin and then we can't stop grinning — we're helpless. Because flying private is new to us. For the past 30 years, travel has meant public transport, with me — "the wife of" — always in tow, because we are hinged together by habit. Also, I could be useful in the many social situations overseas, and act as a buffer in the seat beside him so Isadore could snore in privacy.

A private jet is ridiculously extravagant, but it makes good business

Me and Isadore, Brunei, 1998

sense for someone of Issy's acumen. In the same day, he can do a breakfast meeting in Budapest, a luncheon in Lisbon, and a dinner in Dublin.

Meanwhile, back on that July trip, it's Thursday and we're on the longest leg of our tour, from Hawaii to Brunei, for business meetings and the birthday party of Sultan Hassanal Bolkei. At bedtime, Eric Silva the steward folds out the sofa bed and pulls the room divider across for privacy. We change into our pajamas and climb under the sheets. Issy snuggles in behind me in our usual formation, his left leg between mine. It is tempting to have sex a mile high in the sky, but what if our captain, Duane Holland, should again bump against our bed in the dark on his way to the washroom? We sleep until early light and drifts of toast and coffee and scrambled eggs. Eric has set the breakfast table with white linen and purple pansies.

As the plane taxis down the Brunei runway, I review my schedule:

1 p.m. — mtg. with minister of development & the Sultan
re: new hotel (address him as your majesty)
3 p.m. — Viewing of the Grand Parade, business suit
5 p.m. — Reception
8 p.m. — Black tie birthday banquet

In the blinding desert sun, we descend the few steps from the airplane and into the long black car that regularly awaits us on arrival. Soon we are shepherded into the airport terminal, to an empty sitting room done up in gold damask. The room is cold and wet with too much air conditioning. *Others* have our passports stamped and the luggage loaded while *we* sip a demitasse and watch the news in Arabic on TV. No doubt, somewhere in another part of the terminal, hordes of travellers even now are being coralled in queues from one pen to the next, as each access is locked behind them.

Issy is ushered to his meeting with the Sultan and Prince Alwaleed of Saudi Arabia. They discuss a possible Four Seasons Hotel, Brunei, in a huge mixed-use tourist complex — a questionable destination for the international traveller. Liquor is prohibited in Brunei.

At 3 p.m. we show up at the stadium for the Sultan's Grand Military Parade. The soldiers are dressed in white cotton costumes.

So am I.

As we climb the stadium steps, I notice a sea of black silk dresses. Every woman is in black tunic and trousers, each differently styled and trimmed. In the evening, too, I am out of step in my black dinner dress. Every lady is dressed all in white, apparently the traditional evening colour.

I should have asked more questions.

The ballroom, like the ladies, is rigged out in white, and dust particles glitter gold in the yellow light. Two hundred high-backed banquet chairs, like thrones, are carved in imitation of lace, and gilded. I'm ushered to one of these seats at a table covered in gold brocade, and in front of me are gilt-edged white porcelain plates framed by gold cutlery.

Dignitaries pay homage to the Sultan and his two wives, Anek Saleha and Mariam Abdul Aziz (Bruneian men are allowed four wives). Having presented his gift, each VIP backs away a few steps before turning to leave. A red carpet leads up to the three colossal gold chairs where the royals are seated — the Sultan in the centre, the two ladies resting their golden shoes, with upswept toes, on gilded footstools. One wife wears sumptuous bright green and gold silk and the other is outfitted in red and gold. Tiaras float aloft on their black bouffant hairdos. These two ladies — and I — are among the few women in the room with heads uncovered.

After countless courses, more gift-bearing courtiers, and musical interludes, the festivities conclude and we are escorted to the hotel for sleep and an early departure for Singapore — it's Thursday — followed by a Friday in Bali.

In Bali, Captain Holland, has a rollicking dinner in our hotel restaurant with the two other crew. A large man, the captain is dressed in the full Balinese costume of long flowered skirt and headdress. When we fly on long trips, Issy sometimes invites the crew to have a dinner on us — an extension of the way he treats his hotel staff.

Finally it's Tuesday, and the last leg of this trip carries us 24 hours from Hong Kong home to Toronto. It feels good to snuggle under the familiar blankets of our own bed.

Occasionally Issy travels alone, and then I stay home and sleep with the Issy Bear.

The bear story goes like this: Ty Warner, of Beanie Babies fame, brought out the Issy Beanie Baby, with proceeds to cancer — $2,000,000 was raised. One of these bears lives in our bedroom closet. One night when Issy was out of town, I brought the silky blue bear to bed with me — making a mental note to put him back in the closet before my housekeeper, Emie Buning, should find him in the morning. Of course, next day I forgot and left the toy bear in bed, but thank goodness Emie made no mention of it. However, the next time — and now every time my husband is away — guess who waits for me on Issy's pillow?

Most often, though, we travel together and we can't help but wonder: how did it happen *kineynehore, poo poo* — the evil eye shouldn't think we're too prideful — how did it happen that two schleppers like us are now flying in a private jet when we were both raised in households where one bathroom sometimes served 12, and our parents came from a Polish shtetl with no indoor plumbing?

From horse and wagon on rural roads to paths across the sky.

The Issy Bear — named for Isadore
in memory of Christopher Sharp.
Ty Warner donated $2 million for cancer
research from sales of this Beanie Baby.

CHAPTER ONE

The Shtetl IN NORTH TORONTO

God must have made a mistake when he assigned me to the Wise household. And he also went wrong in matching up my parents. If theirs was a match made in heaven, it must have been on a Friday, just before God's day of rest. I imagine him puzzling over the last two pieces on the table — he couldn't find a match. The leftovers were my parents, Ydessa Birnbaum and Joseph Wise, lately from the shtetl of Ozarow, Poland. The wedding took place on May 26, 1935, in the rabbi's office in Montreal, with little ceremony: "*Ver hot gelt gehat far a khasene?*" as my mother explained. "Who had money for a wedding party?" Right after the wedding, she and her new husband moved to Toronto, and nine months later I came along. Just the three of us till my brother arrived nine years later, when I was already a grown-up.

We were almost the only Jews living in North Toronto. There was one other family, the Goodmans of Fairlawn Dry Cleaners, but no kids my age. We had moved when I was two, in 1938, from 116 Grange Avenue, second floor — from the easy familiarity of the downtown ghetto where

Mom and Dad on their wedding day, May 26, 1935.

our friends and relatives lived, where Yiddish was spoken, kosher food was only steps away, and the Ozrower shul (synagogue) was close by. I admire my father for his courage in moving to the Christian, blue-collar neighbourhood — as it was then — of Yonge Street north of Lawrence Avenue, when he could barely speak English. He taught himself the language by reading the *Toronto Telegram* and later the *Star* every day, as he did until the day he died, five decades later. My dad was an entrepreneur. He opened Wise's Dry Goods at 3248 Yonge Street, an eight-foot-wide shop, and we lived in the back room, eight feet by twelve feet, separated from the shop by a brown velvet curtain. It was a proper shtetl household.

I remember two incidents from 3248. It had to be August or September of 1938, and I was sitting on my mother's lap on a black Queen Anne chair beside the door. The loose chair legs squeaked as my mother rocked me, singing softly. A client came in wearing a moss-green bouclé dress. My mother instantly stood up, rudely dropping me from her lap, and went behind the counter. I pulled at the lady's dress for attention, and she looked down at me with an annoyed expression. I repeated the offence even after being told to behave.

Then there was the time, a couple of years later, I crossed Brookdale Avenue, having been warned never to cross a road unaccompanied. My father gave me a whack and put me down in the scary black cellar. He was not a good communicator and that was the only way he could impress on a four-year-old the mortal dangers of traffic. I loved him nevertheless.

Mom taught me to approach any passerby on the street and ask, "Please, would you take me across Yonge Street?" Most people were slightly taken aback but they rarely refused. *"Az men fregt, blonzhet men nisht,"* Mom would say. "Ask and you won't get lost." These words gave me the chutzpah to be a pest and stop any stranger for directions.

At 3228 Yonge, our next shop, there was a heavy trap door one of my parents had to open so I could use the toilet in the dark cellar with its one light bulb swinging on a wire. I remember the cellar as a *round* dark place because I was afraid to look into the corners in case a rat was lurking there.

This cellar was the setting for a freakish scene. I had called my mother from the toilet when I found something resembling a broad pasta noodle swinging from my rectum. My mother took one look and gave a *geshrey* — a loud call — for my father, who then attempted to pull it out. He pulled and pulled lengths of it until it broke off. This bizarre bathroom scene was to recur twice over the next 18 months, until the worm must have died from starvation. My parents ignorantly put the blame on me for eating too much *khazeray* (junky sweets). Doctors we never called. In the shtetl there was no doctor, only the *feltsher* (old-time barber-surgeon), who dispensed aspirin and epsom salts and mustard plasters and the like.

Not until I was an adult did I work out that the "noodle" had been a tapeworm from the raw fish my mother chopped to make gefilte fish. She then used the same board for other food.

On Yonge Street, we always lived in rooms behind our rented shops, three consecutive Wise's Dry Goods stores in the same block, at 3248, 3228, and 3230, between Cranbrooke and Brookdale. I now buy my smoked salmon at Kristapson's, the other half of the divided shop at 3248 Yonge.

At 3230, if you wanted some fresh air, you carried the one chair outside to the sidewalk in front. The chair was in Marcel Breuer style, covered in peeling red leatherette — the same chair my mother would be sitting on when my dad came in from his piecework tailoring and asked, "*Nu*, were there any customers?"

"*Afile nisht keyn hunt*," my mom would answer. "Not even a dog."

If my dad was alone in the store and a woman came in, my dad would panic, and yell, "Ydess," because he was afraid the lady might ask to see a bra or some other feminine item. Mom was a crack salesman. I recall her in action, opening the box of Weldrest Hosiery (long before pantyhose) and slipping the back of her hand into the top of the stocking so the customer could see how the colour would look on the leg.

In 1940, Dad bought our first car — a 1934 grey round-nosed De Soto, very temperamental. I remember it mostly parked behind our second shop. Whenever Dad turned the key in the ignition, the question was: "What mood will the car be in today?" After a few false starts, the motor would turn over with a roar and the car would disappear beneath a balloon of black smoke. Once when it was not working, the streetcar stopped right in front of our store and Dad hobbled down the steps, schlepping huge cardboard boxes of dry goods for inventory.

Every Sunday we drove the half-hour journey, always via Avenue Road, back downtown to the ghetto. We would have lunch at Goldenberg's Kosher Restaurant on Spadina Avenue near Dundas. It had a high ceiling, black bentwood chairs, and Yiddish-speaking waiters with long white aprons. My parents would order two meals and an empty plate on which they placed offerings for me, sometimes fatty brisket or stuffed miltz (cow's spleen).

After lunch at the restaurant we went weekly to Dad's sister's, the Weinbergs, at 325 College Street, to spend the afternoon. Later we would meander through nearby Kensington Market to stock up for the week on all things Jewish — kosher meat and poultry; *kiml broyt* (rye bread with caraway seeds); *eyer kichlekh* (egg-white cookies known as nothings); cottage cheese bearing the pattern of the cheesecloth it was wrapped in; sour cream; *delikatesen* (smoked meat) for *senevitches* (sandwiches); *schmaltz* herring from one barrel and dill pickles from another.

I ate none of the above. I preferred sliced white bread, toasted, with peanut butter, cereal from boxes, Kraft Dinner, crackers with butter and jam, and Campbell's Cream of Mushroom Soup. This soup would ease out of the can whole, with a suction sound, and I learned to add the water gradually, to avoid a lumpy mess. Anything that came in a tin or a box, and wasn't derived by killing — and especially didn't have a face — was safer. When I ate my Nabisco Shredded Wheat, I would set the box in front of me, and while I munched, I studied the picture of Niagara Falls showing brown lumpy rocks where the water crashes down. I was certain these lumps were the shredded wheat, and I still can't shake the conviction. Besides, what other connection can Niagara Falls have with the cereal?

The emphasis on food and the rituals of a kosher kitchen put me off eating, and I became emaciated. My clothes hung on me. Belts required an extra hole created with the ice pick. I even remember a feeling of dread every day, when I sensed meal time getting near — my mother watching my every mouthful, which sometimes just refused to go down. *"Ess, ess, di bist azoy oysgedart,"* she nagged. "Eat, eat, you're so emaciated." It was sickening to see, on the *zalts bretl* (koshering tray), the blood drawn from meat being koshered with heavy salt. For an hour the blood ran in rivulets down the grooves in the white enamel tray and into the sink. The tray stood on a tilt, filled with all sorts of soft, no-name animal parts — offal. And then there were the chickens, geese, and *katshkes* (ducks). I cringed at the unmistakable sucking sound whenever my mom pulled the entrails out of these large birds.

Certain staples of our shtetl menu come to mind:

- *grashitze* (cow's thalamus, sweetbreads) fried in chicken *schmaltz* (rendered fat) — everything was fried in *schmaltz*
- *p'tcha* (cow's foot), a sandy-coloured, jelled soup
- *miltz* (cow's spleen), stuffed with bread crumbs, *schmaltz*, and onions
- *tongue* (cow's tongue), which looked like a cow's tongue
- *lung un leber* (cow's lung and liver) fried in *schmaltz* and onions
- *kishke* (cow's intestine) stuffed with bread crumbs, *schmaltz*, and onions

- *hun fus* (the foot of a chicken), like the hand of Dracula, with long unmanicured nails lying palm up in a bowl of dense green pea soup
- *heldzl* (skin of a chicken's neck), stuffed with breadcrumbs seasoned with schmaltz and garlic, and sewn up with a needle and thread

These and other animal parts I had to face every day at noon, for our main meal. The evening meal, according to tradition, was dairy, so every night my mom asked me the same question: "*Vos vilste esn?* What would you like to eat?" The choice was always the same: "*Cheese mit cream oder benenes mit cream?* Cheese with sour cream or bananas with sour cream?" In all the years, she didn't seem to notice that I never chose either, and I have yet to eat a banana.

When Eileen Bernstein, a family friend from Ozarow, was emigrating and arrived in Paris by train in 1935, everyone was offered a brown-bag lunch of a sandwich and a banana. No one from Ozarow had ever seen a banana, so Eileen asked her mom, "How do I eat this?"

Her mom answered, "Wait and watch what the others do."

We visited Poland in the 1960s, and found Polish food to be similar to Jewish food. I understood then that menus are defined by the produce that's available locally — potatoes, onions, flour, cabbages, and apples have always been the staples of both Polish and Jewish recipes.

A dish peculiar to our house and a favourite of my father's was *golkes*, made from potatoes that were finely grated, wrung dry in a tea towel till they turned pink, then mixed with an egg and a little flour, formed into balls, and boiled. Mom served these chewy balls in soup or sometimes hot milk, which my father preferred. *Golkes* were dark grey and probably would have bounced if dropped, like the India rubber balls they resembled. In early days, my mom would save money by serving an *opgebrente zup* (burnt soup). She stir-fried flour into small balls in *schmaltz*, then added fried onions and hot water. This was dinner for pennies a serving. Sometimes she added *kliskalekh* (small pasta squares). *"Oreme mentshn kokhn mit a sakh vaser,"* she would say. "Poor folk cook with a lot of water."

Kashe zup was another watery menu. One time at Goldenberg's Restaurant there were white maggots floating in the *kashe zup*. Unfortunately I had already started eating it, because the grain and the maggots were the same colour. For the next 50 years, I skipped the soup course at home. It might have been the maggots or perhaps it was simply because, during the Depression, soup was sometimes all there was.

I remember so well my mother in the kitchen, singing a Yiddish song while making *kliskalekh* or *lokshn* (noodles). She would pour the flour out of the bag into a tepee shape, take an egg, and, with a circular motion, make a well in the tepee, then crack two eggs into the well. With a knife she would fold the flour over into the eggs until the dough was formed. Now, in a rowing motion, she rolled the ball in an ever-increasing circle with the *valgerholts* (long, thin rolling pin, no handles). When the circle reached the size of a large pizza, she picked it up, supporting it over her fingertips, and began to stretch it with rhythmic movements, as if she were conducting music. When it was stretched suitably thin, she hung the large circle of pastry over a chair to dry, later to be rolled up and cut into noodles.

Mom was a consummate cook of all shtetl recipes. She made them exactly like her mother had — no deviation. Each piece of gefilte fish was encircled with the skin of the fish and had a carrot slice placed precisely in its centre. (I was ornery as usual and have never tasted a piece.) She was known for her veal *kotletn* — which I still serve as Ydessa's veal patties — made from ground veal, an excess of garlic, dampened bread, onion, egg, and — my own touch — rosemary.

My parents were serious about buying quality food at kosher stores. My dad went into Naftuly's Butcher Shop and pointed out the very piece of meat he wanted, and my mom would embarrass me in Perlmutter's Bakery, where she would designate a particular challah (egg bread): "Give me the brown one in the corner. No, not that one — the second loaf from the left. No no no, not that one, the one beside it. Yes, that's it."

Everyone who entered our house was fed, and I still follow the same procedure, whether it's the plumber or a visiting sheik. I am reminded of Dr. Samuel Johnson, who once declined an invitation to a house where, on an earlier visit, no food had been offered. He said, "I don't go to a place where I come out the same as I went in."

At seven years old, though, it seemed to me that I was in the wrong house. I hated the un-Canadian food, the cut-down handmade clothes, the Jewish religion, and the constant warring. My parents spoke Yiddish to me, but I always stubbornly answered in English. I imagined life being quite different, if only I had been born in the "right" house — with the life I, as a Canadian, deserved. For example: parents who knew how to swim. Although it is written in the Torah that a father must teach his child to swim, my father could not swim. And besides, we spent only about two Sunday afternoons a year at Belle Ewart Beach, where he would typically sink into the water up to his armpits and sigh, "*Ah, vos far a mekhaye* — what a pleasure," and do the breast stroke — his feet never leaving the bottom. I can't swim because there was seldom a body of water available. Nor can I skate. Ice skates and roller skates were not in the vocabulary of our house, so it was simply out of the question even to try to explain such *narishkayt* (foolishness).

I daydreamed about a household like those in the books I read, where people spoke to one another in quiet voices, with friendship and interest, love and affection, and changed their underwear at least every day. I remember walking past the houses on our block at dusk, when the windows were glowing with lamplight, and peering in, always wondering just what went on behind those windows. Were those shadowy moving figures loving and civil or were they quarrelling and troubled like us? Did all families have two personas — one within the home and one outside? Were they real or were they fake, like me?

I felt like a fraud because my life was a pretence on so many fronts. I was masquerading as an eight-year-old yet I was only seven, because my mom had enrolled me in school early and asked me to lie about my age. Since I didn't have a middle name like everyone else, I claimed that I was named after the English princess Margaret Rose and that my middle name was Margaret.

My parents didn't know about my other life as a Christian. My schoolmate Lorna Chisholm had invited me to the Sandys' house for a weekly Bible class. As we arrived, Mrs. Sandy was on the verandah of her red-brick bungalow, polishing the gleaming brass door handle and letter box. She was short, seemingly very old, her white hair woven into a neat figure-eight bun on the back of her head. "Come right in, young ladies, you're early — just in time for tea and a wee slice of Christmas cake." She had a cockney accent I found new and appealing. We sat at the kitchen table with "Sandy," as she called her husband. Newly retired from the Bell Telephone Company, he was wearing his flannel "combinations" — pinkish one-piece long johns with a trapdoor at the back. Mrs. Sandy brought down from the cupboard a pretty tin decorated with garden flowers, which she said her sister sent every year from England with the fruitcake. She meted out four small rectangles of the holiday delicacy. "How," I thought, "can a cake last a whole year when our family has little respect for yesterday's baking?" The next week when the tin was brought out again, I said, "No thank you, Mrs. Sandy," like a good shtetl child — but also because I didn't want to be responsible for using up the stuff before the year was out.

When a few other girls arrived, we all sat cross-legged on the oriental carpet in front of Mrs. S., who played the black upright piano, and we sang hymns like "Onward Christian Soldiers." Whenever we came to "Jesus," I mumbled, because I couldn't bring myself to blaspheme. "*Reboyne Shel Oylem* — the King of the Universe" would come down on my head.

And then there were the glorious songs of Christmas. When I first heard the Swedish tenor Jussi Bjorling sing "O Holy Night," I was tempted to switch religions. The words and music of Christmas carols are part of the nostalgia of my youth. Every Christmas at Bedford Park Public School, there was a holiday concert. Parents — not mine, of course — would be seated in the auditorium with the doors left open so they could hear the carols sung from all parts of the school. Students from each grade were stationed in the corridor outside their classrooms. Grade 1 always sang "Away in a Manger" from the main floor; Grade 2 sang "It Came upon a Midnight Clear" from the second floor; Grade 3 "Bring a Torch Jeanette Isabella"; and so on. Every year I sang from a different location. Now, in winter, when my feet crunch on new-fallen snow, I recall "Good King Wenceslas" — "When the snow lay round about, deep and crisp and even." I can still hear in my mind's ear those echoing songs that came from near and those that came from far.

Once, in those elementary-school years, my mom sent me to Wilson's Fine Foods for a bag of Five Roses Flour. Wilson's carried neat stacks of pickles, jams, spices, and brick-sized packages of tea leaves wrapped in foil with white labels — only packaged food, no fresh produce. The long, narrow shop was empty as usual, but I caught a glimpse of Mr. Wilson in the back room, sitting at his dressing table, applying rouge over the tan-coloured foundation he always wore. He was a tall, slim man with a peroxide-blond pompadour, and he took more interest in his makeup than in his merchandise. I asked him for a five-pound bag of *mel*, using the Yiddish word. For some reason Mr. Wilson could not understand me, and when he kept asking me to repeat *"mel,"* I thought he was dim. Finally I pointed out a row of white bags, each decorated with five red roses. "Oh, I see," said the grocer, "you mean *flour*." I was embarrassed not to know the English word. "Flour" to me meant "flower" — like roses. How can a rose and *mel* be the same word in English? For that moment, I felt like a foreigner.

In the '40s, Yonge Street saw many goods delivered by horse and wagon: bread, milk, and ice among them. The bread men would whoa the horse, then take a heavy weight attached to a rope and drop it on the curb, so the horse wouldn't wander away while he gave us our unsliced bread. Sometimes the horse would mindlessly drop on the road steaming mustard-yellow turds, which, when dry, looked like chopped hay. The street cleaner later swept these into a folding receptacle that he emptied into his wheeled cart. Downtown, one still saw the occasional ornamental cast-iron water trough on the side of the street, for the horses. The milkman brought milk in a bottle with a double-gourd shape — the upper third was yellow cream. Homogenized milk was not available till the mid-'40s. The coal man, with blackened face and hands, would empty jute sacks of coal down a window that opened, from the street, into the cellar near the furnace. And on steamy summer days, we would run behind the iceman's truck for handouts of slivered ice.

In the Wise household there was a marked absence of things — no clutter, only clean tables. No books, no magazines, no ashtrays, and few *tshatshkes* (trinkets). There was no liquor, wine, beer, or pop — except one bottle of the obligatory Crown Royal *bronfn* (whiskey) and one bottle of Manischewitz sacramental wine: 33 per cent sugar. To date I've never had a beer and I drink no pop or liquor except a very regular glass of red wine.

The Wises never bought any kind of paper — no writing paper, toilet paper, napkins, tissues. We never tore open a gift but rather carefully picked it apart. Then we re-used the gift-wrapping paper by removing the creases with a warm iron. To this day, like my mother, I keep cardboard from shirts to write on, and the cardboard from pantyhose, with its rounded corners, makes an ideal bookmark for jotting down notes or splendid words I come across in my reading.

At our first store, we used old telephone books as toilet paper — logical, because we didn't have a telephone. I recall, in 1943, an alarming summons to the shop next door — a telephone call from Montreal that

Mom's brother Shloime was dead at the age of 43. Phone calls came seldom in those days, but when they did, they were serious.

In 1944, I attended the Borochov Jewish Academy on College Street, a walk-up just west of Brunswick. This was after school, which meant travelling for an hour on the Yonge streetcar in the winter when it was dark. The trolley stopped right outside our shop. Since my parents often needed my help after school, I went only about a dozen times.

On one occasion, when I was almost nine, my mom asked me to pick up a chicken in nearby Kensington Market on the way home. "Get a *yunge meydl* — a young girl, not a capon," she said. Glicksman's Kosher Poultry was dark and smelly as I walked in. When my eyes grew accustomed to the gloom, I saw that the shop was completely empty, not a chicken in sight — just some distant shadowy cages and two people seated up front. The deck of the plate-glass shop window was bare but tarred and feathered with greyish-white glued-on feathers. I faced an old couple, short and dumpy, their clothes the colour of a sepia snapshot. They sat on two kitchen chairs, the man with a long grey beard and a *kipa* (skullcap), and the woman wearing the *sheytl* (wig) decreed by Jewish law. They sat like twins, slumped, their knees loosely spread.

"A gutn tog, meydle. Vi geyt es?" said the old woman. "Good day, young lady, how are you?"

"Fine, thank you," I replied, trying to remember my mother's instructions. "I'd like a lady chicken if you have one?"

Mr. Glicksman, the chicken dealer, still seated, slapped his thigh and roared with laughter. This was apparently a new one on him. Still chuckling, he raised himself slightly by pushing his palms against the seat of the chair, fell back down, and tried again. This time the old man managed to pull himself up to his full height — not much taller than me. *"Kim sheine meydle*, come" he said, and we waded together through the sawdust to the back of the shop where the chickens were housed in grungy wooden cages (the light was purposely dim so the birds would think it was night and be less active, therefore plumper). We selected a chicken with copper-coloured feathers, and the chicken-dealer carried the squawking bird under his arm out of the shop and disappeared across Baldwin Street into a laneway. A few minutes later he reappeared with the bird now featherless and missing its head. From the deck of the front window, he picked up a hose with a nozzle that became a Bunsen burner when he turned it on, and he sprayed the noisy blue flame over the chicken to remove any stray feathers.

I carried the body, wrapped in pink butcher paper, to the streetcar and made my way home. It was rush hour and the trolley lurched and halted. I didn't need to hold on, because the wall of people around me kept me from falling. The chicken in my arms, still warm and gamey, began to work its way out of the package. I could feel its bare, warm rump in my hands, and that and the odour, together with the lurching of the trolley, made me nauseous. Suddenly I had an irresistible urge to vomit, so I cried out, "Excuse me, sorry, but I think I'm going to bring up." At that, the wall of people opened like magic and I gratefully plunged into the fresh air, and took the next trolley home.

No wonder I had to leave the kitchen and the smell whenever raw chickens were being hacked to pieces. But I did enjoy the chicken *gribene* (cracklings). These were the bits of fried chicken skin and onions left over when Mom rendered chicken fat into the ubiquitous *schmaltz*. Also I liked the *pipikl* (gizzard), which was dark purple and leathery. Mom would open the raw gizzard and, with a small knife, scrape the yellow feed of the chicken's last meal from the corrugated pleats of its rubbery stomach. When roasted, it became so chewy it almost defied the teeth. I suspected the *pipikl's* former function was probably revolting, but I preferred not to know.

I didn't bring any of my school chums home, in case any gross blood ritual was going on in the kitchen. My friends' mothers didn't spend their days handling dead animals. They had bridge games, went shopping, played Debussy on the piano, listened to their daughters practice their music lessons, pored over crossword puzzles, and read the latest best-seller.

My parents never read a book or went to a movie. My mom could not read English. Later I discovered she needed glasses and couldn't have read the small print of the newspaper anyway. She would never have spent money to have an eye examination, and magnifying glasses were not then available from the corner drugstore. She always needed me to thread her needles. "It's so dark in here, Rose, please *aynfedeme mir di nodl*," she would say. "Thread the needle for me." She wrote a phonetic Polish–English in letters half an inch high so she could see them, and when older she got all her information by telephone or television.

Since I could read and write English, my parents considered me a genius, a kind of prodigy. Dad's English was confined to reading, so I became the family scribe, writing business letters and all the cheques. Dad would pen his signature, *J. Wise*, very slowly and deliberately on each cheque — proud that he had the money to cover it. It was the only writing I ever saw him do. When I produced his business letters, which always began, "This is an agreement between Joseph Wise and," my mom might say, "*A lebn af dayn kop*, well-done. A long life on your head."

I wanted to belong to a family where I could take lessons, like my friends. At least I should have had ballet lessons, like Marjorie Mackenzie, who could do the sword dance over crossed strings laid on her patterned carpet, or perhaps piano lessons, like Carol Welsh. I played on a piano keyboard I made out of cardboard and sang along as I fingered Beethoven's *Concerto in A Minor*: "Da da dum — da dum dum dum — da-dum — da-dum." In our house, lessons in music and dance were dismissed as *narishkayt*. Dad never sang a note, but Mom and I sang Yiddish songs in the car all the way to Chicago and all the way to

Montreal — ones I still sing, like *"Oyfn Pripetshik"* ("Near the Fireplace"), a ballad about the rabbi teaching tiny children their ABC's around a warm hearth. A sad song because children of the shtetl were delivered into the hands of the rabbi and the bondage of school at just four years old.

And another song we sang was *"In a Lodzher Enge Shtibl"* ("In a Humble House in Lodz"), a folk tale about a Polish Jewish hero, Zishe Breitbart, nicknamed "the Iron King" because he could bend iron, raise a car in the air, and even lift a small elephant. He was six-foot-two, 225 pounds, with pale blue eyes.

Zishe performed in all the major cities of Europe and America, and international news clippings called him the strongest man in the world. In 1924 he wrote a book, *Muscular Power*, which advertised his innovative "Progressive Muscle Builder," available only with his course — all for $26 sent to 1819 Broadway Avenue, New York. Breitbart planned to go to Palestine to train a Jewish army to fight for their homeland, but, unfortunately, he accidentally drove a railroad spike through his thigh during a performance, and died of blood poisoning in 1925, when he was 42. Marmish, my mother's sister, had sent us from Ozarow, in 1930, this four-page ballad about Breitbart, which I still have.

Ydessa loved to dance and sing and be with friends. She liked it *lebedik* — lively. Joe was solemn and slow-moving and preferred to be still. My dad walked with a limp, and only behind the wheel of a car did he feel equal to any man. A car to him was not a luxury or a status symbol. A car was his legs. To the end of his days, he drove a "Kedilek car." Dad was very sensitive about his limp. Mom would always walk two steps ahead of him because she was very quick on her shapely legs and had no patience for his slow gait. She would laugh and say Dad walked "*arop un aroyf* — up and down."

My dad's worst fear was that someone would call him a cripple — which apparently some guy once did, ending up with a fist in the jaw. According to his two sisters, Dad always limped as a child. He gave me the story that he was in an elevator accident, but my guess is that he was born, like one of our sons, with one-third of a club foot. Our third son, Chris, had a corrective cast on his leg for two months when he was about 10 months old and that solved the problem perfectly. We called him Thumper as he crawled along the floor with a big smile on his face, dragging the cast behind him. He was happily oblivious and not at all bothered by the extra weight, which he carried as if it had always been part of him.

Music lessons were *narishkayt* in our house, but book learning was paramount: "*Yiddishe ganovim ganvenen nor bikher* — Jewish thieves steal only books." Dad would slowly examine every report card, and if he found one B among the A's, there would be hell to pay. In his clumsy but caring way he would rant, "What's the meaning of this B? What do you want to do? Be a saleslady and work at Woolworths? Study harder —" he spoke in Yiddish "— so you won't be a tailor like me." Or "Get a Saturday job so you'll know the value of a dollar." I never did learn. I worked at a Chinese greengrocer before I was 12 years old, but I learned little about economy, since I would easily spend my $3.65 daily wage on a belt or some other frivolous item before I took the bus home. Once I was waiting at the bus stop in front of the window display of Lewis Howard Casuals and I noticed a colour combination that made my heart quicken — a coppery chocolate flared velvet skirt topped by a shell-pink sweater. I bought the sweater on the spot, later found some brown velvet fabric, and fashioned my own skirt on our Singer sewing machine.

Mom thought my boss, Mr. Young, was *karg* (stingy) and threatened to phone him and demand that he raise my salary to five dollars. I begged her, "Please, plea-ea-ease, Mom, please don't call — I'll never be able to face him again," but she called nevertheless, while I covered my ears in mortification. My wages were duly raised.

I can still name and enjoy the rare vegetables we sold at the Ah Young Fruit Market — kohlrabi, collard greens, rapini, and okra, among others

— and I learned that rutabaga is just a yellow turnip. Working at the market, I felt very satisfied, because I came to know the merchandise so well. One day the boss had to ask *me*, the part-time clerk, "Where do we keep the Certo?" Telephone clients would wait on hold until I had time to take their order, because I would steer them right and point out the freshest or best bets of the day — one Saturday, we had huge jet-black strawberries such as I have never seen since.

My mother warned me never to go into the back of the store, even to use the bathroom. All the time I worked there, I waited till I got home to pee. I quit after two years when, on a rare occasion when I did venture into the back of the store, Mr. Young rubbed my nipples with his knuckles. And to add to the insult, he smirked as he did it, because my chest was still flat at age 13 — another cross to bear.

The friction between my parents and me stemmed from our shtetl household. The food, the customs, the ethics, the dress, the asceticism — it was as if we were still living in Poland. Yiddish was the language at home, and I felt like an outsider since we were almost the only Jews for miles around, surrounded, in my mother's paranoia, by hostile *goyim* (gentiles). One of these *krists* (Christians) once brought me a gift of a Mother Goose book, which my mother dismissed as *narishkayt*, dampening the joy of owning my first book. The damage ran deep, and I was married for 20 years before I saw any sense in buying books when they could be had free from the library.

Today, I look back with respect on the austerity of my upbringing. A lack of the world's goods, I now believe, fosters creativity. I have seldom bought ready-made toys for my own children, and they tell me they are grateful.

The only doll I ever had was Susie, a homemade rag doll with a ruffle for hair and flat features embroidered on flowered fabric. I longed for a real doll with a human face, with eyelids that opened and shut, and pink lips parted slightly to show pearly teeth. Marjorie Mackenzie, the girl next door, had a Baby Wettums that peed into her diaper after taking water from a bottle. My mother told me that I had once seized a doll's carriage from a strange child during a Sunday outing in Queen's Park. The closest I got to real dolls were the ones I drew on a shirt cardboard and cut out. I enjoyed making complete wardrobes for them, sketched out on paper, coloured, and attached to the doll with paper tabs that folded down over the shoulders. Issy, my husband, says it's because I never had a proper doll that I now collect 18th-century porcelain ones.

I made many more things out of cardboard — the piano keyboard, a sewing machine, playing cards, signs for the store advertising specials like "Children's corduroy overalls — reg. $2.98 now $1.98."

It wasn't only toys that were rare in our house: clothes we also had few of — just enough for three or four changes, and those we had were often made by my parents and later by me on the Singer treadle sewing machine, a central fixture in our house. (That very Singer is here in the room where I write, the machine folded down, a photocopier on its surface instead.) Mom would pump away on the noisy treadle with her slim ankles. Dad was very vain about her shapely legs. She always wore high-heeled shoes, claiming that low heels put her off balance — which she often demonstrated by feigning a backwards fall. Dad sewed as deftly as if he were playing pizzicato on a violin. He would wrap the edge of the hem over his left forefinger, then pick three nimble stitches at a time before he drew the thread through.

Once, Dad bought two huge bolts of red corduroy fabric to make children's overalls to sell in the shop. He cut through two layers at a time of the licorice-red velvet fabric, and he and Mom stitched up dozens of overalls. I sewed on the buttons and pinned on the price tags. To save fabric, my dad had cut the legs dovetailed, with the nap running in opposite directions, but that resulted in an unfortunate colour effect. When the overalls were made up, one leg appeared pink, the other red. The garments had to be marked down, a loss my mother never let my father forget: "*Gelt in drerd* — money down the drain."

It's true that all immigrants straddle two cultures, but in my case the culture of the Old World was to end with me, because of the Holocaust. Elvio Del Zotto tells me that when he returns to the small town of Cordenons, north of Venice, from which his parents emigrated in 1930, he can visit cousins whose lives have changed little since his grandfather's time. I've been back to Ozarow. Not a single Jew survives there or in any of the more than 2,000 shtetls in Poland. With the murder of the Eastern European Jews, a way of life intact since the Bible has vanished in the space of one generation. My grandkids can have no connection to or race memory of that shtetl culture, other than through my stories.

In North Toronto we were occasionally called dirty Jews. Why was this, I wondered as I looked into the mirror, trying to fathom what was wrong with me. I searched my features for signs of dirt, or for some distinguishing feature like a long nose. Maybe we didn't wash as frequently as the gentiles. Mom had a habit of spitting on a hanky, and as she went to wipe my face, I would recoil and squirm out of her reach. I seem to remember bathing only once or twice a week in the bathroom we shared with the family of six who owned the house where we rented rooms. Anti-Semitism was a mystery to me, and I felt diminished by it. After all, I thought, there must be a reason to dislike Jews. I even became somewhat anti-Semitic myself — everything goyish looked better to me.

How was it that anti-Semitism in Poland could evolve from persecution to pogroms, from the gradual denial of rights to expulsion and complicity in murder? Most countries in the Eastern hemisphere at some time banished their Jewish residents. This pattern of welcome and rejection was usually repeated, as I discovered this year while preparing the Passover readings: at first Pharaoh invited the Jews to Egypt during a famine in Palestine, and then he enslaved them. And so it was to be repeated in every land. Initially the Jews were welcomed to the host country, often to improve the economy — because Jews historically were traders, with the courage to travel and learn new languages, and were by law the bankers. In 1066, for example, William the Conquerer invited the Jews from Normandy to England to act as moneylenders, because the Christian Church preached that usury was immoral and illegal. In the 14th century, King Kazimierz the Great welcomed the Jewish people to Poland, offering them the same rights and privileges as the Poles. But after a few generations and a few new regimes, the systematic pattern of discrimination began. Then the "guests" were made to return any land, and were denied work in the artisans' guilds, or in school or government jobs.

It's as if the Polish people looked at the prosperity of the Jews and said, "Why should these strangers own our land? They don't belong here, and their rights should therefore be restricted. Besides, they are infidels, and, as the New Testament states, they killed our saviour." I remember my mother visibly quake when a customer came into our store wearing a cross, a symbol that reminded her of beatings and a religious killing in Ozarow. I felt the same discrimination in North Toronto. As in Poland, we were the unwelcome guests who might be asked to leave.

I had always thought my mother was unfair in branding all *goyim* as anti-Semites. I cringed when she used the word *goyim*, which sounded almost as demeaning as *nigger*. During the war, I thought her tales about death camps were exaggerated and I discounted her rantings that she would never see her family again. From the time I was six to the day I turned nine, I often heard my mom say, "Hitler has killed my parents, my sisters, and my brother. I know it! I'll never see them again." The house reeked of fear. I went about the business of being a child and hid the spectres that haunted our home. I tried to pass as a Gentile. And then in 1945 came the grisly news that the Birnbaum family in Ozarow had indeed been suffocated in the gas chambers. Edith (Ydessa) was the last

Birnbaum. She didn't have even one first or second cousin. The greater family of Birnbaums had evaporated as if a steamroller had crushed them.

All this while my friends were taking tap-dancing lessons and playing the flute and swimming in sunny country lakes. There was an unreality about going to school with kids who *belonged* in the neighbourhood — whose grandmothers were not gassed but took them to see the *Nutcracker* ballet at Christmas.

Where was the real world? I led a double life.

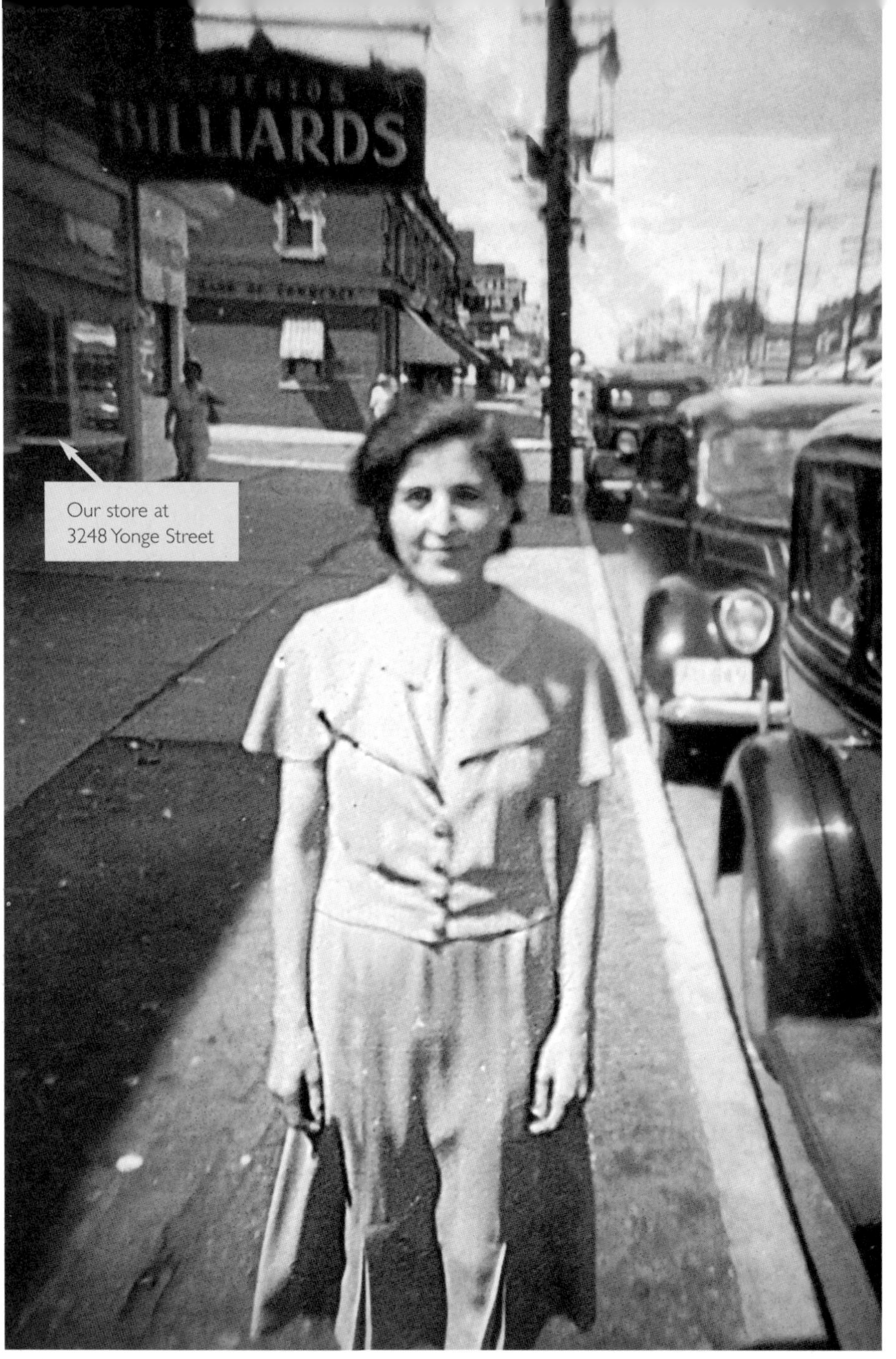

Mom in front of our store on Yonge Street, 1938, wearing a dress from the Polly-Anna Dress Company, the Montreal factory where she had worked from 1930 to 1935, as a new emigrant from Poland.

Me at the time of the tapeworm.

The streetcar stop was just outside our shop at Yonge and Cranbrooke. Notice everyone wore a hat in the 1940s.

Kensington Market near the home of my aunt Khayele. We shopped at the market Sundays to stock up for the week.

The back alley of our apartment at 3267 Yonge Street. Our entrance is the staircase on the extreme right.

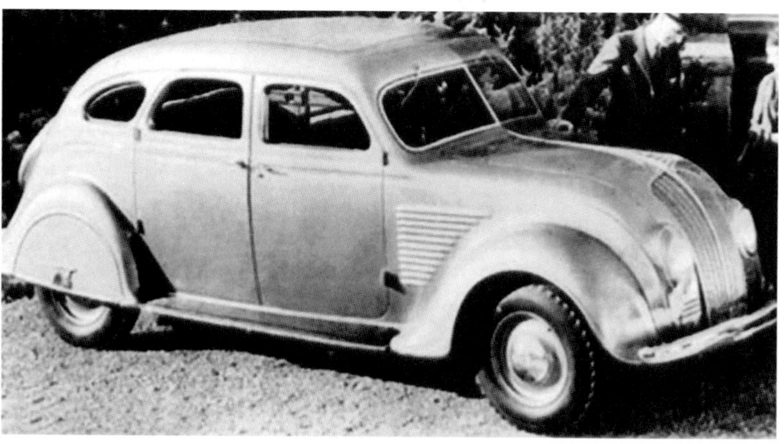

Dad's sluggish 1934 De Soto.

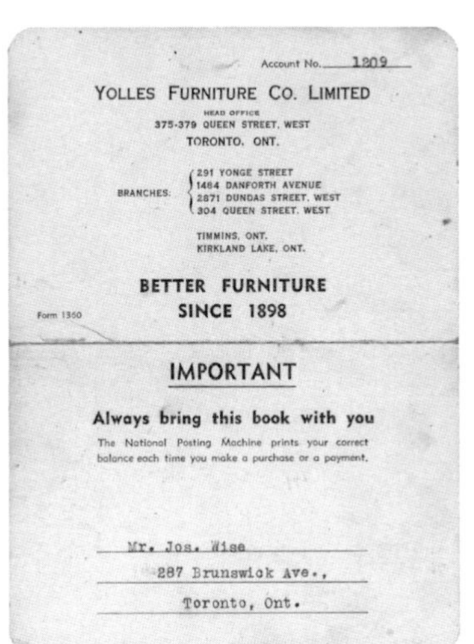

Account No. 1209

YOLLES FURNITURE CO. LIMITED

HEAD OFFICE
375-379 QUEEN STREET, WEST
TORONTO, ONT.

BRANCHES:
291 YONGE STREET
1484 DANFORTH AVENUE
2871 DUNDAS STREET, WEST
304 QUEEN STREET, WEST

TIMMINS, ONT.
KIRKLAND LAKE, ONT.

BETTER FURNITURE SINCE 1898

Form 1350

IMPORTANT

Always bring this book with you

The National Posting Machine prints your correct balance each time you make a purchase or a payment.

Mr. Jos. Wise
287 Brunswick Ave.,
Toronto, Ont.

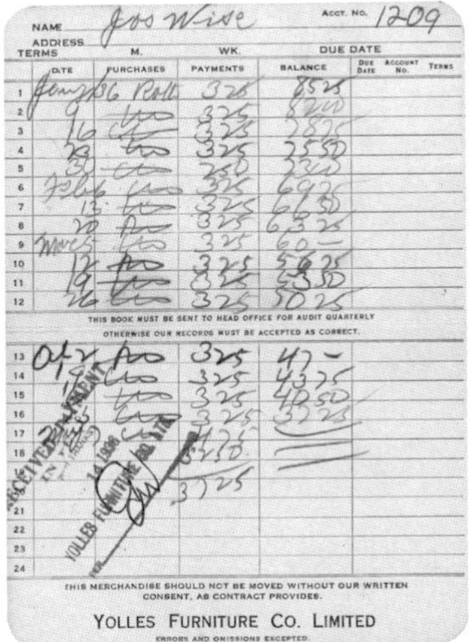

NAME Jos Wise ACCT. No. 1209
ADDRESS
TERMS M. WK. DUE DATE

	DATE	PURCHASES	PAYMENTS	BALANCE	DUE DATE	ACCOUNT No.	TERMS
1	[illegible]	[illegible]	325	8525			
2	9		325	8200			
3	16		325	7875			
4	23		325	7550			
5	30		250	7300			
6	Feb 6		325	6975			
7	13		325	6650			
8	20		325	6325			
9	Mar 5		325	60 —			
10	12		325	5675			
11	19		325	5350			
12	26		325	5025			

THIS BOOK MUST BE SENT TO HEAD OFFICE FOR AUDIT QUARTERLY OTHERWISE OUR RECORDS MUST BE ACCEPTED AS CORRECT.

	DATE	PURCHASES	PAYMENTS	BALANCE	DUE DATE	ACCOUNT No.	TERMS
13	Oct 2		325	47 —			
14			325	4375			
15			325	4050			
16			325	3725			
17			[illegible]				
18			[illegible]				
19							
20			3725				
21							
22							
23							
24							

RECEIVED PAYMENT
14 1936
YOLLES FURNITURE
PER

THIS MERCHANDISE SHOULD NOT BE MOVED WITHOUT OUR WRITTEN CONSENT, AS CONTRACT PROVIDES.

YOLLES FURNITURE CO. LIMITED

ERRORS AND OMISSIONS EXCEPTED.

My parents' dresser, part of the six-piece bedroom suite they purchased in 1935 on account from Yolles Furniture for $185 with $25 down. Dad took the streetcar every week for two years to make the $3.25 payments.

I never had a real doll until lately. These porcelain ones are from the Chelsea Factory, England, circa 1755. The small figures are 5 inches high.

CHAPTER TWO

Hak Mir Nisht Keyn Tshaynik

DON'T BANG ON A TEAKETTLE

In the film about my young years that runs through my mind on fast forward, only a few frames insistently come up as stills.

It's 1942, I'm in Grade 1, and on my way home from school in late November. A dark day and I'm wearing my rubber boots. I come to a puddle that's frozen over and pleasantly slippery, and I notice that the water trapped beneath it moves as I slide. In a stupor, I glide from side to side for I don't know how long, as if there were no me — only the puddle existed. And that following spring, on the first day we didn't need boots, my feet fairly flew off the ground with such ease that with each step my shoes seemed to need weights to bring them back down. The shoes were proper lace-up ankle-high oxford boots, because Dad was careful that my feet would not be misshapen like his were, from the shtetl; the second toe of his right foot sat curiously on top of its neighbour.

Not until I was almost six did I at long last have a pair of regular low oxfords like the rest of the kids. I had begged for these and remember the

The happiest kid in Grade 2 — wearing a favourite red and white blouse.

day it finally happened. I skipped out of the store in my new shoes and pranced back and forth ahead of my mom on the sidewalk, as she cautioned me, "*Gey nisht azoy geferlekh shnel, di vest zikh nokh tsehargenen* — watch out, not so fast, you'll kill yourself." Today I still wear new shoes out of the shoe store.

In another frozen frame from my childhood film, I'm about seven, and I am folded at the waist over a pipe-railing balustrade, with my knees drawn in, holding on with palms up. An irresistible urge comes over me, to let my body freefall over the railing in a somersault, swinging on my hands. I grapple with the urge for a few days, trying to summon up the same kind of courage one might need to parachute out of a plane. After a struggle, I let go and swing headfirst over the bar and upside down. What a victory!

Another recurring frame finds me, at the same age, on our apartment's fire escape, which was our balcony. I am sitting on the gravel roof and tearing bits of waxed paper into a pile. My friend Marjorie comes over from next door and asks me what I'm doing. "I'm making Maple Leaf soap flakes to surprise my mom so she won't need to buy them at the store," I reply.

"Don't be a silly goose," she says, laughing, "that's just waxed paper."

"No, it's not waxed paper," I argue, "because if you can't tell the difference and they look exactly the same, then these must be soap flakes."

I had developed the strange superstition that people had the power to change objects. If a fruit looked like a cherry, then you could bite into it with assurance that you were eating a cherry. And if you could produce something that looked exactly like soap flakes, then they were just that. "Surely Marjorie must be mistaken," I thought, but nevertheless my resolve was shaken and the world was flawed.

In the next image I am in the schoolyard, the first to arrive. I swing mindlessly round a pole and wait for the others. After a while I wonder where the others are. And then it dawns on me — could it be that everyone is already inside? They are.

Schooldays, to me, were the *narishkayt*, the foolishness forbidden at home. School was my private Emerald City. There were stories and games and a tray with balls of Plasticene, a tongue depressor marked with our names stuck in each ball, each looking like a candy apple. We all had a turn striking the triangle, while standing up front beside the piano. In the sunlight I saw the piano's shadow as chocolate on the gleaming caramel-coloured linoleum. It seemed to take forever until it was my turn on that precious silver triangle; if the names were called alphabetically, I was always last. At school, there was a boys' playground and a girls' playground safe from boys, "GIRLS" carved in stone over the door. I always felt privileged to be there, even if I feared that my membership could be cancelled at any moment, because I was a Jew. And I knew enough not to mention to my parents just what went on at school, apart from reading and arithmetic — like art and other *narishkayt*.

I clearly recall the June day when school was let out, kids all around me jumping and whooping because the summer holidays were beginning, and I trudged home with a funereal step to wait out the endless summer, until the fun would begin again. Summer seemed forever.

From age three to six, 1939 to 1941, I lived with my parents in two rented upstairs front rooms at 176 Bowood Avenue, a house we shared with the Kennedy family, who had four boys. The nine of us used one bathroom. Recently I took a look at those rooms, with the kind permission of the present owner — who I probably offended when I said, "It's so much smaller than I remember." She asked if the house in the 1940s had been divided somehow, so that each apartment was private. "No," I answered. "Every night we felt like intruders, as we tiptoed up the Kennedy family's staircase."

One November night when I was four, my dad and I walked the four blocks home to Bowood Avenue after working late at the store, and an almost full moon was up. It's my only memory of just the two of us out together, Dad protecting me against the dark and the unknown. He was walking with his uneven up-and-down gait, huffing with the effort. I was holding his forefinger. As we made our way along the street, which was so quiet we could hear our footfalls, I remarked, "Look, Daddy, the moon is following us." My dad did not say, "Don't be silly," but just murmured quietly and affectionately. He was a very dear and gentle man, except on those rare occasions when his dybbuk surfaced in a flare of rage.

Another night on Bowood, I woke for no apparent reason, climbed out of my brown metal crib — quietly so as not to disturb my sleeping parents — and walked to the window. It was almost first light, and there was an eerie bluish haze like the calm after a thunderstorm. As I turned to go back to bed, I noticed my father was sleeping naked, and in the blue half-light I noticed his genitals, which at first I thought couldn't possibly belong to him — they were scary and of unimaginable design. Another night I woke to find my father on top of my mom under the greyish-purple blanket. I called out, "Daddy — stop! You're hurting Mommy!" I couldn't make any sense of the muffled laughter that came from under the blanket.

I slept in that brown metal crib until I was six, even though I pleaded repeatedly that I needed a big bed because, "See, I can reach the end with my toes."

I have two other Bowood memories, both sexual: one where I am sitting in a tin bathtub on the white enamel kitchen table and resist when my mom, laughing, tries to wash my genitals. Another from when I was about four. I was in the shared bathroom with the youngest Kennedy, Bruce, where I was sitting on the toilet while he washed at the sink wearing only a T-shirt. I noticed that he had an interesting hook attached to the bottom of his stomach. "Brucie," I asked, "do you think you can you lift me off the toilet with your hook?" We worked on this until Mrs. Kennedy discovered us.

Soon the Wises moved up in the world, to a three-room walk-up back apartment, and I embarked on a fantasy life inspired by Hollywood.

When I was four and a half, Mom would drop me off every Saturday at the Bedford Theatre — whether the movie was appropriate or not — to keep me occupied, because it was the busy day at Wise's Dry Goods. For the 11 cent show ticket, there was the Movietone News, a western serial, and a cartoon, perhaps a Tom and Jerry one, which I found wanting because only the feet of the housekeeper were shown. After the movie when you pushed out the heavy doors onto Yonge Street, the sunlight was blinding. Once I saw the romantic comedy where Ann Sheridan plays George Brent's witty secretary. So I became one. I made a typewriter out of a Weldrest Hosiery box from our store. Then I arranged a red sweater on my head, just hiding my hairline, and tucked the sleeves in so it would fall like a shoulder-length 1940s pageboy, styled like Miss Sheridan might wear. I would sit alone in the middle room of our dark walk-up and type on my box and talk to the boss — his girl Friday, like I was to my dad. My desk was Mom's transatlantic steamer trunk, always covered with the same diagonally placed embroidered tablecloth from Ozarow. (I still enjoy going to the movies alone. At the Toronto Film Festival one year I saw 14 films, in empty theatres, masquerading as a member of the press, because Issy had a patron's pass for the previews. One critic asked me during intermission, "Who do you write for?" and when I answered, "*City and Country Home*" — I had written a piece for them on our cottage — he was stymied and made no comment.)

Altogether we lived in six places in North Toronto from 1938 to 1948 — from one room behind the first shop to a five-room bungalow on Cranbrooke Avenue, all within six city blocks, the extent of the world as I knew it. Whenever I stepped outside this domain, it was as foreign as a neighbouring town.

I still live in the same area, about six blocks north, and shop in some of the stores, like Young Bros., that are still around. My present home, however, has more rooms than five, some even grand. From our living room you have a pleasing long view a hundred feet through the arched doorways of five rooms, to the kitchen beyond.

Our walk-up apartment at 3267 Yonge Street, rear, which we lived in from 1941 to 1945, had three tiny rooms off a slim hallway, each with a window closely overlooking the building next door, from which it was separated by a grey gravel alley less than three feet wide. This was our first private home and I loved it. It seemed that every night when my mom and I came home from our store across the road, we would find a pool of water on the yellow and brown linoleum kitchen floor because the *shisl* (bowl) under the icebox had overflowed again. *"An andere umglik* — another pain in the neck," she would grumble as she rolled down her silk stockings, which sat above her knees over round elastic garters, and got down on all fours to mop up the flood.

It was in that apartment that I begged for a party to celebrate my eighth birthday, in 1944. This was the only birthday party my mom had attended, ever. Birthday parties were unheard of in the shtetl; my mom herself didn't have even a birthdate. But she humoured her Canadian daughter, in a rare concession, and followed instructions. She bought a cake, and I invited two friends to our dark apartment. The cake, however, turned out to be standard-issue chocolate, about six inches in diameter and plain — no Happy Birthday, no name — and when I said, "There ought to be candles," Mom brought out one fat Shabbat light.

I slept in the middle room, which doubled as the sitting room during the day. I would be put to bed every night first in my parents' bedroom, and then later my dad, breathing heavily, would lift me, still asleep, over his shoulder, depositing me on the living room couch, which had now been folded out. This sofa was as firm as a table and would not lie flat, and I had to choose the upper or lower section, so as not to roll off the step in the middle. My mom carped about the defective couch because my dad had bought it from a cousin and paid too much. *"Mit meshpokhe zol men nor in shul arayn,"* she said. "With relatives you should go to synagogue only." The couch was always covered in a pink plaid flannelette blanket. The day we moved, when I was nine, I remember sitting on that couch and tracing my finger repeatedly up, across, and down one of the darker pink squares of the blanket and vowing that I would remember that moment, that square of pink flannel, and that apartment forever.

It was not uncommon during the war for stores to be used as living quarters, and the shop below our walk-up apartment was occupied by a Mr. and Mrs. Bentley. The inside of the Bentleys' shop windows had been painted over for privacy. My mom would make snide remarks about Mrs. Bentley, calling her a *kurve* (loose woman), because she reputedly had relations with Mr. Worley, the barber in our block. I had also had relations with Mr. Worley — at the age of five. I visited the barber shop regularly to play with the barber's daughter, Dorothy, and their bright green pet parrot who would gaily proclaim, "Polly want a haircut, two bits." Mrs. Worley was grey-haired and grumpy, with a hard-done-by expression — *farkrimt* (sour). One day I came to visit when Dorothy and her mom were out. We were in the back room when Mr. Worley invited me to sit on his lap, and afterward slid his finger inside my panties; I waited a moment registering the surprise sensation, then impulsively slid off his lap and ran out. I don't know how I knew not to tell anyone.

There were other shops in our area with blanked-out windows. My school chum Lorna Chisholm lived in one where the glass was painted light grey — painted glass gave a unique effect. I would sometimes stop by to collect Lorna on the way to school. Her mom would be listening to the radio in her backless fur-trimmed mules, her hair in pink sponge curlers, a bowl of dry puffed-wheat cereal on the broad arm of the maroon velour lounge chair. Lorna had an older sister who was soon to marry a policeman, but I never saw or heard about a dad.

I preferred to pick up chums rather than have them come to my place. Sometimes I would collect Carol Welsh, whose father was principal of a public school. I would wait while she finished her piano practice. Carol had the goyish good looks I envied — platinum hair and green eyes. But apparently I did look goyish, because my relatives nicknamed me "the little *shiksele*" (gentile girl). I read the subtext: Think Yiddish and look goyish, but better not to have a *goyishe kop* (Gentile mind).

Carol lived in a red-brick house with a central hall. (Curiously, my current driving route downtown takes me past this house and also Bedford Park Public School.) The Welshes' front room had an upright piano, golden lamplight on nice old furniture, and there were always flowers — in our house there were never flowers. Carol wore smocked dresses, and her parents met in the sitting room before dinner for a drink and quiet conversation. My parents' conversation was usually confrontational. True to the shtetl, I never saw my parents drink any spirits, other than Passover wine. And *shikers* (drunks) were not respected. Someone once told me she married a Jewish man because Jews don't drink, and it may be true that alcoholism is not as common among shtetl Jews as in other groups.

It was wartime.

To me it had always been wartime.

Some foods were rationed and there were coupons for tinned salmon. Somehow Mom made me use the issued coupons illegally to procure extra tins we were not entitled to. I recall being uncomfortable asking for these in Loblaws. And this gave me a mixed message about stealing and ethics. Once I stole a small paring knife from the five-and-dime as a gift for my mom. I thought she'd praise my ingenuity, but instead she made me return it. I did not give the knife back to the sales clerk as I was bidden, but just secretly put it back in its bin.

Mom sent me daily to Macdonald's Bakery a few doors away, for milk buns folded over and sprinkled with flour. Mrs. Macdonald, the plump proprietor, always wore a white short-sleeved uniform that revealed her dimpled, doughy elbows. In the window were trays of fragrant cinnamon chelsea buns, two for a nickel. I used to love the corner ones that had a carbon glaze. Margaret Macdonald, the daughter, would wait on me. I saw Margaret as a curiosity, because Mom said she was an old maid, which I understood to be a stigma. On the counter, the Macdonalds had a huge roll of aluminum foil to be donated to the war effort, peeled one piece at a time from the customers' gum wrappers and cigarette packs. Dad listened daily, on the edge of his seat, to the newscasts of Gabriel Heater reporting on the war. During the broadcasts, no one could speak without Dad making a loud "shush."

And every year the Buy Victory Bonds man came with his wooden silkscreen box that measured about three feet by four. At every block, he would put his box down on the sidewalk (sometimes even on the glass of a store window with permission) and pull his roller across. When he lifted the box, an image in blue paint would read: THIRD VICTORY BOND or, the following year, FOURTH. The paint would fade a little with each rain, until it disappeared. Also during the war, the government issued to every shopkeeper tags labelled "Wartime Prices and Trade Board," to be pinned on every item, price included (before this, items were not priced individually). It fell to me to perform the tedious job of folding what seemed like thousands of the prickly, staple-like pins.

At school I was lucky to be chosen to sing in the choir. Miss Brethour, our coach, was as pretty and benevolent as Olivia de Havilland in *Gone with the Wind*. She was short, round, and, when she conducted, red-cheeked with enthusiasm — as proud of us as a mother warbler is of her chicks. Miss Brethour would sing along, silently shaping tall round tones outlined by her shiny red lipstick, while her arms swelled and ebbed — first beckoning the altos and then drawing in the sopranos — tilting up and down on her toes with each upbeat.

But Miss Brethour and the Bedford Park choir were to come into dishonour when we competed in the 1945 Annual Kiwanis Music Festival at Eaton Auditorium. Every school was to be judged on the same program of two songs: Offenbach's *Barcarolle* and the folk tune "When Johnny Comes Marching Home."

When it came time for our school to sing, I was second in the lineup, waiting in the wings of the colossal stage with its black-and-gold-striped curtains framing the Art Deco proscenium. How did it happen that I came to be here on the stage of the grandest theatre I had ever seen? In front of me was the audience — two floors packed with doting parents. The adorable, bright-eyed Miss Brethour bounced backstage for a quick review of the troops. A white gardenia graced the collar of the navy and white polka-dot dress that swung above her curvy calves, each leg defined by a centre seam that rose from the heels of the silk hose above her platform shoes. When the signal came, we marched out to centre stage and formed a double line — I was second from the left in the front row, in the alto section with the boys. Miss Brethour raised her arms for the downbeat, and we were off:

> *When Johnny comes marching home again, Hurrah! Hurrah!*
> *We'll give him a hearty welcome then, Hurrah! Hurrah!*
> *The men will cheer and the boys will shout,*
> *The ladies, they will all turn out …*

It was spring and the war was nearly over. People longed for their sons and lovers to come home from overseas, so the patriotic words rang out into the crowd, and everyone clapped along.

Now it was time for our second song, *Barcarolle*. We waited for the cue from the piano intro, but something went wrong with Miss Brethour's downbeat and a few of us had a false start, so we had to begin again. The Bedford Park choir placed last in the festival.

If my parents had known I didn't spend the day at school, I can imagine the dialogue:

"Rosie, *nu*, where *were* you today?"

"I was at Eaton Auditorium."

"You mean you went shopping at Eaton's instead of going to school?"

"Well no, on top of Eaton's there is a concert hall. You see, it was the Kiwanis Music Festival."

"Kiwanis — what means Kiwanis? Kiwanis Shimanis. Never mind *narishkayt* — school is where you need to go." Words like "festival" and "choir" simply did not translate into Yiddish.

Soon after the concert, the war was over and "Johnny Came Marching Home." I was about nine then, and I became a different person — the one I am today.

I remember the very moment.

I was walking east along Cranbrooke Avenue, where we had just moved into the first house we owned, a small bungalow. I was on the north side of the street just passing number 40, half a block from Yonge Street, wearing white shorts and a form-fitting white T-shirt with narrow sky-blue stripes. For the first time I was very self-conscious and cocky about how I looked. It was as if I were two people and one of me was on the other side of the street appraising the new me. I had lost my oneness, my innocence. I could no longer lose myself on a frozen puddle without being self-conscious. I miss that puddle.

My mother made it clear that she was not happy in the Wise household. She was always threatening to leave. "If I had any family here," she would say, "I would have left long ago. *Ober ikh hob nisht keyn breyre* — but I have no way out." The first time I heard this I trembled with fear, but after a while I knew she didn't have the guts. One minute she would be carping about her sad life and the next she would break into a Yiddish song.

I was often frightened in the night by my parents arguing in bed. Sometimes I worried that it was about me, but although I strained to hear, I could never make out a single word, only a rumble. Then the rumble got louder. My stomach would roll over with fear and my heart would pound and I would wait for my father's words to come to a crescendo and listen for the thud of his feet as he got out of bed. Then I worried that he might come into my room and hit me.

He came into my room only once, and I think he only yelled at me, but for some reason I spent many nights afraid that he would do something to one of us. And now I cannot even remember what my crimes were. I know my mom kvetched about how little help I was around the house. Every complaint began with "*Di keyn mol* ... You never wash the kitchen floor like other kids, you never help with the dishes," and so on. It was true I should have helped more, but her attitude was not persuasive.

My dad's limp was, for him, a source of shame. He didn't feel he was a whole man and he had little confidence or self-love. Some support and a little praise from Mom would have helped, but she seemed to agree with his appraisal. The house was a battleground, and I felt obliged to take sides. So I sided with my father; everything became black and white, and I found fault with Mom on all counts — I was quite unfair. She would carp and complain about me, her sad lot in life, her separation from her family, whose *yiches* (pedigree) was above that of my dad's family. They argued a lot over small things, and she never said anything good about any of his accomplishments, nagging instead about his failures. She simply did not appreciate him. She maintained she would have been happier back in Ozarow with her "genteel" family.

My mother and father hurled insults at each other — more like hollow barks. Mom would shout, "*Du zolst vaksn vi a tsibele mitn kop in drerd un mit di fis aroyf. Mit dir iz mir fintster in di oygn!* You should grow like an onion with your head in the ground and your feet in the air, and with you there is a black cloud in front of my eyes!"

He would counter, "*Lig ayngeleygt, ver derharget!* Shut up, drop dead!"

My dad would be very jealous if Mom danced with another man at a party, because he couldn't dance, and there would be loud words and recriminations the next day. So she took to dancing with women, which was a perfectly acceptable practice in the shtetl. (I always danced with her at parties, which on the first occasion took some courage on my part.)

Mom complained that Joe was no fun, he was a fool with money, and besides, he smelled bad. He didn't smell bad to me — I remember him limping one step at a time down to the cellar, the most remote bathroom. The ultimate blow was when, after 22 years of marriage, Mom moved out of their bedroom and began to sleep in the spare room, claiming his snoring kept her up. This was a painful event for Dad, a rite of rejection, a further slam to his self-worth.

I never once saw my parents kiss, touch, embrace, or even place an arm around the other's shoulder or waist, although I found unexpressed warmth when I sat on my dad's lap as a youngster. It is no surprise, then, that I cringe when a couple in the movies kisses open-mouthed on their first date. And I'm not easy with public displays of affection, such as when the groom pledges his love over the microphone — I much prefer wit. I'm impatient with all the tiresome social kissing that is expected today, too, especially the double-cheek business. Some shtetl people are not demonstrative, but this doesn't mean they lack feeling.

We were living at 3267, across from the store, when I was six, and it was then that I made a discovery of the most major importance — books, my great escape.

Books were my world, my friends.

It was easier to stay home than suffer the anxiety of making real friends, and at home it didn't matter that I wore funny clothes. And with books I could block out the noise of my parents arguing. Storybooks especially were my passion. The earliest one I remember is Kenneth

Grahame's *The Wind in the Willows*, read to the class a chapter a day by our Grade 1 teacher, Miss Sharpe. I could hardly wait to get to school to hear the next episode in the adventures of Mole and Toad and Water Rat.

Then I joined the most important club — and the only club, besides a tennis club, to which I would ever belong — the library. St. Clements Library was a one-storey green and white cottage set well back from Yonge Street in a wide lawn — like an enchanting English storybook house. It was a mile and a half walk from home, but for me it was a regular stop.

Reading was my refuge. One time I got a book early in the morning, read it, and returned later the same day for another. The librarian refused with these bone-chilling words: "See here, it is plainly stamped on the card pocket at the back of each volume, 'A book may not be returned on the day on which it is borrowed.'" I left the library that day very downcast. But it was a good lesson in learning to accept those things you cannot change.

The *Doctor Doolittle* books were favourites of mine. I remember exactly where they were in the library: on the second shelf up from the brown linoleum floor in the southwest corner. This series of narrow volumes, taking up a space on the shelf as long as my arm, was illustrated with simple pen-and-ink line drawings by the author, Hugh Lofting. (Pen and ink is still today my own medium of choice.) When Doctor Doolittle was played on the screen by Rex Harrison, I stubbornly refused to see the film, because I would not exchange *my* Doctor D. for a Hollywood impostor.

Another book I loved was *The Princess and the Goblin*, by George MacDonald. The princess travels through subterranean caves on craggy ledges but is always safely guided by a magic gossamer thread she follows with her forefinger. The goblin community has some laughs at her expense when they discover that the ends of her feet are divided into five parts, called toes, while real feet like theirs have only two parts.

I read like a mad fiend, my face often safely hidden by the book. I read at the dinner table, while walking to school, and late into the night. As a teenager, I stayed home to finish my book instead of going out on a date.

My mother would implore me to stop: "Rose — please — put the book away already. You'll ruin your eyes." In fact, I did wear glasses, because I had one lazy eye that strayed and from time to time my nose would loom into view. My parents explained to friends that unfortunately I was *shikldik* (cross-eyed), a *kalike* (damaged goods). My dad, who had little faith in doctors, tore off my glasses and said, "These glasses are doing no good. Your eyes will be stronger and straighten out better without them," and he proved to be right. I never again wore the ugly wire-rimmed glasses.

I'm still a reader and I always have a book on hand. Books are still comforts and friends — unlike people, who you have to get to know too well.

When I was eight, I began to nag and beg my parents for two things: a bicycle and a baby brother. I got both. *"Hak mir nisht keyn tshaynik.* Don't nag. Don't bang on a teakettle," Mom would say.

"But, Mom," I argued, "Dad rode a bicycle in Ozarow, so it's not *narishkayt*, and I can ride to school like other kids."

New bikes were expensive because it was wartime, so my dad bought me a rusty used one that once must have been a maroon colour. He paid $35 for it, and for once I agreed with my mom that Dad had been taken. Of course, I didn't give her the credit. I bullheadedly maintained my censorious stand against her. My bike soon had a flat tire, and when the mechanic at Gerber's Gas Station uncovered the inner tube, it was so plastered with small rubber patches that it looked like Joseph's coat of many colours.

One day Mom wore a small guilty smile when I again brought up the subject of "Please, why can't I have a baby brother like other girls?" Although she loved pretty dresses, she now seemed to have lost all sense of fashion and had taken to wearing the same stained dress day after day — a shapeless wraparound affair in a faded teal blue. Then I caught her giggling on the phone that her daughter was teasing her about this dress. Later, when my brother was born, I figured it out — this was her version of a maternity dress. She also told her friends that she didn't need to tell her daughter anything about sex because the brilliant kid already knew everything.

"Everything" had been explained to me by Florence Bongard, who lived upstairs from my aunt Khayele, Dad's sister. On one of our Sunday visits to 325 College Street, in the Jewish ghetto, Florence told me about men and women, and which part of each body went where, a stunning and preposterous manoeuvre. But she also told me that men menstruated monthly like women, but that the stuff that came out was white. I held on to this misconception until I was 16 and almost gave away my ignorance in health class, which I quickly covered up when I caught on.

Stanley Barrie Wise was born when I was nine, and he was named after my mother's brother Shloime. In the Jewish tradition you are named after the closest deceased relative, a person you therefore will never know, and the name recurs every few generations. Mom recuperated from the birth, complainingly, in the Western Hospital, where she stayed for two weeks. When I visited, she was wearing her black "wrapper" with the bouquets of bright flowers and was walking very slowly, bent over and holding her *rukn* (back) and kvetching, *"Oy vey iz mir,* oh pain." Since then I have always liked textiles with florals printed on a black background.

Whenever my mom found my behaviour trying, she would remind me of the many torments I had caused her. She never tired of telling me the story that she had been in the hospital for "three days and three nights" giving birth to me and also that I was the only child in the city to have contracted chicken pox and measles simultaneously. She would often use standard Yiddish curses that made me laugh. They seemed harsh but were more benign than they sounded: *"Ikh hob dikh in bod"* — literally "I have you in the bath" — or *"A fayer zol ir trefn* — she should meet with a fire" or *"Shlog mitn kop in vant* — go bang your head against a wall" or *"Dayne kinder zoln dir breyngen di zelbe tsores* — you should have the same troubles from your own children." Oh, gladly would I settle for the same troubles from my boys.

My new baby brother, Stan, arrived home with a greenish complexion from a touch of jaundice — not the pink doll-baby I had hoped for. But soon his colour improved and he began to smile. Mom said it was just gas. Now my life changed forever as I took charge of the baby. There is a shtetl tradition that a sister should look out for a brother, because women should always defer to brothers and husbands.

Which brings to mind Isaac Bashevis Singer's shtetl story where an elderly wife dutifully wants the best of everything for her husband and buys only the best cut of meat for Him, and cooks the best soup for Him, and ultimately procures for Him a younger woman so He should have the sex that He deserves.

Stan should be grateful, because he owes me a lot: I saw to it that he had swimming lessons, that he can roller skate and ice skate, that he has a middle name, that he's in this world at all, and that he has one single photo of himself before the age of nine. For this photo, I took him downtown on the streetcar to Starkman's Chemists, who had offered "a free baby photo with any small purchase." We waited in line the whole day with all the other mothers and babes.

I was also charged with taking care of Stan from after school until bedtime, and on weekends. I was forbidden to stay after school. According to my dad, who had never attended school, only bad kids had to stay. One day the teacher kept the whole class in. I went up to her and pleaded that I was expected at home to take care of my brother — *or else* — but she refused to make an exception. My father was screamingly angry and would not accept my story. (Another time the teacher asked that everyone buy a paperback math workbook for 59 cents. My father said, "No, the school provides all the books." So I was the only one in the class without one and had to read a story while the others entered sums in their enviable math books.)

Meanwhile, my brother and I became inseparable. We are still best friends — he and his wife, Martha, live just a short bike ride away. As a baby, he was plump and cuddly, often wearing a pair of soft, homemade pale blue flannel overalls, and I loved his trusting weight in my arms. What was he thinking, I wondered, when he stared with such an unblinking gaze at the wind rustling the leaves? He would sit, easygoing, in his carriage with his dark chocolate eyes and brown curly hair, looking like an Arab prince.

One Saturday a friend and I wanted to go to a movie in the early evening, but Stan didn't go to bed till about eight, so I hit upon a plan to make him sleepy. My friend had a bottle in her medicine cabinet with the label "Contains ether," and I had read the Nancy Drew mystery novel where ether figured in one of her crime cases. So we opened the bottle and put it near Stan's nose. Well, he squirmed and refused to sniff, and as we followed his nose with the bottle, some of the liquid may have dribbled into his mouth and he began to scream. I called Webb's Pharmacy, as my mother always did for all medical advice, and Mr. Webb prescribed milk as an antidote. So we plied Stan with milk while he continued to protest. That evening, Mom came home early from work and gave Stan a bath, during which he tried repeatedly to tell her the story of his bad day. Luckily, I was the only one who could understand his baby talk. "*Vos zogt er* — what is he talking?" said my mother. "I can't understand one word."

On one of our long walks, Stan and I passed Loretto Abbey, a girls' boarding school. It looked to me like a fairytale stone castle, with its towers and crenellations — as Victorian as the one in *Wuthering Heights*. I boldly walked up to the door and rang the bell. A nun in full skirts answered the door. "Please," I asked, "may I come in and look around your beautiful mansion?" She graciously invited us in. I parked Stan and his carriage in the front hall, put on the brake, and followed the nun for an hour-long tour of the place. When she showed me the bedrooms for the boarders decorated with floral fabrics and white furniture, I gladly would have converted and moved right in.

Even my own school, Bedford Park, was fascinating because it was palatial, with its Doric columns, broad staircases, and so much light from the six tall windows in each classroom. The ancient date of 1911 was carved into the stone lintel over the entrance.

I suppose gracious old buildings will continue to fascinate me. Once recently in Palm Springs, I was riding my bike to the market as usual when I passed a handsome early-'30s house. Of course I was curious to see the inside, so I knocked on the door. The beautiful blond woman who answered was at first a little wary when I said, "We have a house of similar vintage and I'd love to have a look, and perhaps you would like to see our place just around the corner." This was my introduction to two former Hollywood people who are good friends to this day, Pamela and Irvin Green, the founder of Mercury Records. They often remind me of how we first met.

Perhaps my love for old buildings came from my dad — he had the mind of an architect-designer. In Ozarow he had settled for the profession of tailor because there were few opportunities open to Jews, but in Canada he reached his full potential. The man was gifted. He took our storefront on Yonge Street from the ordinary to the extraordinary. The existing store window was flush with the sidewalk, and my father redesigned it by pushing it back into a glamorous U-shape, so there was twice as much window display. The glass was curved, in three sections, with a terrazzo entrance floor and a black sign in Vitrolite (a glass material) with silver letters.

Business improved because there were now more items on display to entice passersby. My dad dressed the windows and I made all the signs advertising the specials: LADIES' HOUSEDRESSES, MEN'S WORKING SOCKS, CHILDREN'S COATS, HATS & LEGGINGS, and BOYS' BRITCHES. Mom would look at my work and say, "She has *goldene hent* — golden hands." Customers often wanted only that item in the window, especially if it was the last one; then Dad would have to crawl, mutteringly, on all fours into his carefully arranged display.

It struck me as curious that Dad — super-tailor that he was — did not make his own suits but had them cut to measure (with two pair of pants) at Tip Top Tailors up the street. Of course, in the 1930s, a man didn't count for much without a nice suit, silk tie, and felt fedora. And then, each spring, a Jewish old-clothes peddler would come by and bargain for Dad's suit from the previous year.

One day when my father was downtown buying inventory, two policemen came into the store while I was sitting on the lone chair reading. When I called Mom from the sewing machine in the back room, one of them told her, "Mrs. Wise, we're sorry to inform you, but there may be some bad news about Mr. Wise. An hour ago we found a dead man near the Danforth and he was wearing a suit jacket with the name 'Joseph Wise' printed on the lining."

Mom was hysterical: "Nooo, noo, *oy gotenu*, oh God, it can't be. It's not possible — he just went down to Matlow's on York Street to get socks and underwear for the store. It must be a mistake, *reboyne shel Oylem*, God help us."

"Mrs. Wise, I hope you're right, but just to be sure, please come along with us to the morgue. We'll need you to identify the body."

The officers took her arm and the three of them climbed into the curbside cruiser, leaving me on the red leatherette chair to mind the store and to wonder. Maybe it was just a few minutes later when I heard the click of the back door, and who should it be but Dad, schlepping his brown-paper packages by their string handles.

When Mom returned, she gave us the story. Apparently a vagrant (i.e., "the body" — I regret I never did ask her what he looked like) had jumped or was pushed from the Bloor viaduct to the road 200 feet below. An embroidered label on the inside pocket read, "Joseph Wise, Tip Top Tailors." When we remembered the peddler, the story began to come together.

My father graduated from tailor-shopkeeper to builder-landlord with the construction of a cement block one-car garage behind the store. It happened like this: A truck arrived and dropped about 200 ten-inch cement blocks in the yard. Then Dad went off to the Selective Service, a government organization that provided pickup work for unskilled labourers. He recruited John Brennan, a new immigrant. Brennan was average height, young and muscular, with reddish curly hair, blue eyes, and an Irish brogue. He looked like the actor Albert Finney. He had some experience in building — we didn't know how much — but he knew more than Dad, so he became the adviser.

"Well, to be sure now, Mr. Wise, first off, we'll be needing to dig us some footings four feet deep."

"Four feet, John? But the building is only seven feet high. Maybe two feet should be okay?"

"Well, to be sure now, Mr. Wise, 'tis the regulation, and if you don't dig a four-foot foundation, the building will be heaving, it will, come the first frost."

Dad reluctantly agreed to the unplanned-for extra cost and Mr. Brennan soon finished the handsome block building. This one-car garage was not for *our* car, but to be rented out at $15 per month. Privately I thought, "Dad has a lot of chutzpah to ask such a high rent — who would pay that much for a garage?" When that cheque rolled in regularly, even Mom and I were impressed, and she made the $15 go a long way. And Dad thought, "What a simple way to make a living — no inventory." So from that time on, 1944, when my dad was 33, he became a builder-landlord, although we still kept the store another five years.

Business was brisk at Wise's Dry Goods, so we bought our first house when I was nine. It was a five-room bungalow at 165 Cranbrooke Avenue. Steps ran up a steep hill to a path that led to the front door. Dad cut out the hill, jacked up the front of the house, and put a garage under the front porch, with flagstone steps curving from the driveway, which was now on grade, up to the front door. A piece of genius, although we were never sure if the jacked-up house was safe from collapse, because Dad knew nothing about engineering or building, and again relied on John to do the job. The neighbours next door, whose bungalow sat on the same hill, soon copied Dad's architectural design and made their house a mirror image of ours.

I recall Dad and John Brennan at the kitchen table over coffee and a cheese Danish, poring over plans for the next project. John continued as my dad's right-hand man for his next few buildings — one at a time — stores with one or two apartments above them. Then there were three stores in a row at Eglinton and Keele, and with the purchase of a ten-plex on Wilson Avenue, Dad's life on the third cushion of the living room sofa began in earnest. Ever since Dad had become a landlord, his routine never varied. He went out for coffee at six, came home, sat on the sofa all day, read the newspapers, watched the news on TV — sometimes the wrestling program, a favourite of Mom's — waited for the mail to bring cheques from the tenants, and maybe went out to the bank or shopping for food with his wife. On these occasions, he always waited in the car — so no one would see his limp.

One time I was shopping on Eglinton Avenue near Oakwood, about 1950. Three red fire engines, each following the other, came screeching down the street, so loud I could feel it in my solar plexus. One of my dad's stores was located a few blocks in the direction the fire trucks were rushing. The thought came, "Could it be that Dad's store is on fire? No, it couldn't be — it's never the *known* evil that gets you."

I headed in that direction. It was our store that was on fire.

Our store — before and after — designed by Dad, who made the children's wool coats, hats, and leggings (right) from his own patterns.

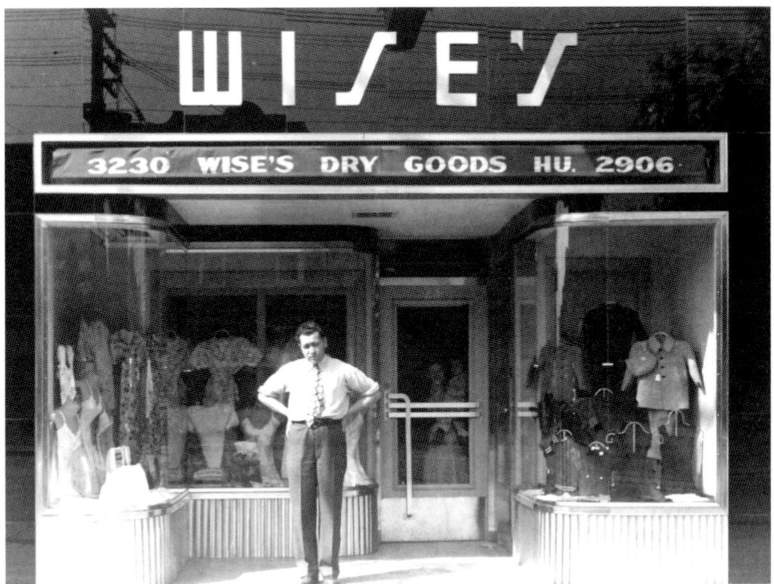

I watched forever (a year) while stone masons laid row after row of limestone blocks. Would it ever be finished? I missed the opening in Jan. 1949 by a few days, when we moved out of the district. Not until 1962 would I step into this grand library. Then Jordy and I became card-carrying members of the George H. Locke Library at Yonge and Lawrence.

Me and my constant companion, Prince Stanley, at Lawrence Park with all the other mothers and babes.

Stanley Barrie Wise marries Martha Kohn. Stan says he and I were very lucky in our choice of mates.

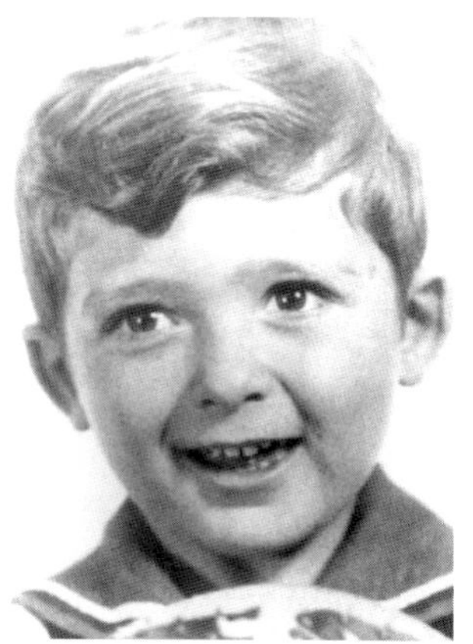

We lined up the whole day at Starkman's Chemists for this free photo.

Loretto Abbey, the castle I longed to see inside.

At 176 Bowood Avenue, we rented the upstairs front bedroom and the room behind.

The Wises in front of our car on Cranbrooke Avenue.

Our first house, 165 Cranbrooke Avenue — before and after. The upstairs window was fake. Dad was a self-taught designer. This house, the store, and a rear garage were the beginning of his career as a builder.

CHAPTER THREE

Teler Fun Himl

THE SAUCER FROM HEAVEN

I was almost a year younger than my high school crowd because my mom had needed me out of the way when I was little and had enrolled me in kindergarten early, at age four. Her last words as she had dropped me off at the Bedford Park School were, "Now, *gedeynk shoyn, Rifkele* — remember, Rosie, your birthday is November 23, not February 23." Thankfully no one asked for my birthdate till Grade 3, though, and by then I forgot to lie. But I quickly recovered and told Miss Robinson, the teacher, "Sorry. I made a mistake. February 23 is my cousin Norman's birthday." God was on my side, and luckily my teacher did not challenge me further. Miss Robinson was small, narrow, with a mannish haircut from the '30s, and she never smiled. I remember she was sometimes preoccupied with blowing her long nose into her hanky, closely examining the deposit, folding the hanky fastidiously to a clean spot, and repeating the process.

Second-year high school.

So with my two dates of birth, in Grade 9 I was younger on average than the rest of the class, and also the smallest. Needing an explanation, I gave out that I had "skipped." I got along well with the boys in high school, but I wasn't a great social success with my crowd of girls. One of them called me a "kook," which I didn't even know how to spell but knew was no compliment. In high school, being a freak is a disadvantage at first, but soon it becomes a distinction; to be named a true eccentric is praise indeed. In later years of school, I began to see the value in being a kook. Thereafter I didn't feel the need to fit in, to be like everyone else, as I had so longed to be as a child.

The girls in my class had more of the world's goods than I did. Once I was visiting a classmate, Elaine Levine, and she showed me all her "cashmeres," which was another new word for me and I had to ask for an explanation. I felt no envy because I didn't want to change places with Elaine. I considered my meagre wardrobe only an inconvenience. I owned just a couple of skirts I had made on our treadle machine, and every morning I ironed one of my five white cotton blouses, which I had washed by hand the night before. We had no washing machine — Mom washed the clothes on a washboard that sat inside the laundry tub down in the cement-floor cellar, where the 40-watt bulb gave little light. Just as I never helped her with the housework, Mom never washed my shirts. Each morning I would decorate my blouse with a scarf or a ribbon to try to compete with the other girls who wore a new outfit every day.

Two years later, when I met my future husband at 16, my entire wardrobe consisted of about three Singer skirts and five blouses swinging freely in my closet. The skirts I sewed were wool plaid, box-pleated, the pleats stitched following the lines in the plaid. Even my formal dress for the high school prom was a tulle homemade evening skirt topped by a store-bought bustier, costing a total of $14.

My boyfriend — Issy — bought me a red cashmere skirt-and-sweater set for Valentine's Day, and the next day he sent the same outfit again, in a cognac colour, for "the day after Valentine's." These items were firsts for me; like my mother and her sisters in the shtetl, I had few store-bought clothes. But I did not feel deprived. I would not have traded places with someone who had a fancy wardrobe because I preferred the package that I was and felt resourceful enough to put myself together with flair.

My raw materials for the sewing machine were sale fabrics from Eaton's, where I sorted through the table of remnants folded in squares, each labelled with its price and yardage. Once I bought a yard remnant of chartreuse green chiffon printed with tiny multicoloured flowers. I ran up a sleeveless sheath-style dress for the price of one dollar and wore it that same evening. And — early signs of my interior design flair — I also found a length of printed pink fabric with a small black-and-white figure, to cover my armless bedroom lounge chair. There was not enough material for the back, and one side of the chair was also missing some covering. The chair had to be stationed in a corner with its back against the wall, and I was always conscious of this fault. I protected the chair by standing on its weak side — nervous that visitors to my bedroom would discover the deception.

Although I might have occasionally carped about my few clothes and the many other limitations of our shtetl household, there is a value in privation. I used to tell my kids that I was sorry the one thing I could never provide for them was deprivation.

I might have been a social flop with the girls at school, but the boys nominated me for Prom Queen. I lost. Truer to my interests, I took the initiative to direct the decorations for the dances. For the prom, I conceived a tipping champagne glass 15 feet high, fashioned from chicken wire. I wanted to try out for cheerleader, but didn't, because I couldn't do a cartwheel — I'm a congenital physical coward. On the debating team I was involuntarily propelled to make my case centre stage instead of from behind the lectern. Finally, there was some status from being the third member of a singing trio that included Carol Weinstein, our music coach and pianist, and lead singer Dorothy Goldhar. We called ourselves the Three Graces, and for the school's variety show we dressed in matching tight white sweaters and flared black quilted skirts. I recall standing in the wings just itching to go onstage to sing "Chattanooga Choo-Choo." (These days I tremble whenever I speak in public — although no one has detected this so far.) Our trio even had an audition for television's *The Denny Vaughan Show*, with a repertoire that was mainly Cole Porter's "Just One of Those Things," punctuated with a lot of *doo-ahs*. We never heard from Mr. Vaughan.

I also had an interest in languages. On the first day of French class, from the moment Mr. Mckewen entered the classroom, I was fixated on his fly, and it was a year-long struggle to keep my eyes on his face. A fly struck me as too obvious a device to hide something functional yet so secret and mysterious. Mr. Mckewen introduced French by giving us a short dictation in this language we knew nothing about. The dictations were marked and returned the next day. I noticed I had three mistakes, which didn't look good until he announced, "Miss Wise had the top mark by quite a margin." And so it went through high school that I was top of the class in languages.

Monsieur Casaubon, my final-year French teacher, suggested I try for the scholarship in French. I declined because I had no interest in becoming a translator or a teacher. He was disappointed. Nevertheless, I decided to take four languages in Grade 13 so I wouldn't need to study, and so I could avoid math. But I was missing two subjects, Latin and German. So I borrowed the Grade 10, 11, and 12 textbooks and taught myself three years of Latin, studying one lesson every lunch hour. I had never attended a single Latin class before writing the Grade 12 Easter exam, and I got an 82, a mystery because I was just trying for a pass. Mr. Tough, the principal, congratulated me over the school P.A. system and I was surprised he even knew my name.

German was another language I taught myself, again writing the exam without going to classes. (Here I only had to make up two years, and German was simple because it was related to Yiddish.) My facility for languages was more a matter of remembering vocabulary and spelling than of speaking. I've never been adept at speaking French, or any other second language, for that matter. To my parents I owe the determination and work ethic it took to learn two languages on my own.

But math was another matter. I had no mind for it at all. Higher math is still a mystery to me. Geometry and trigonometry I would surely have failed, and I've quite forgotten how to do long division. Spelling and calligraphy are still my two best skills, but both have become archaic arts, having been capably mastered by the computer. It would have been more useful to know how to swim.

Handwriting back at Bedford Park in the 1940s was considered an art — important enough to be marked by the principal of the school. Somewhere among my papers I have my penmanship workbook signed by R.C. Cameron. I could hardly wait for Grade 3, when the empty inkwells in each desk were filled with the risky blue-black ink that could not be erased. We were taught just how to hold the wooden pen and each stroke was to be evenly parallel at an angle of one o'clock.

One day in high school, Monsieur Casaubon announced that there would be an opportunity to live with a French family for the summer in Trois Pistoles, Québec. I wanted to go more than anyone in the class; it sounded so exotic, as wonderfully strange as one of Margaret Mead's field trips to New Guinea. I would have been willing to suffer any privation to go. But I never even mentioned it to my parents because, as with skates, they would not have understood. It would have been tantamount to asking for "*dos teler fun himl* — the saucer from heaven" — like asking for the moon. My parents would not even let me sleep at a friend's house, or baby-sit, so how would they let me go to Québec?

Another trip came up the next summer, when my friends Merle Shain and Carol Weinstein were going to Europe for two months. I would have killed to go with them, but of course I made no mention to my parents of this trip either. Merle, I remember, bought an entire wardrobe of drip-dry clothes in black and white, so they would mix and match.

These unresolved yearnings to travel somewhat dampened my eventual first trip to Europe, because the reality could never compete with my dream — a concept I later found a name for in V.S. Naipaul's book *The Enigma of Arrival*. Naipaul describes making the trip of his dreams to India, the land of his forbears, only to find garbage floating in the harbour. If I had gone to Trois Pistoles, my expectations would probably have been dashed then by the "enigma of arrival." As I recall, Sandy Title, one of the girls who did go, got bitten by a dog and had to return home.

The summer that Merle and Carol went to Europe, I went to work in a sweatshop that looked like a Hollywood set for a Lower East Side factory before the advent of unions. Mom had found me the job at her cousin Meyer Riba's sweatshop Reliable Embroidery on Adelaide Street West. He was a third cousin, her closest relative. On the Monday morning, I arrived at 7:30 and walked down the steps to the factory, which was below ground. The air inside was steamy. About six men were operating pressers covered in wet grey cloth and a dozen or so women were bent over sewing machines, embroidering "His" and "Hers" on guest towels. No one looked up.

Uncle Meyer showed me how to punch the clock and ushered me to my summer station — cutting a roll of men's handkerchiefs one at a time, with a huge pair of scissors. The hankies were pulled along a table from a bolt on a roller. After the first hour, I was ready to leave. "How," I thought, "can I possibly last till lunch? Well, I'll definitely quit at the end of the day." But I came back the next day with my blistered hand bandaged, and stubbornly worked that mind-numbing job for eight endless weeks, before school resumed. When once I forgot to punch the clock till noon, I lost the morning's wages. My summer's earnings would later finance two dental bridges to replace baby teeth that should have been pulled.

Back at school in September, my friend Merle, home from her summer in Europe, sat behind me in class. She wanted to be a writer, but I doubted she could achieve this, given that she couldn't spell. Disdainfully I watched her write uphill with her left hand, a wavy indecipherable scrawl, smearing the ink with her arm as she went. *Some Men Are More Perfect Than Others*, the first of her three books, written when she was in her 30s, was a bestseller. But as fine a writer as she was, Merle was very unlucky in love, with many failed relationships. I tried to pick up the pieces, but eventually she became emotionally fragile.

When she was about 40, I took her to New York for a weekend to distract her from yet another lost love. Like most women, including me, the love of a man was more important to Merle than any vocation or prestige.

But back in school, she was a very strong character, imitating the father she had lost at age 14. She was quite overweight, so she went on an apple diet and lost 25 pounds, which she kept off for the rest of her life. We were the same age, but she was much wiser and she became my mentor. Once when I was plotting my revenge against someone who had wronged me, Merle taught me to "heap coals of fire on his head" — a concept I have continued to value. The phrase, from Romans 12:20, translates: disarm your enemy by kindness — feed him if he's hungry and give him a drink if he's thirsty. In so doing, the guilt will be on his head.

Sadly, Merle Shain died when she was 53, of unexpected heart failure.

With high school ending, I had to decide what I wanted to be — apart from married — which was the first thing on my parents' agenda. Was it art school to be a window dresser or sign painter or fashion designer — or English to be a journalist? I decided against art school, because I was in the academic stream and it seemed more sophisticated to follow Merle and my brainy friends to university. At the University of Toronto, the "ologies" appealed because they sounded so esoteric — particularly anthropology. I had read Margaret Mead and fantasized about fieldwork on some undeveloped South Pacific island. But the truth is, I knew I couldn't handle the mosquitoes, the risky food, and the celibate life.

I had reached the age when romance was everything. Ever since Mr. Rochester had cantered down the road on horseback and swept Charlotte Brontë's Jane Eyre off her feet, I was on the lookout for just such a man. Or even Heathcliff from Emily Brontë's *Wuthering Heights*, played by Lawrence Olivier, my movie heartthrob for years. I had that strong prerequisite for romantic love, my love for my father — which is quite a mystery, because he did, after all, *derlang* me — give me a whack — once in a while. But nevertheless we loved each other deeply, and I found him quite sexy.

I recall a few public school crushes. There was Rodney Anderson in Grade 5 until he transferred to Upper Canada College. Rodney was blond, poised, and wore a tie and V-necked sleeveless cable-stitch sweater every day. He didn't know my name. The next time I met him, when we were in our 30s, he was a genius musicologist — and still didn't know me. In Grade 7, I had a serious crush on my English teacher, Mr. Vyvian. He was dark, reserved, and formal. I'm sorry I didn't question why he had asked Miss Wise, the only Jew in the class, to read the part of Shylock.

Finally, when I was nearly 15, Morley Markson asked me out on a date and came to collect me on his motorcycle. On the spot, my father said, "Don't let me see him here now or ever again." Dad screened each boyfriend carefully. He had to be Jewish and studious, with good prospects, and he had to bring me home, in the same condition in which I had left, by 11 p.m. I was not to wear lipstick or makeup, bare-necked dresses or high-heeled shoes. I'm surprised I had any offers at all, because at 14 my arms and legs were like sticks, and I was the only girl in my class with a flat chest — the bane of my existence. I would say to my mom, "How can you be so sure that I'll grow breasts? God can't remember everybody." My mom refused to let me buy a bra. "You're so *mazeldik* — lucky — to be small," she said. "What do you need them for? They just get in the way." So there I was in high school, still wearing an undershirt. Finally I bought a size 30A bra and stuffed it with hankies. I was mortified one day when my dad came into my room and spied a hanky sticking out of my bra. He just scowled and said nothing.

But Dad was pleased when I dated Steve Borins, who became a judge, and Harry Arthurs, who became the dean of Osgoode Hall Law School and later the president of York University. My dad also okayed Howard Levin, a dental student, who came to collect me in his Hudson car. My friend was a bit miffed that I was not impressed with this rare vehicle — today I still classify cars by colour only. Howie left me in the Hudson near Fran's Restaurant on Eglinton and soon returned with two hamburgers and French fries. This was my first-ever store-bought hamburger. Mom ground her own patties, claiming, "You never know what the butcher puts in ground meat." She would clamp the cast aluminum grinder onto the kitchen counter and push the bloody chunks through the top and wind the crank, issuing red meat worms through a disc in the side.

I unwrapped Howard's hamburger, took one bite of the pink non-kosher patty, and pleaded a late lunch.

Which reminds me of a later Hamburger story: in the 1980s, Issy and I were vacationing in Morocco. We were barrelling along an empty highway which wound like a steel blue ribbon through the golden sand of the Sahara desert, and there was nothing in sight — no buildings, no cars, only a solitary speck in the distance which up close turned out to be a Berber in a grey-and-white-striped djellaba, walking along the side of the road with his crooked stick. We came across a small hut with the sign

"Drinks," so we stopped. Suddenly a sleek silver bus appeared and pulled up at the shop. The licence plate read "Hamburg." How, I wondered, did they drive here? (By way of Gibraltar was the answer.) Out hopped about 70 overweight Hamburgers carrying brown-bag lunches and folding chairs. Each bag revealed one fat pink bratwurst.

Once, in high school, with my Saturday-afternoon earnings from the Ah Young Fruit Market, I bought a pair of clunky, low-heeled, beige old-maid sandals. For no apparent good reason, my father's dybbuk rose up in him and he went ballistic. I guess he thought the shoes were too sexy. He opened the front door, stepped onto the verandah, wound up like a baseball pitcher, and threw those shoes so far that they landed in the middle of the road. I thought he had lost his senses. My mom said, *"Gey aroys* — quick, go for a walk around the block till he cools off," our usual routine when Dad got his dander up. When I returned, he was sitting sheepishly on the sofa, as if the incident had never happened.

My father must have been afraid I would get pregnant like his sister Pearl had at age 15, but he didn't have the skills to communicate this fear. He needn't have worried; even in high school I innocently believed that no one had sex before marriage. And I had a mistaken idea of what sex was. I didn't know sperm was involved and had never heard the word "erection" or that such a condition was a prerequisite for penetration. My first real boyfriend, Issy, would convince me that it was unnatural not to have sex, so of course my dad was right about his fears. And I did, in fact, become pregnant, which no one ever knew. This has always been my darkest secret.

It all began when I was going on 17. My high school friend Pearl Lottman was getting married, and I was a bridesmaid. It so happened that the groom, Leonard Godfrey, was Issy's first cousin, so seated at one of the round banquet tables at the wedding was the Sharp family. After dinner, Isadore came to the bridesmaids' table and asked me for a dance. He was wearing blue suede shoes, and with his slim build he carried his clothes like a model.

That night we first met we had a few dances, and I tried my best to keep up with his nimble jitterbug, but he was too quick on his feet and far too good for me. Besides, I like to claim that the boogie-woogie was before my time — he was four and a half years older.

I'm still trying to get the hang of it. Otherwise, we are quite attuned to each other on the dance floor. Invariably at parties people come up and say, "You move like Fred Astaire and Ginger Rogers." Mostly they tell Issy that *he* is a great dancer — to this I should reply as Ginger did: "I do the same steps he does, but I do them backwards." When we waltz, I am transported, sometimes airborne, and devil-may-care about falling. I fix my eyes on Issy's nose to keep my balance — the fixed point ballerinas need when spinning.

The day after the night of our first encounter, I confessed to Merle that I had met "*the* man," but told her he probably would not call. He didn't, for at least a week. Then he invited me out to a movie at the Imperial Theatre: Jerry Lewis in *Sailor Beware*. We took the two aisle seats about 10 rows from the front on the right side. The film had hardly begun when Issy slid down in his seat and promptly fell asleep, even snoring a little. In his construction days, he was on the job by 6:30. I was in awe that he could be so cool on a first date. What an accomplishment! I have yet to fall asleep in public, or take a nap at home, for that matter. Naps are a waste of time. Sleep for me is at night, in bed, in pajamas, in a running position, with blankets to my chin.

Well, after that night Issy and I became an item, a dubious union because we were not at all alike. All my previous dates had been more the nerdy types, while Issy seemed to be a sports person, and sports was a subject about which I knew nothing. From a young age, he had been involved in every athletic activity of the season. He didn't mind body-checks in hockey or broken ribs from football. He was game for anything — even cheerleading and double dutch with the girls.

Issy was always a team player. He still is. I've heard him say in many speeches to his employees that sports taught him how to handle defeat and also how to lead a team. I played no sports. Perhaps that's why I'm usually such a sore loser.

As different as we were, we were magnetically drawn together. I loved his sweet nature — although I did think he was a Casanova and a risky choice for a husband, a likely philanderer. I was right, because Issy did have a few dalliances during the time we were courting and "knew" each other.

But I had no choice. I was smitten.

We enjoyed our differences. I taught him to like Chinese food and black-and-white movies with subtitles, and to read the book I had just finished, and he taught me how to ski and the benefits of physical culture, including sex. And, later, a lot more about wisdom and how to count to 10 before speaking my mind, which I rarely remember. He was wise, kind, and smart — an unbeatable combination.

My dad was not at all pleased with our alliance, though. He didn't think Issy was such a *gantse metsie* — a big bargain. A son-in-law in the building business was not his ideal. He was hoping for a doctor or a lawyer, or at least an accountant.

One day, Dad and I came to an impasse when he decreed that I was no longer to go out with Isadore because one of Dad's cronies had seen Issy in a bar the night before with a shikse. I did, however, go out with Issy one more time after this command, and when I came home from school the next day, my father had locked me out of the house — yet another of Dad's communication problems. So I went to Issy's job site on Roselawn Avenue, where he was building an apartment house, and said, "Issy, I don't know where to turn because my dad is angry at my disobedience and I'm locked out."

"Well, don't worry, it'll be all right. We'll go and talk to him," said my friend, who always faces a problem head on — "sang-froid" is the word that now pops into my mind.

I was embarrassed, but nevertheless I walked meekly behind Issy up the concrete path and the four steps to my front door, hoping my parents would let us in. I can still see, in front of me, Issy's rubber boots with the grey lining worn where the boots were folded. He looked very handsome. He wore an open shirt. His sun-bleached eyebrows and curly copper hair matched his rust suede sports jacket, which hung loosely on a lean, hard body — the body he still has.

We found my dad reading *The Telegram*, sitting woodenly on the couch, where he could always be found. Issy began making his case politely and quietly in his positive, winning way, and my father was obviously impressed. As Issy spoke, I saw my father's expression transform from haughty self-righteousness to the subdued demeanour of a humbled child. From that time, my father fell in my eyes. At that Freudian moment when Issy took charge, I transferred my allegiance from my father to my lover.

Issy has always felt that sex is as natural and vital in a relationship as any other form of communication. He still does. So he persuaded me that premarital sex was the norm. This was a big surprise to me. I was absolutely certain that all good girls were chaste until the marriage bed — and that virginity was the gift a girl saved for her husband. At school there was gossip about the one bad girl, Barbara of the big breasts. It was rumoured she was easy, and had known Jim and John and had done the lot with Henry. But Issy told me that my Victorian attitude about sex was outdated, and after all, he was 25 per cent older than me and seriously persuasive. So we took to driving to romantic lanes after the movies, and he showed me how it was done. The steering wheel, I remember, was always in the way. But, although I admit I was a promiscuous teenager, I have only ever known one man, which makes me what — a virgin, once removed?

Now I was 19, and my parents and I were invited to the Sharps' house for Shabbat dinner. During dessert Issy surprised me with a magnificent diamond ring, platinum with a large round stone. I was thrilled, although at some level I would have preferred a ring he had made by hand out of some humble material like copper wire, because I was a declared snob about clichés like diamond rings and mink coats. Nevertheless, I remember sitting on our stairway landing later that night under the chandelier and marvelling at the prismatic colours in the stone. It was spring and we were to be married in the fall on a *mazeldik* Tuesday. We decided on a Tuesday because on that day, according to the Book of Genesis, God was particularly pleased with his creation. Not once, but twice, he smugly "saw that it was good." (On the Monday, he had not given his new-made world even a mention.)

Issy's mom, Lil, was very pleased with me. I was Jewish, and her boy loved me, and that was all she needed to know. I remember the first time Lil and I met. I came into the house and there she was, standing on the landing at the top of the curved staircase. A house dress as big as a tent flowed to the floor over her tall, more than substantial, figure. When Issy said, "Mom, this is Rosalie," she practically lifted me off the floor, clasping me to her big bosom, which was unfettered by undergarments, and said, "Velkom to di femily." (I try this phrase with all the girls my sons bring home, but it hasn't worked yet.)

But now disaster struck in the Issy-Rosie romance. Our worst fear. Somehow I was pregnant, even though Issy was taking precautions. For kids today, this would be no problem, but it was the '50s. Jewish children were expected to bring only *naches* — joy and gratification — to the family. We didn't belong to ourselves, after all. We were our parents' children.

There was no question — we simply could not do this to them. My father might have killed himself.

I tried some pills that made me ill. I recall that as I got out of bed the day I took them, the floor turned upside down and hit me on the head. I remember feeling nauseous at dinner facing a bowl of my mother's dense green soup. So at 19 years old and three months' pregnant, I had an abortion at a stranger's apartment in Rosedale. It was an irresponsible act, because at the time I believed there was a risk I might not be able to conceive later. Giving birth hurt like hell, but an hour after the soap-and-water douche on a kitchen table, and wobbly on my feet, I took the bus — not even a taxi — home. A few weeks later I anxiously went to see a Dr. Doris Barkley in the Medical Arts Building. I felt the hostility in my skin the moment I walked into the imposing granite lobby of that WASP bastion — Jewish doctors were banned. An elegant bronze sign on the architrave over the door read: "Entrance to Motors." Dr. Barkley, wide with the face of an owl, looked like a spinster who had never known a man. When I told her what I had done, she said, "You have committed murder," and she was right. We have always felt that guilt, but at the time there was absolutely no other way out.

The wedding was scheduled for the prescribed *mazeldik* Tuesday, September 6, 1955. So my parents took me to Buffalo to buy a trousseau — largesse I had never seen from them before. I bought a bouffant cotton organdy dress that wasn't meant to be a wedding gown. (I have never followed the rights and wrongs of fashion, preferring the *moyshe kapoyer* — upside down — approach.) I also bought 56 towels in grey and peach to match the tiles I had selected for the bathroom in our new apartment — early signs of the decorator. Dad did not approve of my wedding gift registry for Jensen Pyramid pattern silver, handmade pottery dishes, and modern crystal glasses with cubes instead of stems. He preferred ornate goods that looked the price.

Issy and I had a traditional dinner-dance wedding at the Club Kingsway. Soon after the wedding, the place burned down, which I took to be like breaking the champagne glass after a pledge, or Joshua breaking the walls of Jericho. Five hundred guests attended, mostly invited by the

Sharps — as my mom would point out often, because my dad footed the bill for everything. The Sharps paid for the flowers only, which my mom thought was *karg*, even though traditionally the bride's father paid for the wedding. And we received the customary wedding gifts from all the guests — $15 on average, the cash pressed into our hands at the wedding, along with the *mazel tov* handshake. Issy's pockets were bulging.

Dad didn't know how to dance, so before the wedding he took lessons at Arthur Murray's and learned the box step for the photo-op family dance exchange. During the dance, I remember his strained smile and sweaty brow as he tried to simultaneously count steps and make conversation with Lil Sharp. His right foot dropped down heavily on each corner of the box.

The truth is, I would have found it more romantic to elope. I don't enjoy having to smile on cue, and my mind was so scattered and stressed during the wedding that I couldn't appreciate the moment we took our vows.

Later I found Dad's cache of invoices:

Wedding cake — 16 lbs., 8 pedestals, and vase — $27
Rental of silver cake stand — $1.50
Menu: appetizer, tomato stuffed with chopped liver, main course, half spring chicken with kishke, knishes, and peas
Music by Ellis McClintock and his orchestra
2 songs by Manford Steer — $15
Gratuity for limousine driver — $1

Issy and I had a nine-day honeymoon in New York, Miami, and Cuba. It was such a luxury to stretch out and have sex in a bed. On our wedding night, we stayed at the Skyline Motel in Toronto. Mysteriously, we were wakened in the late hours by the click of someone's heels in our bathroom;

apparently we had a connecting room with a shared bath. In the morning Issy carefully filmed the building's mediocre exterior with his dad's 16mm movie camera. About half of our honeymoon movies pan tediously up, down, and across hotel buildings, including a long stretch of underexposed footage of the gaudy interior of the Fontainebleau Hotel, which had just been built in Miami Beach. Even then Issy was dreaming about the hotel business.

The next morning we were having breakfast in bed in our New York bedroom on the 38th floor of the Hotel Taft when Issy suggested we should call home. Max Sharp answered and we said our hellos.

Then he asked me, "So how do you like New York?"

"Great," I answered.

"And how is married life?"

"It's better than New York."

At the time I was wearing my short yellow cotton nightie from Buffalo, with the matching bloomers, and my new curly hair. My poker-straight hair had been permed before the wedding because I thought a wife shouldn't be seen in curlers. Someone in New York asked if we were brother and sister with our matching short, frizzy hairdos.

Issy and I had affectionate pet names for each other. I called him "pooch" (I hate to admit). And since he preferred petite girls with good legs, he sometimes called me "little one." Little did he know that after the wedding I would qualify on only one of these counts since I would grow a half inch to just under five-foot-five — not much of a difference, I'll admit, but how many people grow after they're married?

Havana I found more exotic than I later found Spain. The women were broad-hipped and sensuous, and the poor were very picturesquely poor. Our hotel was lavish, reserved only for the upper classes in pre-revolutionary opulence. One night we signed on for a bus tour of nightclubs. At the open-air Club Tropicana we were seated with an ancient colonel and his wife, probably taking their last vacation. The showgirls dancing on the distant stage looked nearly naked, but we couldn't be sure since our table was about a football field away.

Issy excused himself to check out the gambling tables, saying he would be right back. I tried to make conversation, but the colonel was quite deaf, so after a while the shouting became tiresome.

Still Issy did not return.

After what seemed forever, he finally showed up, flashing his square, toothy smile. Later he confessed he had lost $300. I immediately rose to the occasion, played the selfless soap-opera wife, and dramatically declared, "What's done is done and we can manage just as well."

After the night life of Havana, we spent a few days at Veradero Beach — still the most beautiful fine white-sand beach I've ever stepped on. I could see my toenails through the transparent turquoise water. It was the off-season and we were the only guests, just the two of us that evening in a huge red plush nightclub filled with descending tiers of empty tables and chairs.

What surprises me, though, is the way my marriage turned out. I expected that Issy would continue his premarital Casanova capers and carry on at the dice tables — after all, he did lose half our wedding-gift money on our honeymoon — but he's never gambled since, and to all appearances he's remained faithful.

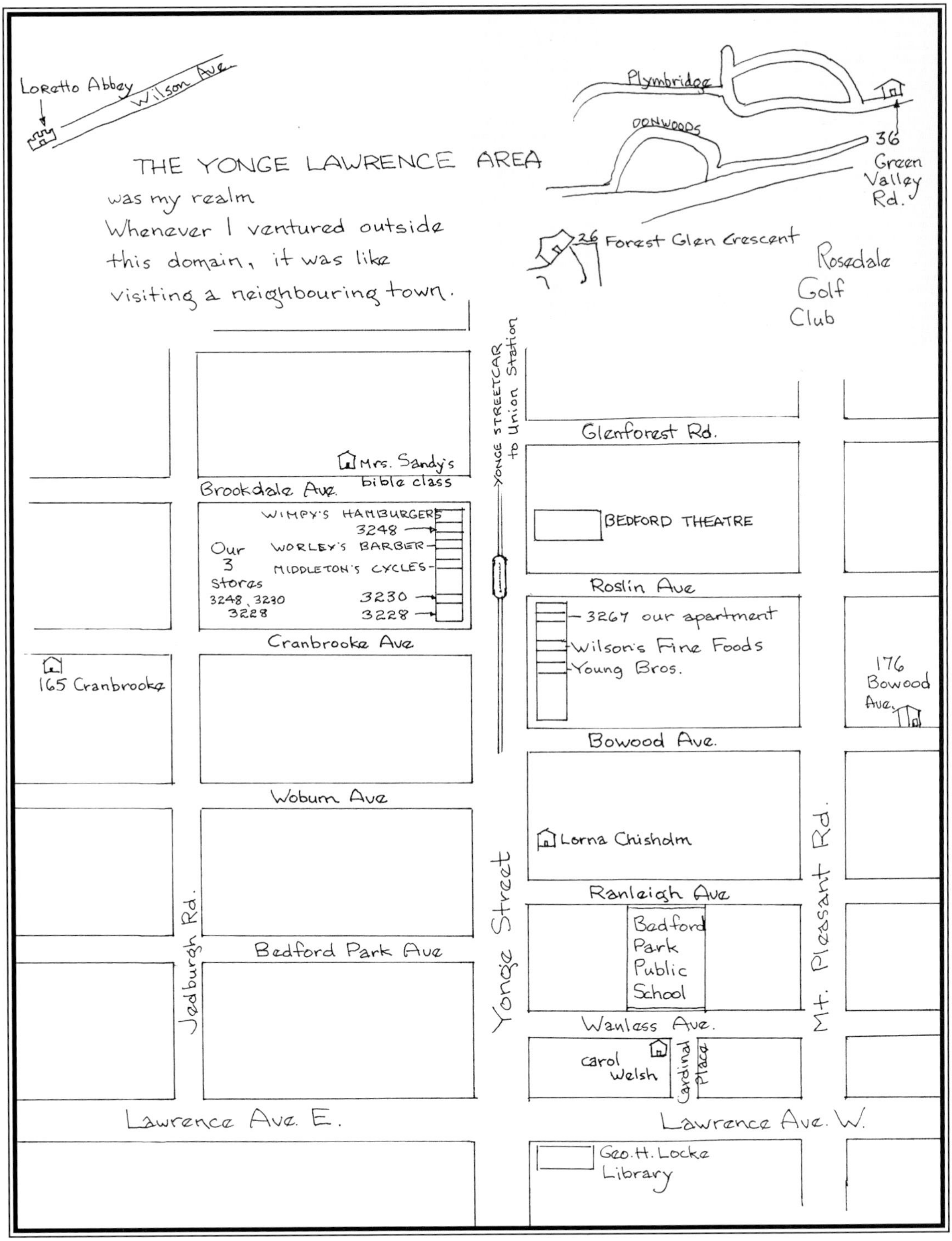

THE YONGE LAWRENCE AREA
was my realm
Whenever I ventured outside
this domain, it was like
visiting a neighbouring town.

Loretto Abbey
Wilson Ave.
Plymbridge
Donwoods
36
Green Valley Rd.
26 Forest Glen Crescent
Rosedale Golf Club
YONGE STREETCAR to Union Station
Glenforest Rd.
Mrs. Sandy's bible class
Brookdale Ave.
WIMPY'S HAMBURGERS
3248
Our 3 stores
3248, 3230
3228
WORLEY'S BARBER
MIDDLETON'S CYCLES
3230
3228
BEDFORD THEATRE
Roslin Ave
3267 our apartment
Wilson's Fine Foods
Young Bros.
Cranbrooke Ave
165 Cranbrooke
176 Bowood Ave.
Bowood Ave.
Woburn Ave
Lorna Chisholm
Ranleigh Ave
Bedford Park Public School
Jedburgh Rd.
Bedford Park Ave
Yonge Street
Mt. Pleasant Rd.
Wanless Ave.
Carol Welsh
Cardinal Place
Lawrence Ave. E.
Lawrence Ave. W.
Geo. H. Locke Library

The Three Graces perform "Zing Went the Strings of My Heart." From left: Carol Weinstein, Dorothy Goldhar, me.

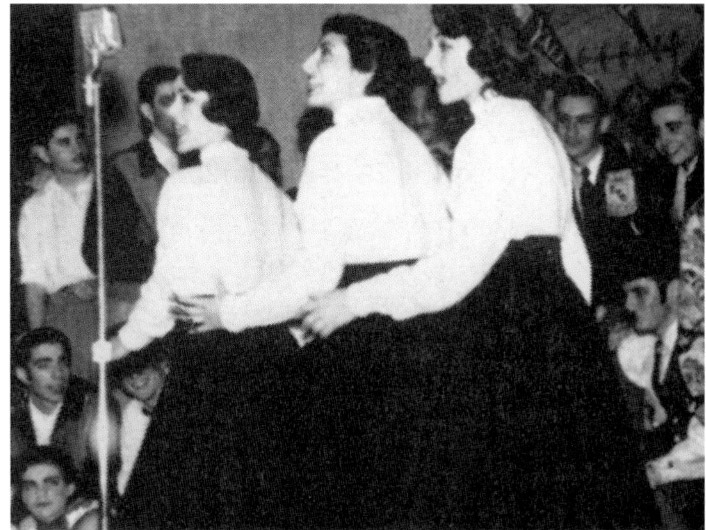

With Dick Dunkelman. I'm wearing a green plaid skirt I made on our Singer, which hummed often in our house. The sewing machine is now closed and holds the photocopier.

On a date with Morley Markson, October 1952, before Dad banished him from our house.

Our honeymoon and my first store-bought dress, $35, more than twice the price of any purchase till then. I kept the dress for years, but not the waistline.

Issy, the Ryerson football star, 1952. He was athlete of the year and won the silver medal for proficiency in his studies. In high school he had scored high marks with sports and girls — not schoolwork.

The *kale* and her baby brother.

My hero at the time he went gallantly into the frey with my father. He still has the same slim build.

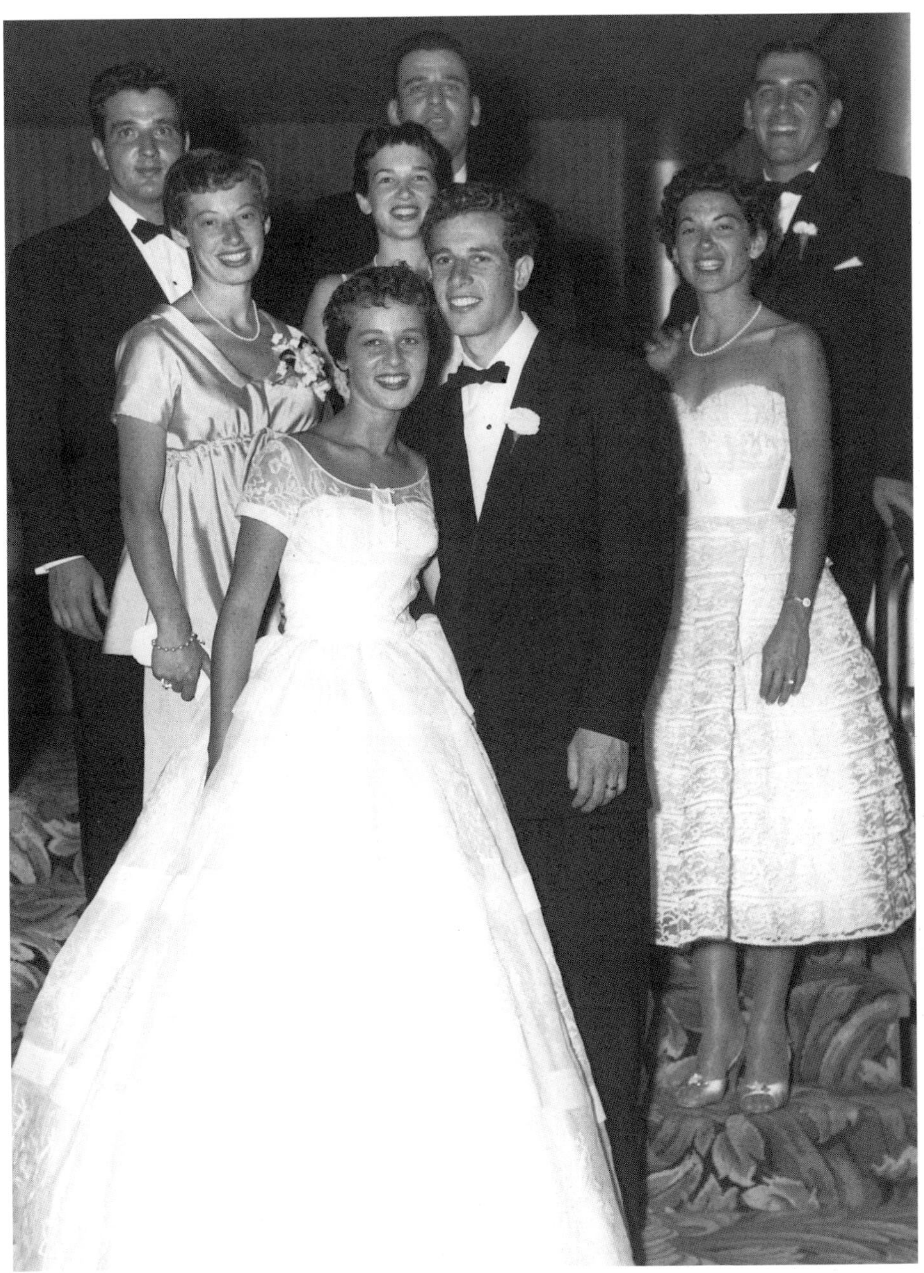

The wedding, September 6, 1955. With Issy's three sisters and their husbands, from left: Bea and Fred Eisen, Nancy and Siggy Levy, Edie and Eddie Creed. The three girls are saints, visiting or telephoning their parents every day.

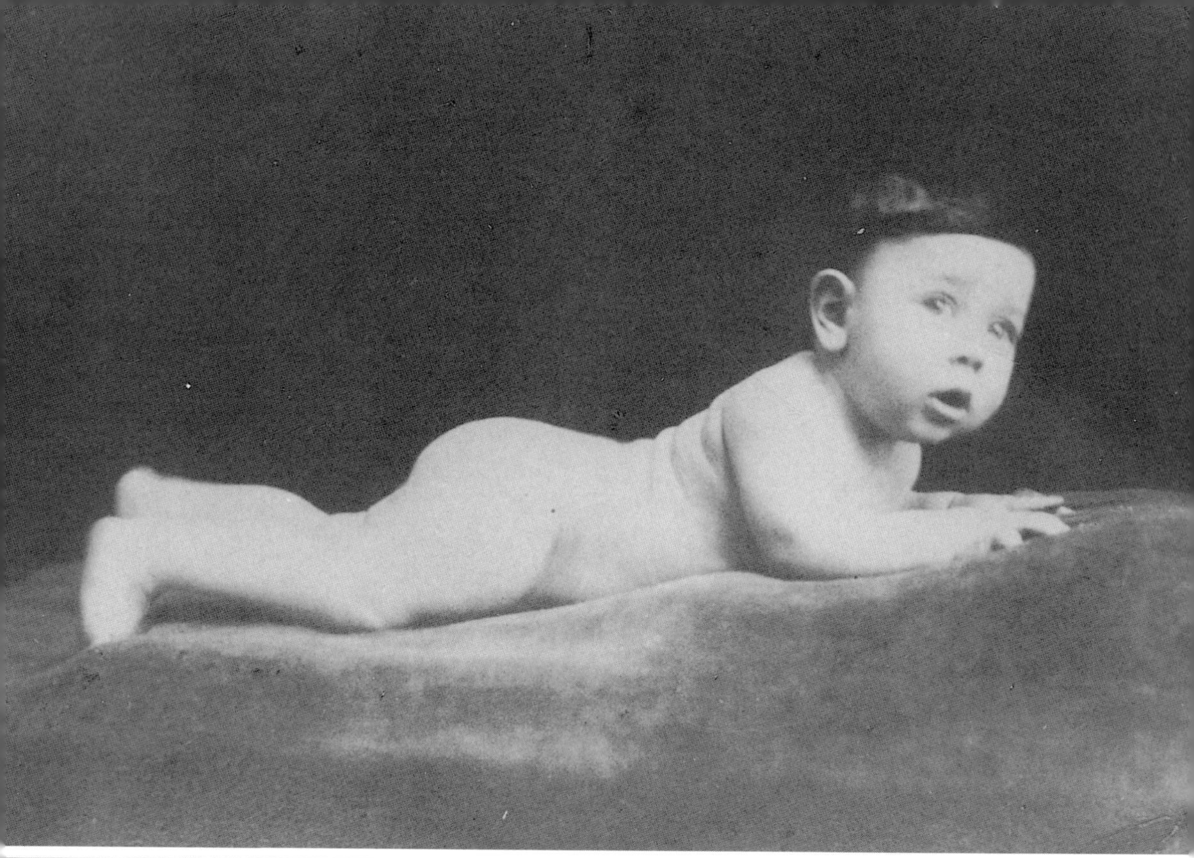

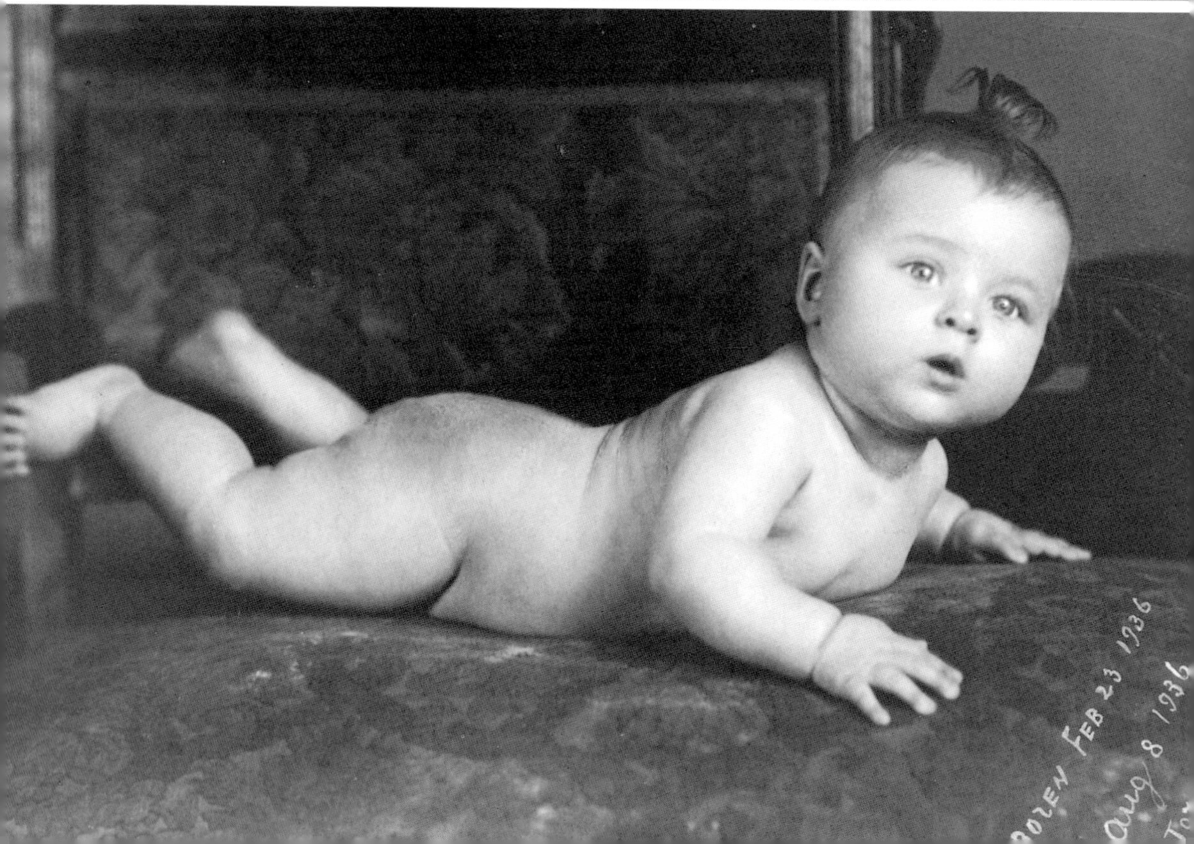

FEB 23 1936
Aug 8 1936

CHAPTER FOUR

Di Kale

THE BRIDE COMES HOME

It was late afternoon when we opened the door to find the apartment completely empty except for a mattress and box springs leaning against the bedroom wall, still wrapped in brown paper. The honeymoon over, we had arrived at our one-bedroom home at 130 Eglinton Avenue West, in a building Issy had helped his dad build. Our shoes left light footprints on a dark sooty floor that hadn't been cleaned since the last tenant left. Thanks to Lil Sharp, there were two brown bags of groceries on the kitchen counter. But the counter was also covered with a layer of grime, and the fridge needed wiping out. I slowly realized that for the first time it fell to me as designated housekeeper, and not to my mother, to do the cleanup.

A month later I magnanimously invited the whole family for a Shabbat dinner, as I thought a good wife should. I had no cooking experience because I had *never* helped my mom in the kitchen. But by following recipes I thought I could do better, a more *goyishe* meal. I got out my

The bride and groom. ABOVE: He has the same slim build and canny demeanour. BELOW: She has the same hips, was the first in her crowd to use hair gel, and wears an expression later described in her kindergarten report card as "alert, interested, talkative."

Gourmet Cookbook Vol. 2 and planned an ambitious and pretentious menu, including some dishes I had only seen in print: blanquette de veau, petit pois, French fries, noodle kugel, braided rolls, carrot *tsimes* (beef and carrot stew), and for dessert, baked Alaska. And since it was nearly Halloween, a huge orange jelly mould filled with black licorice ropes (ugh!). For the table centrepiece, I had a carved pumpkin with a small candle inside, the top decorated with a crepe-paper afro.

I began preparing all this bright and early on the Friday morning. Little did I know that my five-course menu was a two-day job for three people. By 4 p.m. I was panicky and only halfway done, so I reduced the number of courses but refused to give up on the stiff egg whites needed for the baked Alaska's meringue. The guests arrived, dinner was served, and we were well into the dessert — the meringue at half-mast — when the pumpkin exploded in flames and the crepe-paper hairdo hit the ceiling with a boom.

Days later, small black particles, like fruit flies, were still descending.

I didn't have much to do every day when Issy went off to work except throw out the apple core he had left on the bedside table. Why was this *my* job?

I had quit university, which I should never have done, on the advice of my mother-in-law, who said, "*Meshugas*! Craziness! A wife doesn't go to school — a wife takes care of a husband." So off I went to work for six months as a salesgirl at Creeds, Toronto's poshest ladies' clothing store, thanks to an offer from Eddie Creed, who was married to Issy's sister Edie. The pay was $25 a week, plus 1 per cent commission.

There was a big room downstairs at Creeds where we salesgirls would have coffee. The "girls" were a group of former society doyennes, divorcees. They were the classic 1940s "little woman" who, with apron on, dinner ready, and candles lit, would hinge her day on that moment when the front door would open to: "Hi, honey, I'm home." But as the husbands aged, some of them experienced mid-life crises. Then these husbands would adopt the best defence they could find against complacency and old age: younger women. It was not that they didn't love their wives — they just wanted to do the same life all over again.

In the '50s, women didn't take the college courses that trained them for anything more than matrimony. So the girls at Creeds were all cast-off spouses selling clothes in the shop in which they had formerly had charge accounts — except for my friend Mrs. Vandermeulen, who was working to supplant the income her husband had lost in the stock market. She was frail, elderly, and wrinkled from smoking. She once confided, between coughs, in her raspy voice, drawing on the cigarette she carried in a long holder, that her mother-in-law blamed her for being childless, when in fact it was her husband who was sterile. Mrs. V. had taken the blame forever and never told her husband or his mother the truth. She didn't want to bruise her husband's ego. You'd think she'd been born in the shtetl.

The girls at Creeds often asked me to join them for lunch at the Fifth Avenue Restaurant where they had the Businessmen's Lunch for $1.10. No way would I spend 25 per cent of my wages for food, so I stayed at the store with my hard-boiled egg from home.

I was a crack saleslady at Creeds, one of those aggressive types that accost you on the way in, like my mother at Wise's Dry Goods. Hapless shoppers were no match for her. They would come in for a pair of stockings and go out with a housedress as well. But I remember something unethical I did at Creeds. A young girl came in looking for a sweater that was to be charged to her mother's account. She was wearing jeans, saddle shoes, and bobby socks, and no makeup to cover her blond, freckled complexion. I should have shown her a casual cardigan, but since I was working on commission, I talked her into buying an inappropriately expensive cashmere evening sweater. The mother was furious and the garment was returned.

At last, our new apartment on Bathurst Street at Roselawn was ready, in an 11-storey tower Issy had built, and I quit Creeds because I had a new job — decorating and furnishing our home. It was a two-bedroom suite on the 10th floor, 1,500 square feet, with one wall of windows facing the hot western sun, and it was just one floor below my in-laws, who lived in the penthouse. Issy left the decoration to me, and the results were considered fresh and dramatic. I took out the nub wall that typically formed the entrance hall and instead left the column exposed. This gave an open diagonal view from the front door of the L-shaped main room, and our apartment looked larger than others of the same model. I put a modern mural wallcovering with a black ground on one wall. Otherwise, the sheer striped curtains were white and the walls were painted white, which in those days walls never were — dark colours like wedgwood green were in vogue. My friend Marion Orenstein commented that our too-white walls reminded her of a hospital. The carpet and soft goods were pearl grey, and the dining room set was a black wrought-iron-and-glass oval table and chairs, copied from a photo in *House Beautiful* magazine and made for a song, to suit our budget.

One day a four-seater sofa arrived from Eaton's, a gift from my mother-in-law. I never let on that the sofa was a great disappointment — I would have preferred to keep the space empty until I could afford to choose my own couch. Our bedroom suite, rather awful in retrospect, was custom-made in clunky oak stained a pale turquoise, and the curtains were in the same palette.

I kept this apartment spotless, quite unlike the sloppy teenager my mother always complained about. Once, in my teens, I had come home late and just stepped out of my stiff skirt and crinoline and left them standing on the floor. Anna Pupulin, our cleaning woman, came the next morning and vacuumed all around the clothes and the bed while I pulled the covers over my head and slept till noon.

Life in our honeymoon apartment was idyllic. The 56 colour-coordinated towels were folded in exact stacks of pink and grey in the closet beside a hundred rolls of toilet paper, bought from Eaton's at a quantity discount and also neatly stacked. In my yellow kitchen with its white vinyl floor inlaid with small black diamonds, I produced Polynesian stir-fry dinners for two, presented on our arts-and-craftsy handmade pottery with unglazed bottoms and rims. With dinner we had loganberry juice — we didn't drink wine until our first trip to Europe in 1963; in Paris, if you didn't order wine, you got no service from the waiters.

We often watched Issy's favourite TV program, *NFL Football*, on Lil's four-seater sofa, my husband lying down and me sitting at the end, always knitting, because I had no interest in, or understanding of, football. From time to time, without taking his eyes from the TV, Issy's hand would drop down into the potato-chip bowl on the floor. The bowl was striped black-and-white pottery to match the décor, and did years of service for chips. Beside the bowl stood the crystal candy dish, with its stale green and black jujubes — the rejected flavours. We ate only the red, yellow, and orange ones.

(We no longer have the black bowl, nor do we eat chips. We're great snobs about any food that's "fast," and make a fuss about brown rice, green tea, golden flax seed, and anything organic. Should anyone suggest herring oil is better than cod liver oil or that psyllium husk cures constipation, we add yet another potion to our after-breakfast lineup. I can't swallow pills, so I make a vile cocktail by emptying all the vitamin capsules in water. My mom taught me how *not* to swallow pills, like she did, crushing aspirin in water.)

Back in our honeymoon days, I was happy to have Issy relaxing on the sofa, a necessary respite from his long work hours — up at six and out on the construction job, building twin apartment towers at Avenue Road and Heath Street. Isadore was a gentleman landlord, and I loved to watch him in action, dealing in his courtly manner with the demands of the apartment tenants. In our own building, whenever we met anyone in the elevator, they would invariably remember a leaky faucet or some other defect. My husband would disarm them with his smile and assure them that the item would be fixed a.s.a.p.

Of course the ladies all melted. They loved him.

When our honeymoon apartment was suitably decorated, I needed a new project, so I thought, "Why not learn to swim?" When Marilyn Bell swam across Lake Ontario in 1954, I was awed and inspired. She had stepped into the lake that day with three other veteran contenders who soon quit, put off by the strong winds. The intrepid teenager Miss Bell plunged on despite squalls which carried her so far off course that she ended up travelling twice the width of the lake when she finally stepped onto the far shore. Her swim coach, Gus Ryder, had pushed her the whole way from his boat, shouting, "Come on, Marilyn! You're almost there, Marilyn!" Later I looked him up in the book and called. Gus gave me a lesson a week for six months — just him and me in the small indoor pool at Glenview Terrace. But it would prove easier for Mr. Ryder to coach Marilyn across Lake Ontario than to coax me to swim across the pool. I lost six pounds, swallowed gallons of water, occasionally had to be rescued with a long stick, but never quite got the hang of it. Nevertheless I water-skied once and took one canoe trip.

For my next project, I began begging for a baby, as I had formerly begged for a bicycle and a brother. Even though we had decided earlier that we would wait two years, so we could enjoy the carefree life, Issy gave in. In my anxiety to have the first baby quickly, I consulted a fertility book, which advised keeping my hips high on a pillow after sex, so the egg and the sperm would have a better chance of colliding. It also said that the first sperm to arrive were the boys, because girls were slower swimmers.

It must have worked, because I got pregnant on the first try and was always to produce the fast swimmers.

I loved being pregnant. It made me feel slow and satisfied and complete.

Jordan Jeffery was born in September 1957, two years after the wedding. He emerged from the womb on the run, and he hasn't slowed down since. Jordan was always getting into trouble. He was fascinated by the box of liquid shoe polish with round felt tips that I kept a stock of in many colours, so I put it out of reach on the top shelf in the kitchen. One Sunday, I rose late to find his white furniture decorated with graffiti in indelible shoe polish. The enterprising Jordy had simply pushed a chair to the kitchen counter and nimbly reached his prize. I did not spank him, which was my first urge, but declared in my best mother's rendition of the child-rearing book's advice, "Shoe polish is for shoes, not furniture, so we'll have to take it away." Another time he was curious about my hair dryer, plugged it in, and left it on High, sitting the nozzle down on his plastic-covered crib mattress. By the time I discovered what he'd done, there was a square hole in the mattress filled with flames. I quickly took the smoking mattress down in the elevator, hoping to reach the ground floor before it exploded.

Nineteen-fifty-eight was the year of the great car accident. The press that day reported, "A 16-month-old baby and his pregnant mother, 22, escaped serious injury in a head-on collision on Roselawn Avenue east of Bathurst. Glass from the windshield showered Mrs. Rosalie Sharp [who was] treated for head and face lacerations.... Their auto struck by William Basha.... A passenger in the Basha vehicle required 10 stitches when he was pitched through the windshield."

Jordy and I were "Basha'd" while returning from our daily visit to my parents a few blocks away, where routinely Mom and I would share a cup of coffee while Dad played with the baby. On our way home, Jordy in his child's car seat, we had been waiting in a line of cars, just a few yards from our apartment-house driveway, for the traffic light to change at Bathurst. The next I knew, there was a flash of lights, a crash, and the steering wheel hit my nose like a sledgehammer. In a split second, our car was on someone's lawn facing in the opposite direction. Jordy had fallen forward in his car seat, and his face had hit the dials of the radio (later he would be a disc jockey for a time). He was screaming, and I was afraid to look at his bleeding face for fear he had lost an eye. Thank God he was okay, so I stormed out of the car and started yelling at the idiot truck driver, who was drunk of course. The point of impact was nine feet from our side of the 30-foot road. I must have looked a sight, eight months' pregnant with blood running from my nose down the front of my tight hooded jacket. I had to have the smashed cartilage in my nose replaced so I could breathe — my nose has been crooked ever since — and Jordy still has traces of the scars. In court some months later, William Basha — what an improbable name — was not charged with reckless driving, the story went, because he would have lost his livelihood. Besides, I looked beautiful and could not prove that any damage had been done.

And then one day in 1960 our honeymoon apartment was all but destroyed. An *andere umglik* — another misfortune! It was a grey day but we needed milk, so before the rain came I set out quickly with the two kids in the carriage. I always bought jug milk, because you got one quart free, a welcome economy on my $35 weekly household budget. (Shtetl people always manage. I never asked for more.) We hurried, under black rain clouds, the six blocks to the supermarket, retrieved the 35 cents for the empty jug, and put the milk in the basket under the carriage. As we made our way back home, I noticed that the rain had come and gone. But when I opened the door to our apartment, I was confronted by a bizarre scene. There was broken glass on the carpet, but no glass in the windows. The curtains were mostly missing, the tops hanging in shreds. The place looked like Miss Havisham's room in *Great Expectations*. My light grey carpet was soaked dark, and most of our wedding crystal — which my father didn't like — had been swept off the shelves and lay in shards on the floor. During the 20 minutes we had been in the market, a 100-mile-an-hour wind had driven through our home.

Gregory Jay had been born in March 1959, 18 months after Jordy, and Christopher Hugh another 18 months after that. Since we had only two bedrooms, Greg bunked with us until Chris came along and took his place in our room. It seemed like there were always three kids in diapers, one of them sleeping in our bedroom. Night feedings were a nightmare, because with breastfeeding you never knew how much food the baby was getting. To make matters worse, if the baby cried, Issy would invariably say, "He's hungry; go feed him." So I took to weighing the baby before and after feedings. The difference indicated the number of ounces he drank. But if he peed while he was nursing, this threw off my calculations.

Breastfeeding is one of life's special offerings, though. There is an earthy scent to a newborn baby that is like that of a new puppy. I loved the sexual sensation when my babies drew milk from my nipple, their silky heads resting against my bare arm. I recall the beads of sweat on their noses pressed against my breast. They would take about eight gulps, rest for four, then take six more, all with eyes shut, worn out from the exertion. Moist eyelashes would grace a damp cheek and one tiny hand would spread like a flower and hold on to my breast for balance. Those were moments I cherished, and I think Issy felt somewhat impotent that he could not feed the kids.

But Isadore was a wonderful dad. He always changed the kids' heavy early-morning diapers before he went to work, a joy he says he wouldn't have missed. He would open the door to find the baby standing in his crib, his pink face beaming with anticipation for the day to begin, oblivious to the urine-soaked triple diaper hanging down around his knees. Issy felt that changing diapers was important to share with his sons — it was the only dialogue available at the moment. And on weekends, Dad would make the boys porridge (he hasn't cooked since). In later years, I would hand out a pile of towels to five naked guys — Dad and his boys together in the big walk-in shower.

Isadore responds to all kids and all dogs. He'll get down on the floor and romp with a strange dog and let him slobber all over his face, then roughhouse and play a game of dodge. He'll toss the kids in the air or wrestle with them on the floor. He'll scratch the dog behind the ears just like he rubs my head and playfully musses my hair. When our old dog got frisky, Issy would often say, "She's still like a pup" — which I know is the way he thinks of me at 70.

After five years of marriage, at Issy's suggestion, we took our first vacation. Vacations had never been part of my life or expectations. Our honeymoon had been my only holiday. Shtetl people did not take holidays, nor did they even know the word "entitled" — in fact, "entitled" is not in my Yiddish dictionary. For our first vacation, we drove to Niagara Falls and spent three days in the Midtown Motor Inn. We thought the place was so-o-o glamorous; we raved ad nauseum to each other about everything. We opened the sliding glass doors and stepped out to the patio, a concrete square placed on the grass, just large enough to hold two webbed plastic chaise lounges on which we promptly stretched out, in the sunlight, as we thought all good vacationers should. That night we both had such wicked sunburns, we couldn't even touch.

A year later Issy would open his own, very much nicer, midtown motor hotel.

In 1962 I also took a holiday on my own, because I had missed back-packing as a teenager and still had never been on a train. So I resolved to take the overnight train to New York and stay at the YWCA. Issy wouldn't hear of the Y and browbeat me into staying at the Plaza Hotel. In retro-spect, I should, of course, have stayed at the Y. The plan was that I would shop and go to galleries for two days, and then, at five o'clock on the Friday, we would meet up in the Palm Court Bar. I went to three museums and Bergdorf Goodman, my first shopping experience alone and as a grown-up, the first clothes I had bought in seven years — and the most at one time. I found a dramatic white chiffon skirt and black top and also a shoulder-length Marilyn Monroe-style blond wig. Since I have a problem with punctuality — I'm always early — I showed up in the bar 15 minutes ahead, rigged out in my new gear and platinum hair. I took a table near the string quartet that may have been playing "Some Enchanted Evening."

Issy arrived, looked around, and sat at a table for two across the room. He ordered a drink, probably a rye and ginger ale. (Now he drinks very old Scotch.) Our eyes met and he gave me an appreciative flirty glance but no sign of recognition.

I ordered a club soda.

He made no move.

I sipped my drink and waited.

Still no move. He didn't know me.

So I finally got up and walked in his direction. He jumped up, kissed me, and said, "Sweetheart — sorry, I didn't recognize you. Your hair looks great and you look fantastic in that outfit. I didn't know it was you. Your hair looks great. So sit down and tell me — how was your trip? Your hair looks great." And so on.

He, of course, thought I had dyed my hair blond, which I didn't contradict during his declarations that the colour looked great. Meanwhile I must have bored him as I gave him a breathy, minute-by-minute account of my time in New York: tedious descriptions of the paintings of Turner and Boucher at Henry Clay Frick's beautifully scaled museum home and still more about Picasso's horrifying 24-foot-long masterpiece mural, *Guernica*, at the Museum of Modern Art. I told Issy that the Germans' bombing of the ancient city of Guernica, as allies of the Spanish during the Civil War, had been their test run for World War II.

While I went on and on — in a voice that reaches an unpleasant, off-putting pitch when I'm excited — I slowly raised my hands and reached up as if adjusting a hat that has slipped back, and pulled my wig slightly forward. Issy fell back and collapsed in laughter. The Palm Court musicians played on while we caught up. And the evening and night were splendid — as good as it gets.

Living in a two-bedroom apartment with three kids had its difficulties, but only in retrospect. In the winter I had to dress all three and myself and then summon the elevator, by which time we were all in a sweat. After six years at Bathurst and Roselawn, we moved to a spacious, modern four-bedroom house in Hogg's Hollow in 1962. I was pregnant with Anthony David, who arrived the prescribed 18 months after Chris. Four boys in five years! Only the first one was planned — the others materialized in spite of all precautions, including the pill, a diaphragm, an intrauterine device, and the withdrawal method. It seems we should have used two birth control methods simultaneously. But four kids were fine, because in my fantasy life I had planned to have six kids — two adopted, since I considered this a *mitzvah*, a virtuous deed. In fact, I was to have six pregnancies — the last one was a miscarriage, induced because I was wearing a birth control device. While I was at it, I had my tubes tied, because Issy was threatening to have a vasectomy.

Isadore was working on his second hotel and we enjoyed a new measure of prosperity. Our Hogg's Hollow home was designed by Peter Dickenson, who had drawn up the first Four Seasons Hotel in Frank Lloyd Wright style. The place he did for us featured wood and fieldstone accent walls both outside and in. It wasn't the style of house we had wanted at first. Before Peter drew up the plans, we drove him around the corner and insisted he see our idea of a dream house. He was not impressed. After studying the building for a few moments, he sniffed, "Oh, I see you have a fondness for mock Georgian."

Of course, we were enlightened by this dismissive remark and gave Dickenson the go-ahead. Issy collaborated with Peter and the result was dynamic. (Recently we went back for a look at the "mock Georgian" house we had shown Peter and found a dinky pedestrian place.)

A few months before we were about to move into the house, though, Issy had gotten cold feet and thought, since the place had exceeded our budget, that perhaps we should sell it and move into something more modest. I was game; I was up to the challenge to make any place look good. Every house we looked at was fine with me, but in the end Issy capitulated and we moved into 36 Green Valley Road after all.

Peter died of cancer a month later. He was 6 feet 5 inches tall, 35 years old, and one of Canada's favourite architects, with many good buildings to his credit, notably the O'Keefe Centre and the Beth Tzedec Synagogue in Toronto. The Inn on the Park was built from a sketch Peter made in his hospital bed while Issy was visiting him.

The house Dickenson designed for us was spaciously spread on one level, with stone floors, cathedral ceilings, and rich, oiled cedar panelling that Issy designed, with one-inch square vertical strips covering the seams between two-inch boards. Floor-to-ceiling picture windows gave onto the grassy dunes of the then-restricted Rosedale Golf Club. We covered the plaster walls with natural burlap, and on my mother's Singer sewing machine I ran up full-height drapery for the windows out of the same fabric. Seventy-five yards of burlap, a dollar a yard, prickly with splinters, but I was determined to have the windows covered, even though there was little money.

We had no furniture, so that first New Year's we had a square-dance party for 75 friends. I ordered in rectangular bales of hay for seating and hired a square-dance caller from the Yellow Pages, a source that rarely lets me down. We enjoy having people in for dinner — me fussing with the food and the flowers — which is curious because I'm not a social animal, not at all gregarious. And our next party caused some confusion among our friends because the invitation read: "Please come to dinner on Saturday April seventh, And Or, Saturday April fourteenth." This was my democratic way of handling so many guests without designating an "A" crowd and a "B" crowd. No one knew how to interpret it, but the numbers were about the same both evenings.

At this time, in 1963, we took our first *real* vacation, to Europe. (How did we ever leave the kids for five weeks? When we returned, Tony, then 18 months old, wouldn't speak to me for two days.) What a great trip we had driving our rented Fiat, "the Reluctant Fifi," who was something of a mule and had to be prodded to climb hills. At dusk we would begin our lookout for the closest hotel, usually the seedy kind where you brought your own toilet paper and soap. We chose either fleabags or luxury hotels, following the star ratings in our faithful Fodor guide, always philosophically avoiding the in-betweens. In Paris, we splurged and stayed at the five-star George V Hotel. We had a very sexy night, after which we ordered caviar and pommes frites at 3 a.m. I recall we were wearing the white terry-cloth hotel robes when the room service arrived. Who could have imagined that in 2002 the George V would become a Four Seasons?

Our drive through the Italian countryside was magnificent, and so was the sex — no kids banging on the bedroom door. There was one memorable day at the Ritz in Lisbon when we were in bed for so long that when we woke up we didn't know if it was yesterday or today. "How," I wondered, "can we discover if it's Tuesday or Wednesday?"

"Maybe there's a newspaper in the hall," said Is.

"I know, let's call the front desk and ask for the date."

I can't remember anymore which day it turned out to be. I do, however, still have the ashtray I took from the bedside table as a memento.

We've always preferred travelling in the off-season. In November 1967, we spent a glorious sunny week in Venice, after the hordes of tourists had left St. Mark's Square. I can still recall the hollow echo of my heels in the streets by the canals, where there was no noise of cars. We were also once the only guests at Il Pelicano, a limestone villa clinging to a cliff 90 miles north of Rome. The pink-clay tennis court was ours at any time, but the kitchen was closed, so there was no food available. At night we would leave the staff having a fine meal in the dining room as we headed out to look for a restaurant, where we were again the only guests. Adventurous, I chose the least recognizable item on the menu, which looked like some sort of fowl. When later I consulted my Italian dictionary, I found I had silenced a song thrush.

Twice in the winter of 1968, we skiied in Chamonix, France. Issy was always a big-time skier — "intrepid" is the best adjective to describe him. He has been dropped off from helicopters onto rocky mountain peaks in British Columbia, and skied down virgin slopes between the close trunks of tall trees, in the Bugaboos and the Monashees. He describes his whoops of joy when, with each steep turn, he drops 30 feet with the powder snow in a cloud around his head — a thrill he says is as good as any orgasm.

Issy taught me to ski when I was 17, but as with the jitterbug, I never quite got the hang of it. I somehow learned just enough that I could pick the easiest way to the bottom, mainly across rather than down the mountain. My goal was a cappuccino in the warm chalet just as soon as possible. With each turn, could I risk lifting a leg to step around? I imagined being torn up the middle while doing the splits headlong down the hill. I also remember the moment at Mont Tremblant when I gave up while I was speeding down, doing a snowplough, and released my desperate grip on the hill — hanging on by my toenails through the ski boots. I broke my ankle.

Instead of skiing twice in France, as scheduled in 1968, I suggested that we go skiing once in Zakopane, in the Tetra Mountains, while we were in Poland. That was the time I schlepped Issy to Ozarow. I wanted to see if my grandfather's house was still standing. We arrived in Warsaw in the frosts of February, the temperature 25 below zero. At the Hotel Europesci we were assigned a room with two cots lined up against the same wall. There was frost inside the windows and on the sill — my mom had described similar frosty windows in her youth. When we called down for help with the draft in our room, the engineer came up and took our bathroom towels and stuffed them along the window sill. So we called the desk clerk and asked if he had a suite. "A suite," said he. "By us that is much bigger the price — six dollars a night." Our suite turned out to be 10 times larger than the five-dollar room. Across the road at the Hotel Bristol, we went to see Hitler's bedroom. The décor was fascist-style Art Deco with a dark mahogany bedroom suite, the blankets covered in a grey-blue silk counterpane with a see-through circular hole in the centre, like my mother's Polish bedcover.

From Warsaw, we took the train to Crakow and then a taxi to Ozarow, where I shot a few photos in a snowstorm. The Birnbaum house had been taken down. We set off for the journey back, and the car rattled along a rural country road bumpy with ice as hard as concrete. It began to snow more and more heavily, until we were floating in a whiteout with no horizon. We panicked in frantic English and the driver answered in Polish as he kept bouncing along the invisible road. Issy and I were frightened half to death and I thought how ridiculous it would be to die on a country road in Poland, leaving four kids at home — and it was my fault. Suddenly, one of the windshield wipers flew off and the driver left us in the car as he went out to look for that needle in the snowdrifts. By now Issy and I were not speaking to each other, sitting well apart in stony silence, wondering how this unnecessary adventure would end.

Miraculously the driver returned, gleefully holding up the windshield wiper, and we thought, "This is a sign that this man will save us." We came to a village, hoping to find a train to Kielce. At the post office, I made a fool of myself with sound effects imitating a train, to ask, "Where is the choo-choo?" Issy recounts this story too often. Our good friend the cab driver then drove us to the safety of the train station, where Issy handed him a bundle of American money in an amount I'm sure surprised him later when he unrolled a year's wages.

Safely back at our idyllic home on Green Valley Road, we were living in luxury. The kids and our Samoyed dog had a garden that led out onto the golf greens. In winter they snurfed on the snowy hill (a snurfer was a board with a string attached — forerunner of the snowboard — and Greg was an expert on both). I did my best to be a good mother, but my kids say I sometimes made a mess of it.

They were right.

The boys complain of too much support and too little attention. I know I made a lot of mistakes, but it was my first try. Unfortunately, you don't get a second. I'm hoping, as Arthur Miller did, "to end up with the right regrets." And the apple, as they say, doesn't fall very far from the tree.

I wish I'd had lessons in parenting. We'd had lessons in bridge and tennis, but for our most important job — parenting — we had no training. I consulted many books, by Dr. Spock and Dr. Blatz, about understanding the young child. What I failed to comprehend is that children should be allowed to be obnoxious. I would say to Chris, "If you're going to be revolting, you can't stay here with us. Go to your room until you can behave." I'm now guessing that kids who are not permitted to be antisocial grow up with too strong a need to please. The best advice came from the book *Parent Effectiveness Training*, which taught you to say, "I need help with the garbage" rather than "You take out the garbage" or, as my mom would have said, "You *never* take out the garbage."

It was a frenetic time, with four boys under the age of five, the hardest period in my life. I was frantic, going from one diaper to the next, because first it was the older three wearing diapers, then the younger three. Sometimes, when I had no help, I had to leave the kids safely in the playroom while I tidied the kitchen and threw in the laundry (two loads a day).

It was a zoo. When Tony started to walk, I was so harried I went numb. Four rambunctious boys were too much for me. Tony was very curious — he was to become a mechanical engineer — and took apart every clock and removed the springs from all ballpoint pens, so there wasn't a working pen in the house. I had to be very vigilant because, although he was a picky eater — mainly apples and cheddar cheese — he seemed more interested in sampling the poisonous cleaning solutions under the sink. All of these had to be moved to high shelves. But the kids were too quick for me. Chris swallowed a whole bottle of baby aspirin. I found him lying in a stupor on his bed and immediately checked the bottle of St. Joseph's pills, where I had hidden it on the top shelf of the closet. It was empty — another trip to the hospital Emergency.

One time a friend, Wally Cohen, came over unannounced on an average hectic day on Green Valley Road. He was cheerful as usual, but he noticed I wasn't myself. I just couldn't fake it. It's the only time I can recall losing the power to smile and pretend all was well.

I was a very teacherly mother — we had painting sessions on the kitchen floor, each bottle of paint with its own brush. Once Tony was painting "a very bad animal" and he accidentally dribbled some paint across his paper. "That's just the way I wanted it," he said with his father's penchant for positive thinking. I took the boys to the library regularly and enjoyed reading to them, very keen that they learn to read for pleasure and feel the comfort and magic of literature. I've noticed that a common factor among great thinkers who speak and write well is that they are great readers — the brilliant Churchill, for example. Good readers unconsciously collect data that might later surface as wit, ready badinage, or a more sympathetic grasp. Readers meet unconventional characters, which instills flexibility. And books bring out a broad sense of irony.

We didn't send our boys off to camps or nursery schools much. I raised them like I was raised — to be self-reliant and self-motivated. Like their parents, they successfully followed their own passions, with the guts and resources to fearlessly face a blank page.

From the press, 1960, working on a fundraiser for the Mount Sinai Hospital.

On the back of this photo is written: "Sept. 6th, 1960, our very happy fifth anniversary." I ran up the red dress on the Singer. The photo was taken by a stranger at the CNE, where we celebrated annually, touring the International Building to soak up foreign cultures. Little did I know that Riyadh and Langkawi would someday be regular stops.

On the French Riviera, when we were young and gorgeous, 1963.

In a Paris nightclub, 1963.

Dancing, which we still like to do at every opportunity.

36 Green Valley Road, our first house. The roof on the right is my studio with northern light.

With Jordy, 1960.

The Four Seasons Motor Hotel opened in 1961 and instantly became the popular hangout for the literati and glitterati. My brother Stan the heart-throb lifeguard had to keep the groupies at bay.

At the Inn on the Park, 1964, where we went Sundays to swim. We changed in Issy's office instead of taking a guestroom, and always sat on the grass to leave the lounges for the guests.

The boys in the dining room. LEFT: Jordy, Tony, Chris, and Greg. The first time I served a buffet, Jordy said, "Mom, it's just like a party," so we had buffets every night, which was a lot easier.

With the boys on Green Valley Road, 1965.

CHAPTER FIVE

A Melokhe Iz a Melukhe

A TRADE IS A KINGDOM

When Tony was three, I borrowed a life-changing book by Betty Friedan, the most influential book I have ever read. In *The Feminine Mystique*, Ms. Friedan challenges women to escape their "trapped lives" as housewives and go out into the workforce and be people, not just helpmates. She asks, "Where will you, the housewife, be, when your children leave home?"

The feminist movement had begun in England with Mary Wollstonecraft's A *Vindication of the Rights of Women* in 1792, and had some successes among the suffragettes in early 20th-century America. But it was considered a narrow trend and didn't take hold until the 1960s, when feminism was finally embraced by most Western women. At my husband's hotels, there are now seven women in the top cabinet of 22, and the chain's chief operating officer is Kathleen Taylor. It seems lately that when a man in a high position retires, he may be replaced by a woman.

Christopher at age five.

But back in 1964 I was poised and armed with the edicts of Betty Friedan. I resolved to take action. I waited until Tony, the baby, was old enough for nursery school, and charged his older brother Chris to hold his hand the whole three blocks home from school. I once came upon the two of them walking hand in hand on the edge of the road — a heart-warming picture I have stored. With the boys in school, I applied to take some part-time courses at the Ontario College of Art, because I believed it was important for the "wife of" to have her own credentials. My plan was to do some interior design for Issy's hotels. Of course, my mate spurred me on as always.

Well, what a crash of disappointment when I found out that the school absolutely refused to take part-time students. I gave up because there was no way I would abrogate my responsibilities as a mother by attending school full-time. Until Issy talked me into it. I've never been able to resist his reasoning. He is very persuasive, as well as too supportive, as Jordy says. "Why not make your own schedule," Issy asked, "and attend three days a week? What's the worst that can happen? You'll fail attendance, but you'll succeed at what you're looking for — you'll learn design."

So for four years I dropped the kids off at the Toronto French School every morning and went to college, always home when they arrived back at four o'clock. I hardly missed a day of classes and was usually the first to arrive. During the first three months, there were many days when I almost quit, but I would make a deal with myself: "Just hold on for another week — maybe it will get easier." Between homework and home-making, my days were frenetic and fractured. The worst moment was the day my colour studies were due. Here I was locked in the bathroom at home — the only room where I could work undisturbed. The boys were banging on the door: "Mommy, when are you coming out? What are you doing in there? Mommy-y-y-y!" My paints were spread all over the bath-room as I tediously painted 100 postage-stamp-size squares of colour, each a tint, tone, or value darker than its neighbour. "Mommy will be out soon," I yelled back at the kids, thinking, "God help me, what do I do now? Should I simply pack up and quit or give it one more day?"

If I *had* quit, I would never have found out that after Christmas the work came almost to a halt, as if the first semester was simply some sort of test. By January, a lot was left up to the student's initiative. Never again would I need to do schoolwork at home. The following three and a half years were a breeze, sometimes a joke, with lots of time to spare. Typically every project had a three-week due date. Unlike the other students, who would pass their days in the cafeteria socializing, then complete the project the night before it was due, I would stay alone in the classroom and work. In this way, I was able to complete all assignments within the school day.

I picked up many new ideas at art school: Mrs. Lilly Maley, my design instructor, taught us, "Always have the concept before beginning a project."

Eugene Butt instructed us to "check out the works of Josef Albers and Johannes Itten before you think you know anything about colour."

Helen Fitzgerald, who taught us lettering, had designed three Canadian postage stamps (she did the artwork at three times the size of the stamp). She asked us each to paint a poster describing any collective word or phrase, such as "a gaggle of geese." My solution was "AHELLUVALOT," painted in graduated shades of red, from fiery to icy. Miss Fitzgerald told me I had "a feeling for lettering." I didn't mention that I wasn't new to sign painting, having done a hundred "one brush-stroke" signs for the Hadassah Bazaar, not to mention Wise's Dry Goods.

(Jordy, like my mom's brother Khaskel Birnbaum, is also a natural graphic designer — he made a wonderful three-dimensional sign for his restaurant the Santa Fe Bar & Grill and does a lot of his own corporate artwork — and Greg is a software designer.)

In our first painting class, the instructor, Carl Schaeffer, demonstrated — with his arm raised and folded at the elbow — that painting the negative shape of the space between his arm and his head was as important as the positive shape of the arm itself. Schaeffer's own landscapes recall the magic realism of Maxfield Parrish — especially Carl's trees, in the rounded shapes of leaves and branches that owed something to the art nouveau period still popular in his youth.

Even today, when I examine a painting, I check out the negatives. And when displaying my porcelain, I remember Mr. Schaeffer's dictum and ensure that the shapes of the coloured background visible between the pieces are as pleasing as the pieces themselves.

In my last days at art school I had a fantasy: five of us students — a sculptor, a jewellery maker, a weaver, a potter, and a printer (me) — would set up a studio together. The building would be in my garden where we would all work together in joy and harmony in a "Cranbrookian" utopia, a private and spiritual community modelled after the Cranbrook Academy just outside Detroit. We would existentially produce whatever the madness of each mind could imagine. There would be no worries about wealth, because profits would naturally follow from our appealing products. It would be an idyllic working life in a garden among woods, streams, and velvety lawns. In spring, branches of blossoming almond trees would sway across our open windows in the sunlight, and Mozart arias would fill the cathedral rafters above our heads. At lunchtime, someone would bring us a buffet of tofu and brown rice, crisp greens, kukicha tea, and chocolate meringue tarts.

I had the wherewithal to make all this happen, but it remained a dream — in the end, I knew I'd rather work alone in the felicity of home. My father, too, had preferred working alone.

In 1969 I graduated from the Ontario College of Art with two medals — the Lieutenant Governor's Medal and the Art Gallery of Ontario Medal — plus various prizes. Out of 240 grads, I stood second, after Sister Mary Emmanuelle, in marks and number of awards. The boys and Issy came proudly to my graduation.

And now, in 2006, I am Chancellor of that school, a title conferred on me for a few reasons: since 1969 I have headed up many fundraising events, like the CADA Antique Show, which in a good year brought the college $200,000. I also served on the school council for six years and was chair of the OCAD Foundation (the college's board of trustees), and we did give the school $5 million to help build the Sharp Centre for Design — a dynamic leggy box of a building designed by Will Alsop, which opened in 2004 to rave reviews and ruffled the feathers of some traditionalists.

School over, I designed a line of fabrics for house furnishings, printed on a table 30 feet long by 5 feet wide, in a design studio — Green Valley Workshop — we built adjoining the house. It was satisfying painting the designs, usually floral, in black ink on mylar, one 54-inch sheet per colour, photographically transferring each to a silkscreen. I would mix the coloured dyes and lift the 50-pound wooden screens onto the long table. The dyes would be squeegeed across each registered screen to print a four-colour repeat design on about 10 yards of white fabric, which was then cut up for samples.

I cut up and stapled small cuttings of printed fabrics, each topped with a cardboard border bearing its description. For example:

> *Fabric Name: Kinetic*
> *Colorway: 03 claret*
> *Cotton print in 4 colours*
> *Width: 54 inches*

I made up sets of samples and sent about a dozen different designs, each available in many colours, to Eaton's department stores across Canada, then sat back and waited for the orders to roll in. I never received a single reply — from which I learned the value of salesmen. I never did hire a salesman, though, but got most of my orders through Issy's contacts.

When a client ordered any substantial yardage, the goods were reproduced in a factory. I designed a few custom-printed curtain fabrics for

Simpsons Contract Department. They would order thousands of yards for hotels (usually ours) and office buildings, which I would then have printed by the Farquhar Textile Company on King Street East. The two Farquhar brothers, Jim and Bill, became my constant companions as I supervised the colour printing daily. Jim, the younger brother, had never finished high school and was now in his 30s. He and I had a slight sexual thing going on between us, although he was in a time warp: he still wore his black hair in a greasy sophomoric pompadour, striped with the lines of his comb. We had lots of laughs during lunch breaks, when Bill, the older brother, would spike his tea with Scotch (the bibulous tendency was handed down through his family). There were no alcoholics in my background, so I didn't recognize that Bill had a drinking problem, or why, for that matter, anyone would have such a problem. The factory was always dark and grungy, and one day as I wandered among the bolts of fabric, I was startled when Bill Farquhar suddenly loomed up like another roll of textile. He had passed out drunk, draped over a few bales of cloth, with one foot still on the floor.

Once, Green Valley Workshop received an order for 4,000 yards of floral fabric for curtains to be installed in the Royal York Hotel. The brothers Farquhar and I duly filled the request. After the drapes were installed, Simpsons (on behalf of the hotel) asked that I send them the standard two clippings, a piece of the original and one that had been dry-cleaned four times, to prove that the colours were fast. The clipping came back from the cleaner's almost blank — the pattern had come off in the cleaning process. I was horrified and anxious that Simpsons would again request the samples, but thankfully they never did. For some years I fully expected to be sued by the Royal York, when the curtains were cleaned, but by some miracle they never called.

My fabric business had now reached a dead end because no one in Canada produced colour-fast dyes, and it wasn't feasible to travel to Italy or the Orient. I toyed briefly with the idea of opening a factory that would produce such dyes, but that was too far removed from the drawing and painting, which is what I loved.

Later, after we moved to our present house, I installed the printing table in the basement. Here the boys went into the T-shirt printing business — shirts with slogans like Greg's *Save the Environment* and 1,000 shirts for the Toronto French School from a silkscreen I drew up. (The school went on to use the design for 20 years.) Meanwhile, Greg came up with an ingenious solution to a production problem. The issue was that we had to wait for each table of shirts to dry before we could print the next batch. Greg laid a string under every row of blank shirts and, after printing, simply lifted the whole row above the table to dry. I can remember about a dozen of these rows swinging above their heads as the boys printed yet another batch.

We were a productive household. Jordy started his music career, playing the drums first thing after school. He later played the banjo and sang with perfect pitch — which he didn't inherit from the Sharp genes, because the Sharps don't sing. I knew Jordy had arrived home from school when I heard him drumming behind closed doors in his room to "Moon Dance" by Van Morrison. His four-piece band "After Dark" played at school dances.

I marvelled at the boys' ingenuity. They devised contraptions that depended on an advanced knowledge of maths and physics that defied my comprehension. Greg was always rigging up something that would fly. At age seven, he sailed off the roof with umbrellas and his own flying devices. On Green Valley, he devised Tarzan-type rope swings, one that catapulted the rider from the hilltop 50 feet over the roof of our house. Six-year-old Tony was designated to take the inaugural flight and luckily crashed into some bushes. I was cowering in the kitchen with blinkers on, afraid to watch. A neighbour called to say, "Do you know your boys are flying through the trees?" It wasn't easy for a coward like me to mother four boys.

My mom, too, was a coward on many counts, and I still share some of her fears. She was afraid of dogs, cats, cars, lakes, showers, flying, sudden movements, and any occasion that required the removal of clothes. I am still cowardly about my boys flying. Nevertheless I remember driving on Highway 401 to Centennial Park with Greg's hang-glider precariously strapped to the roof and attached to the hood ornament with string. I was scared stiff all day watching the kids fly. Today Greg flies through the city on his bike and in fair weather flies his ultralight, and Jordy has his pilot's licence.

When Tony, the youngest, was age nine through 11, he and I travelled in the safety of a train across Canada from Newfoundland to Vancouver Island and as far north as Moosonee, where the tracks come to a halt. Saskatchewan, from the train window, was astonishlingly ruler-straight — a landscape I found more remarkable than the Rockies, just as Samuel Johnson had found that a tree in Scotland was more scarce than a horse in Venice. The ferry from Sydney, Nova Scotia, to St. John's, Newfoundland, took seven hours. Tony went fishing in both oceans and caught a 34-pound Chinook salmon in the Pacific, even though the guide had said that day the fishing was "slim pickin's." Curiously, Tony eats no fish. The salmon was duly stuffed and mounted on the boathouse wall.

That train trip was the second — after my solo trip to New York — in my long love affair with locomotives. I can sit still for days watching the world gliding slowly past my window on a train. I've always wanted to ride the 4,000-mile train trek from Moscow to Vladivostok. Sometimes on my hotel travels with Issy, I will take the train and meet him at the next stop, as I did from Singapore to Bangkok, a 35-hour trip. Trains are an escape into anonymity, and nothing is expected from me.

Back to work at Green Valley Road, where the four boys challenged the laws of gravity and my courage — with their dangerous flying devices. Christopher was masterful with animals and all moving machines —

motorboats, motorcycles, and bicycles. At four he persevered and taught himself to ride a two-wheeler, although I told him to wait a year and Dad would teach him. I watched from the kitchen window as he sat on the bike for two days and rocked from side to side, from one foot on the ground to the other, until finally he wobbled off, both feet on the pedals. A few crashes and then he had it. He put our dog, Snobo, through her paces, making her mind her manners. She looked up to him. Chris was a take-charge person. Once, in a winter blizzard, a friend's collie got stuck in the ice and couldn't make it up the hill to the house. Christopher came to the rescue immediately and, as we watched from the window, did what needed to be done. Without taking the time to put on his gloves, he held her collar and, one step at a time, they slowly climbed the steep hill in the freezing rain, each footfall breaking through the top layer of glassy ice.

Chris took up cooking and baking, his specialty a fruit-topped cheesecake. He once rustled up a dinner for our friends, on the spur of the moment. "Don't go," he said. "I'll make some pasta with a marinara cheese sauce." And when any of our guests left, Chris had an endearing way of going to the door with them, shaking hands, and saying all the right things, which made me smile. It was good to see him instinctively more personable than I.

But Christopher also had street smarts. He was the only one of the boys who wanted to go into the hotel business. His pragmatic plan was to quit school as soon as allowed by law and learn on the job. My guess is that, if things had turned out differently, he would still be working for Four Seasons Hotels.

In 1973, I began seeing a psychiatrist for a year and a half. For two reasons: because my mother had terminal ovarian cancer and I feared I wouldn't cry at her funeral, and because Chris had been born with the forces that formed him — perhaps an atavistic link to my father's dybbuk

— some kind of no-name learning disability that made us all crazy. Ten years later, we would discover that the condition by then had a name — attention deficit disorder — and there were doctors who specialized in its treatment. In maturity, they said, the condition would fade. It would have saved a lot of heartache had we known this earlier.

Psychotherapy turned out to be a good exercise, though, like taking a course in understanding human behaviour. It made me more philosophical. My doctor very kindly shored me up and we came to admire each other. This backfired when I couldn't bring myself to risk losing the doctor's respect and kept one secret from him. But after almost two years, I came to the inevitable I'm-okay-you're-okay conclusion. Now my son Jordy is my therapist. When I told him that I had withheld a secret from my psychiatrist, Jordy browbeat me into confiding in him, on the spot. He's a good listener. Having finally gotten that matter off my chest, I've forgotten now what it was.

In 1974, Chris called me into his room one day to look at a wart on the inside of his right calf. When I asked if it had changed in the last few months, he said yes. So we went to see a skin specialist, Dr. Marvin Lester, who took a sample and a week later called to report that it was benign. But he had made a fatal error — Chris had an obvious lack of pigment in his skin, and the doctor should have given this vital information to the lab so they would know how to read the sample.

Disaster struck in November 1976, when Chris's school called me to say he had a growth in his groin the size of an egg. This was his first semester at St. Andrew's College in Aurora, where, for the first time since second grade, he was enjoying his studies and had brought home a great report card.

Dr. Lester examined Chris's groin and ordered a biopsy. My first question was, "Will he miss any school?" I was not worried, because I could not imagine that it was serious. Why would the worst happen? As it turned out, it was mighty serious — melanoma. The cancer cells had multiplied madly in Chris's young, healthy body. We did not sue Dr. Lester — who has since died — for malpractice, but we probably should have.

Before he became ill, Chris had been working out in a gym and had developed a toned, shapely body. He had looked the picture of health and beauty, with his peerless complexion, no cavities, and platinum-blond good looks. God, he was so wholesome. He had no use for drugs or cigarettes or coffee. His favourite songs were the sunny sentiments of John Denver, his look-alike. And Christopher had a lovely red-haired girlfriend, Joanne Fogler. (There was gossip that Chris had been seen climbing out of Joanne's bedroom window. I've never asked her, because I prefer to hold on to the hope in my heart.) Chris and Joanne tooled around in the new red TR6 we bought him since we knew his time was limited. When a chum once questioned his having a car at 17, I heard him reply, "I'll trade you. You can have the car, but the cancer goes with it."

Issy's considerable business success gave us the trump card people of means hold — the power to pull strings. We found the best specialist available and arranged an emergency appointment. The specialist prescribed a most hideous, unnecessary operation for Chris, a so-called "exploratory," where they butchered him 10 inches up the middle of his chest looking for further cancer cells. The surgeon proclaimed him cancer-free. I thought to myself, "What's the point of the operation when cancer cells can be microscopic?" For this slaughter we had taken him to Boston. And after the operation I let him down by miscalculating what time he would be back in his room. Arriving late, we found him lying there quietly, tears running down his face.

A couple of months after the operation, we were at the summer cottage in Beaumaris, and Chris, in a superhuman effort, managed to pull himself up to the roof of the boathouse using only his arms. He was determined to get his strength back.

The summer before, Chris had taken up golf and asked if we could join the Beaumaris Golf Club across the water from our cottage in Muskoka. We applied and were refused membership because we were Jews — a surprise because we Jews perennially believe that "it's different now." I recall that when we told Chris why we had been turned down, he was very sober for a few days. He was perplexed and felt diminished, like I had felt as a youngster. He thought there must be something wrong with us.

Now, at the cottage, the cancer returned and chemotherapy was prescribed. For these treatments, Chris and I flew to the Sloan-Kettering hospital in New York every few weeks. Our thinking was that if we travelled some distance and consulted the so-called best doctors, we'd maximize our chances. On one descent for landing, the plane careened dangerously close to the skyline — a view King Kong might have seen — but we just looked at each other and said, "What have we got to lose?" Another time, on our way into New York, our cab broke down and we stood in a heavy rain, hitchhiking on the highway. I was hysterical with laughter and tears — we were soaked, the water pouring down our faces. Was there a God, I asked.

On these trips we would go to the hospital, have the chemo, then make a mad dash by taxi to the Plaza Hotel, getting to our room just in time for Chris to drop down in front of the toilet bowl and vomit his guts out. He endured about six of these sessions, but then he went on strike. He had asked the doctor, "Will the chemo cure me?" and when the doctor replied, "No," Chris said he'd rather take his chances than have another treatment.

In the 1970s, the treatments were much more debilitating than they are now. We tried to talk Chris into more chemo, but he refused and we respected his decision. Christopher and I became ceaseless companions. One time he and I were sitting at Sunnybrook Hospital, not far from our home, waiting once again for some doctor, and he said to me, "Mom, it's just you and me; you're always here." But Issy was always there for him too. He would spend every minute after work with Chris.

The grim time arrived when Christopher was hospitalized for what looked to be the last few months of his life in Sunnybrook's D wing (D for Death? I wondered). We asked could we take him home, and the reply was that the morphine he needed was illegal outside the hospital. But with our power to pull strings, we arranged to get a supply of the "Brompton Cocktail" — a combination of whiskey, morphine, and other drugs.

So we kept Chris at home instead of in the hospital, thinking he might be fooled into a hope of recovery. We like to think it worked at times. Besides, at home he wasn't plagued with hospital tubes and routines. Chris slept in our bed, and Issy and I took turns sleeping with him, while the other slept in Chris's room. I remember the guilt I felt on those nights we had sex in the other room, while he was asleep. I gave Chris his shots myself, which I learned by practising on an orange. While his body atrophied horribly, his face became more beautiful. He suffered the indignities of bedsores and relieving himself in bed, on paper, lying on his side. He said to me one night as I went into the bathroom, "You don't know how lucky you are that you can just get up and get out of bed." There came a time when I had to hold his penis while he peed into a bottle. He didn't seem to mind — there were worse things to mind.

Once, as I was fussing with the sheepskin he lay on because of the bedsores, he asked, "Am I going to die?" and I answered, "We hope you will recover, but it's possible you may not. No one knows for sure."

Once I said, "There can't be a God," and he answered, "Don't say that. There is a God."

Those were black days and black nights: I remember going up the stairs so heavily, with nothing but dread in each step. The night before Chris died, the rest of us ate a chicken dinner in his bedroom. We were chatting normally, hoping to make him feel included. He didn't speak. He just lay there quietly, very still, looking at the ceiling. I marvelled at that stillness that he had maintained during the three months he was bed-ridden — graceful and easy in his body, never a twitch of anxiety — like John Denver's "Serenity of a clear blue mountain lake." That last night he was wearing sunglasses, which he had asked for before dinner. He was removing himself, the way people do when they are ready to leave the world.

The next morning, Friday, March 10, 1978, the day he died, Chris said, "Dad, don't go to work today." Issy stood by his bed and I lay across the bed and each of us held one of his big beautiful hands. He was quiet and still, breathing heavily, and then he gasped, "Doctor — ambulance — hospital." A moment later, Issy gestured to me with his chin toward the slowly increasing wet circle on the sheet. It was almost ten o'clock. Christopher's hand was still warm and I had to let go when the men arrived and put him on a gurney and took him down the stairs. I watched from the top as they had trouble making the turn on the landing because he was six-foot-two and, according to the doctor, not even fully grown.

I had been expecting him to die for weeks, and even at times had wished for an end to his suffering — yet I felt a shattering grief and emptiness. If you ask, would I wish this tragedy had happened to someone else, I can't say I would — I don't know why. Today we confer with Chris in our daily lives, and remember his kindnesses, his follies, his recipe for cheesecake — which we have on the wall, framed — and what his life might have been.

I think I don't believe in God. I am tone-deaf to words like "Messiah" and "redemption." I make my one appearance at synagogue for Yom Kippur. We go to the Shaarei Shomayim, a conservative shul, where the men and women sit separately. When I'm asked why such an orthodox temple, I invariably reply, "It's just as good a place not to go." I'm embarrassed to read the prayer books with their repetitious glories to our King of the

Universe. At shul I'm conscious that I'm standing outside the circle — out of step with my crowd.

I attend synagogue because I'm awed by the certain knowledge that for thousands of years the ancient community of Jews has come together to pray on exactly this day with exactly these words. That's why I spend my one evening at shul — Yom Kippur. I feel a tribal link with the culture of my people, but not with their holy writ. I very much enjoy celebrating the holidays with the family, like Passover, Chanukah, the breaking of the fast after Yom Kippur, and the festival of the ingathering, Sukkot. I respect the time-honoured rites of passage like the bar mitzvah and the wedding ceremony. But I don't buy the dogma. I'm one of those who finds it difficult to reconcile science with religion. The Bible, to me, is a lot of tall tales, based on historical events that were exaggerated over long years of stories handed down.

Apostate that I am, I'm sorry to miss the poetry of the other religious pageants which, in the shtetl, were the cultural life, the entertainment. My grandfather Birnbaum mentions in a 1938 letter that he travelled to Ostrowietz, a distance of some 12 miles (two hours by horse and wagon), to buy, for the fall festival of Sukkot, "thanks to G-d a beautiful *esrog*. It's more expensive now than in the past." No citrus grew in Poland, so it would have been shipped from Palestine. At our house every Sukkot, the Israeli *esrog* (citron) in its silver bowl fills the dining room with a fine pungent scent redolent of lemon blossoms. My grandfather's strong faith that "G-d will surely provide" permeates his every letter.

God and I have a very uneasy relationship. We call on each other rarely. That doesn't mean I don't pray for help once in a while. I do, just in case God can hear me, or maybe because billions of believers can't be wrong. My God is different from the God of other people. My God is not petty and he's not human. Punishment and forgiveness are human concepts. Surely God would consider sin simply as the inherent and fallible behaviour of his merely human creature.

(It is said God made man in his own image — but imagine this: a community of crocodiles meets weekly for a séance on the edge of a bay. When they sing their hymns and hosannas, does their God wear the face of a crocodile?)

When good things happen, I automatically say, "Thank God." But I don't believe in asking for forgiveness for sins I should not commit. Is it right that the Nazis could commit murder on a Saturday and make confession to God in church on the Sunday? How can any holy book — whether the Bible or the Koran — preach prejudice and violence in the name of God? I wish there could be a secular law that forbids such scriptures. And revenge and reprisals simply do not work — the reverberation is endless and the fighting foments generations of hatred and bitterness. To me, the greatest warriors of the 20th century were Martin Luther King and Mahatma Gandhi.

Existentialism, when I first encountered it, made more sense to me than the Bible. At university, the works of Jean-Paul Sartre and Ayn Rand resonated, and I still believe that man makes his own fortunes, good and bad, give or take a little *mazel* — luck.

Every Friday I light the Sabbath candles, and we make the blessings over the challah and wine. I began to do this regularly when my children were grown and I started to value Jewish tradition. I take pleasure in performing those same rites my people have done for centuries. We have the traditional Shabbat Friday dinner with our family, which is now into three generations. I enjoy the Jewish culture and the connection to the past: continuity transcends mortality. So I am a cultural Jew rather than a religious one. I have the greatest respect for Jewish ethics and integrity. Given the choice, I prefer working with Jews, because in my chauvinism I believe I can trust their word and their handshake. (This is not to say that all Jews are honourable: we have our share of scoundrels.)

The contributions that Jews make to society are statistically stunning, per capita higher than any other people. In New York, in 1936, the year I was born, 65 per cent of the lawyers and judges were Jewish, as were over half of the doctors, artists, and sculptors. Volumes have been written listing the contributions of Jews like Freud and Marx and Einstein to science and humanitarian causes. Although Jews number only one-quarter of one per cent of the world's population, 20 per cent of Nobel Prize winners are Jewish. It surprises me that anti-Semites give no credence to how different our world would be without some of the great Jews of our time. It is said that countries that expel their Jews do not prosper.

Anti-Semitism will always be with us but will always remain to me a mystery.

Yes, I really wonder why we Jews encounter such hostility. The answer must be envy. You cannot legislate love. And only in recent years has it become fashionable to invite Jews to join formerly restricted golf clubs. Thankfully we have legal protection now against disabilities like Jewish quotas in schools and hospitals and banks and government, not to mention getting rounded up and being shot. How can there be a God who has had a hand in all this — one with such a human agenda? A deity who reviews his checklist regularly and draws lines through the names of people who don't please him?

How can this be?

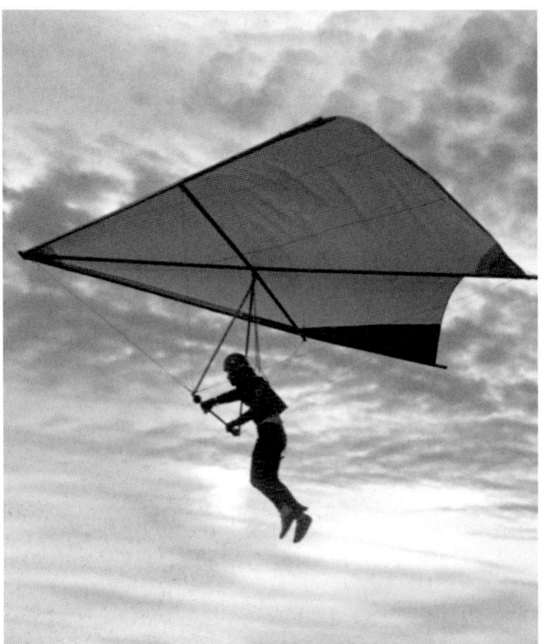

Greg flying the second hang glider he built, 1973. Now he flies his ultralight.

No. 41: Tony, captain of the basketball team, St. Andrews Junior High. PHOTO FROM YORK MILLS MIRROR.

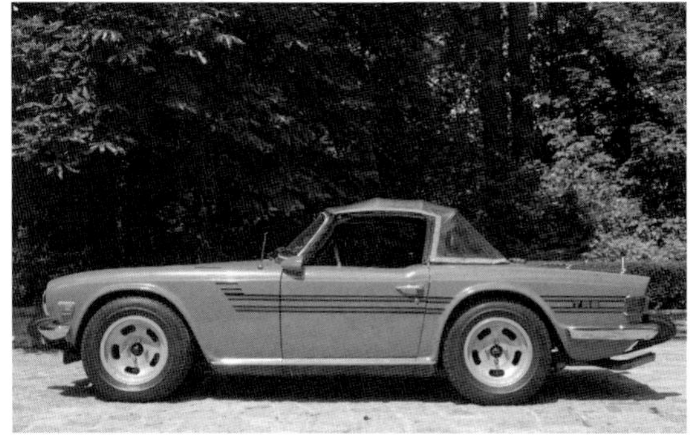

Christopher's flaming red 1977 TR6. The car is still in the garage and Greg takes it for a spin each year on Chris's birthday.

Snobo with her master, Christopher.

Chris needed no instruction on how to operate the boat — he just got in and drove off.

Chris and I at the cottage in Muskoka, 1977.

With his girlfriend Joanne Fogler, 1977.

With Nanny Lil less than a year before he died. He's wearing the tailor-made coral jacket, white pants, and vest of his own choosing. His taste in clothes, like mine, verged on the flamboyant.

The gown, woven with ribbons and string, is now in the textile collection of the ROM.

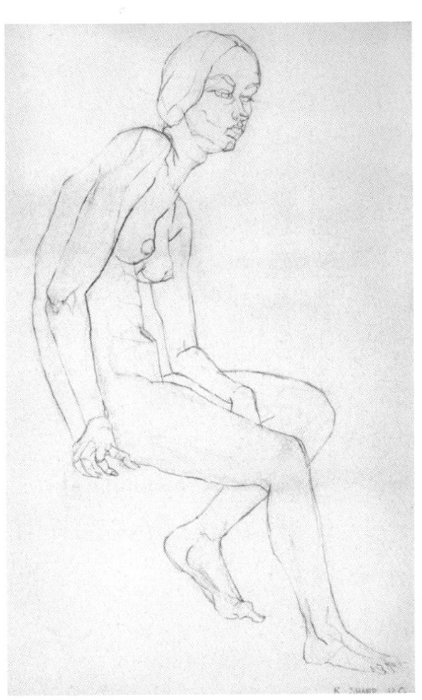

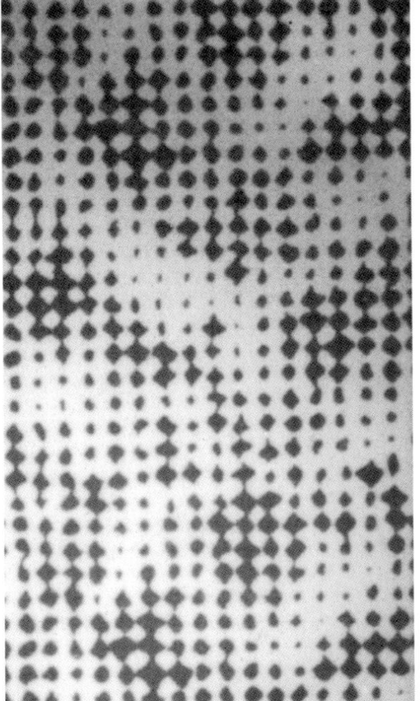

Two drawings, Ontario College of Art, 1965.

Two fabrics and a gown, from my graduating exhibition, 1969. The show took three prizes, including the Lieutenant Governor's Medal and the Art Gallery of Ontario Prize.

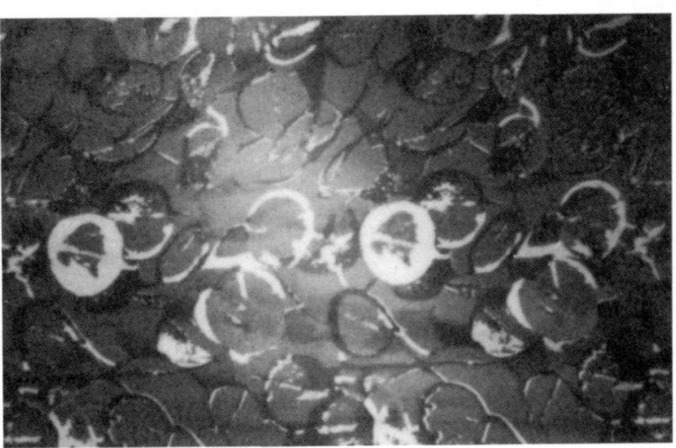

Vi T'su Zibn, Azoy T'su Zibitsik

LIKE SEVEN, SO AT SEVENTY

In 1972, when Chris was preparing for his bar mitzvah, we moved from our unique, sprawling one-level house on Green Valley to a red-brick 1937 boxy house on Forest Glen with four rooms upstairs and four down. (Our son Tony was always nostalgic for the Green Valley house, so when it came on the market again in the '90s, he looked into buying it.) I hoped the move to a conventional house would quiet the frenetic pace of living with four boys. Our previous house had such an open plan that from the front door you could see almost everything going on except who was in the bathrooms. The new house had the privacy of doors. And indeed it did seem more civilized. Jordy immediately claimed the basement rec room as his territory, a private club off limits to adults. My daughter-in-law Ann tells me that I was duped, because there was pot smoking going on and I didn't recognize the sweet scent.

I have never tried pot, ordinary life being heady enough. An art-school colleague once suggested Issy and I join her and her friend for an evening

It's fun to run the house and garden at 26 Forest Glen, and we like having people in.

of indulgence, including pot. Issy said, "Nonsense. There's no reason to try drugs. How would we then have the collateral to convince our kids to be non-users?" He was right, of course. And except for a very rare aspirin, my consumption of drugs to date consists of one diet pill, given to me by a svelte beauty named Denise in the ladies' room of the Four Seasons. This pill speeded me up so much that I couldn't stop cleaning the kitchen and even found myself on all fours washing out the doghouse. I wouldn't take such punishment again.

Jordy's rec room hangout behind closed doors (the doors I soon removed) was decorated with brightly coloured flags — stolen from gas stations. When I noticed a stolen park bench, though, I put my foot down and gave him two days to return it or I would call the police. Like my father, I was a stern communicator.

We've been in this home on Forest Glen for 35 years, half my life. The purchase of it, like many happenings in my life, was a chance event. I heard that the place was to be auctioned, so I brought Issy to see it. He didn't react to the house one way or another, which is like him, but he seemed to respond to the huge garden, which had its own forest. Either I forgot about it or I didn't want to press him, I can't recall which, but about two weeks later, on the day of the auction, I remembered and phoned him at the office: "Issy, this is the day of that house sale, and I really liked that place and forgot to ask if you thought we should bid on it."

"Why didn't you say something?" he asked.

Well, we were lucky. We missed the auction, but the buyers had a change of heart, so the real estate agent called us because we had been listed as interested purchasers. We made an offer of $225,000 and became the owners.

True to its name, the Forest Glen house sits in a leafy glen, unfolding in three storeys down a hill and out to a back garden with almost three acres of sloping valley filled with rolling lawns, virgin pines, New

Brunswick maples, chestnuts, and many other Canadian trees. Some of them have paired off in couples, so by the front door are Mr. and Mrs. Yew, he looking very trim although she has let herself go, and by the back door are pairs of pines and a couple of chestnuts, joined at the hip.

There must be a billion leaves around us, because in warm weather the house is quietly darker and cool. The ancient trees have been permitted, like us, to enjoy their old age undisturbed. Three of the pines may be as much as 250 years old. I miss them in the winter when we go to the California desert, where the 25 varieties of palms are just an excuse for trees. My favourites in Canada are the flowering trees. One year, our flowering almond tree billowed like the pink tulle hoop skirt of an antebellum beauty, but unhappily, that year was its last. I wish I had taken a photo. And when the jolly yellow forsythia blooms, I'm sad, recalling how ephemeral life is: I know the flowers will die in a week.

When we first acquired this large garden, I applied my usual zeal to learning about plants. I made a careful study of a book called *What Flower Is That?* and planted great drifts of rubrum lilies. Every year fewer survived, and then there were none. But that first year, when they grew to six feet, I had life-sized portraits of them painted on panels that now border the fireplace in our house in Palm Springs.

I think plants of a kind should collect in exclusive crowds, as they do in nature. I once saw a whole hill covered in snow-on-the-mountain; it brought a white light to an area darkened by a canopy of trees. So we planted the same species under our own trees. On another slope, in clouds, I planted every gigantic-leafed ground cover I could find in the book. To a dinosaur's toes, the leaves would have seemed the size of periwinkle. The colossal, lacy white sprays of our Heracleum appear unfailingly every July 15, resembling prehistoric Queen Anne's lace. (Unfortunately, some of our chosen plants would have been more comfortable in the climate of South China, as the book suggests.) Once, in

Santa Barbara, I was stunned by a bank of electric-blue cinerarias seen in the magic hour of twilight, when colour is so strong it's almost heartbreaking. I promptly planted a hundred feet of these across the front of our Palm Springs house.

The balance in a large garden comes from the weight of the positive — trees and flower beds — against the negative — the grass. We sometimes need to add some lawn so the shape made by each grassy area is as pleasing and reciprocal as the shape of each flower bed.

As well as flowers, I take equal pleasure in the shapes of leaves, particularly acanthopanox, ginkgo, and the chestnut, which resembles the acanthus leaf found in Greek, and later Georgian, art and architecture.

You might imagine from all this that I love nature, but I don't. I go for a walk in the garden hardly once every two weeks, preferring to survey, through the window, the long shapes of rolling lawns and the golf course beyond with its many shades of green created by the dappled shadow from the tall trees. Mostly I go out for five minutes of sun on the front porch as we used to do outside our shop on Yonge Street.

As for *real* nature, I feel like a fish out of water. As outdoorsmen, Issy and I are a joke. In 1972, we took the boys on a canoe trip in Algonquin Park. The two of us slept in a rented pup tent, little more than a sleeping bag for two, which Issy pinned shut against snakes. I woke in a sweat in the middle of the night and had the most irresistible urge to escape, but I couldn't open the flap because we were pinned in. So I panicked and stood up, dragging my sleeping companion with me. He calmed me down and eventually induced me — I don't know how — to go back into the tent. But in the morning, instead of marvelling at the call of the loons skimming across the glassy water, I had a bout of real claustrophobia and could only think, "How will I ever ride back to the city in a car, with the roof so close to my head, when I'll be compelled to stand up?" I did get over this fear, but I'm not certain it won't happen again.

That was our first and last camping trip. Now I am content to look out at nature from the windows here at home. Recently a pair of robins set up housekeeping in the climbing hydrangea on the brick wall outside our bedroom window, so I took up birdwatching from a chair. The lady robin and I watched each other, eye to eye. She questioned whether I was up to no good. We dubbed the birds Rosadore and Isilie (names courtesy Mirilyn Sharp). Together, husband and wife built a handsome home of exclusively beige materials — not even one green twig — as neat as if they had consulted an Audubon manual. Then Rosadore Robin spread her skirts and settled in her new nest, and after a few days there were four blue eggs. Through thunder and windstorms, she sat implacably on those eggs, until four fuzzy chicks arrived. I wondered if they were all boys, like ours.

In a week they tripled in size, with brown feathers and reddish breasts. Both parents answered their imperious demands by poking food down their throats and cleaning the nest by eating the bird droppings. To teach the boys the art of flying, Rosadore stretched up tall on her toes and flapped her wings, while the young followed suit. One baby would stand on the edge of the nest, stretch to his full height, and sway as if about to take off. While he was deliberating, he pecked his feathers clean like a cat, a trick his mother had shown him. The takeoff would happen any moment, I hoped from my armchair. In a few days, the four baby birds more than filled the nest and had to jostle each other for position, one half hanging over the edge. One morning there were only three, like at our house.

I checked first thing every morning, expecting the nest to be empty, but the boys waited till the day we flew off to visit some hotels, and so did they.

Another armchair nature watch I conduct from our den is my study of the chipmunk condominium in the four-storey rock garden. A few families make their home there, and every spring tiny baby chipmunks venture out to try their luck in the new world of our garden. A red fox, a vixen no doubt, passes through regularly as well as one round fat groundhog.

Tony had a pair of pet ducks that fit into his hand the day we bought them at the farmers market in Stouffville. Soon the large white birds, Donald and Lucy, grew to recognize their master's feet, which they followed. They even came when they were called. The pair had the run of the kitchen and playroom, but whenever they stopped they left droppings. Every evening at dusk, at my prodding, Tony would round them up and put them in a fenced hatch in the garden, safe from the raccoons. But one night when I forgot to remind him, the raccoons got them and Tony was devastated. It was a terrible moment — such anguish and distress. I hardly felt more wretched when my parents died. Here I was, a grown woman, wailing with my forehead pressed against the wall of the dining room, crying, "No, no-o-o-o! Please, God, I want to die!" I couldn't bear to see Tony's pain: my reaction was like that of my aunt Helen when she threw herself on her son's coffin as it was being lowered into the ground. But in the morning I heard Issy's happy voice saying, "Tony, go outside. I think I hear Donald." It was true — one of the ducks had escaped. Tony decided to bring him to the duck pond at the Inn on the Park, the better to forget about Lucy.

Two other birds took up residence at our swimming pool, which I had painted an eggplant colour, giving the water an oceany hue. A mating pair of mallards sat on the edge of the pool and looked at each other as if deliberating, "Is this a swimming pool or a pond?" They decided the pond would suit them and settled there for a few years. We named them Esther and Williams. Williams would arrive first to confirm that all was quiet for the missus. Whenever we saw him coming in for one of his clumsy cartoon landings, we were afraid to look. He would careen and touch down on one outstretched heel, like a float plane on a single pontoon. One year, when the ducks didn't return, we imagined they had set up housekeeping at a proper pond in the golf course.

After the mallards had left, I campaigned to fill in the pool and replace it with grass, since nobody swam in it, including me. I was outvoted for 18 years, until the day that Issy wanted to add a huge, 40-foot living room. I was against the project, but Issy pointed out, "To build the room we'll have to fill in the swimming pool." That guy knows how to negotiate.

When the kids grew up and moved out, instead of downsizing and moving to a condo, in 1990 we upsized and added Issy's large room plus two more, which we find gives us just the right-sized house for two. "Suitable rooms for different hours and occupations," as Edith Wharton wrote in her 1897 book, *The Decoration of Houses*. The added-on rooms now give the house all the charm of a bulging Victorian mansion in which the windows are designed from the inside, placed willy-nilly to suit the furniture, with no regard for exterior harmony. Our new library — entered by a door that was formerly a window — hangs over a cliff, adding yet another tenuous protuberance. Issy and I are both cheerfully mad renovators. While the house was being remodelled, we lived in a small upstairs room for four months as a merry band of carpenters and plasterers whistled and hammered and chopped.

Give us a wreck of a place and we'll light up with the intoxicating possibilities in a new project. We have converted two other places — a summer cottage on Kempenfelt Bay and our house in Palm Springs. Both were white elephants, on the market for two years. We gleefully attacked the 1905 cottage — moved the staircase into the pantry and turned the sitting-room windows into three pairs of French doors opening onto a wraparound verandah. We Victorianized the place with wooden fretwork and trellises like the lacy collars and cuffs of a turn-of-the-century English princess. The exteriors of four buildings on the property were painted in pastel colours of yellow, peach, rust, and turquoise, as beguiling as fairy-tale houses, with names to match — the Witch's House, Seaside, Rose Cottage and Ann's Folly. (Ann's folly turned out to be Greg.)

Our Toronto home is now as much a museum as a house, because we have a huge collection of 18th-century English and French ceramics on display. Every room is chockablock with them — a cabinet of salt-glaze teapots, and open shelves in the four corners of every room featuring a hundred sauceboats, teapots, botanical plates, and porcelain figures five inches high. Each shelf becomes a little stage with its own scenario — on one, a bevy of china musicians play ancient instruments like the zither, the saltbox, and the recorder; on another, a group of actors perform in a contemporary play by David Garrick.

Colour was the initial attraction, ceramic colours — molten glass really — brighter than the flowers in Flemish paintings or the blue of sapphires or the green of emeralds. Ceramic colours that never change through the ages. China can shatter, it's true, but my St. Cloud sugar bowl made in 1710 looks a lot better than people of that date.

At first we collected Regency floral plates, but now our passion is wares made in England between 1745 and 1755, the first decade after the English discovered the formula for porcelain. We still buy rare pieces, now perhaps only a dozen a year, but like a proper chinamaniac I still enjoy the chase — bidding in the middle of the night by phone to London or Amsterdam — for some very rare cup marked with an "A" that may have belonged to the Duke of Argyle, or for porcelain pots from a Chinese junk that sank off the coast of Vietnam in 1690 and was raised in 1992.

I knew I was in trouble the day I was lamenting my chinamania to my close friend James Bisback on the telephone and he said, "Not to worry. At least you haven't started boarding up the windows yet." At that very moment, a carpenter was hammering — making a cabinet out of a window.

Isadore and I enjoy rearranging the ceramics as if we were making a collage. Every time we get a new piece, compositions change. In the early '80s, when only a very few pieces were on display, a dinner guest remarked, "This place looks like a museum." It was a stab in my heart — the one remark I had hoped never to hear. So, with nothing to lose, I began to collect with a vengeance, ostentation be damned. Some guests, uncomfortable with the egregious presence of the china, make a fuss over the few paintings. Museum curators and serious collectors from abroad call every other month or so for a tour when they're in town. Buses filled with ladies come on occasion for lunch from as far away as Buffalo, because we are often asked to host fundraisers. Typically, after touring the china, the ladies will congregate in Issy's large sitting room for a talk by the hostess and a Q&A. Inevitably someone will ask the boring question "Who dusts all this?" and once someone asked, "Is there a catalogue?" Today I can offer my book *Ceramics, Ethics & Scandal,* which I wrote because the curious collector — which I am — cannot help but wonder about the world in which the china was made. Material culture can define an era. So I escaped to 18th-century England with the journals and letters of chroniclers Samuel Johnson and Mary Delany, and to the 19th century of the great collector Lady Charlotte Schreiber, who once remarked, "There's nothing like china to light up a house" — which I wish I had said.

I still have 70 copies of my ceramics book — out of an edition of 4,100. I should never have printed so many. The distributor took half and the other 2,000 copies were stored in my basement. I imagined that the house was listing to the left under the weight of these tomes. To lighten the load, I donated a pile to museums across the country, shipping them postpaid (albeit receiving a tax receipt for each copy). Although the book-keeping was more difficult than the writing, composing that book was a challenge I was almost not up to — I remember masses of notes spread all over the rec room floor. At times I was floundering, not clear on how to pull it all together, but as I wrote in the preface, "The best parts of this book happened accidentally, as I suspect is the case with most creative work. Writing it was, admittedly, a kind of conceit, rather presumptuous, but always an adventure."

While working on the ceramics book, I had a great stroke of luck — I met Esther Evans, librarian extraordinaire at the Jewish Public Library, during my research on Judaica porcelain figures of street sellers in 1760s England. Esther offered to find me a book I was after at the downtown reference library, as she made this trip twice weekly. This was the first of about 30 titles she found for me, including the obscure journals of Charlotte Papendiek, Assistant Keeper of the Wardrobe and reader to Queen Charlotte, wife of George III of England. Mrs. Papendiek had written two volumes with lots of contemporary details on dress design, interiors, and handicrafts. I had expected to spend days in the cellars of Oxford University to access this material, but Esther found the books online in the Yale University library and had them photocopied and sent, for $20. Esther Evans now lives in Israel.

My next project will be a catalogue of our early ceramics only, just for the record, not the challenge. When Issy and I depart this world, the Gardiner Museum of Ceramic Art in Toronto will receive only a few pieces. The family will, I hope, take their favourites. But the rest of the china, if our kids agree, we plan to put back on the market, so others can experience the joy of collecting and regrouping.

Early on, when there wasn't much money, I bought yard-sale china for both use and display, because I prefer things with a past — and besides, new pieces were more expensive. If I didn't have the means, today I would still have just as much fun collecting on the cheap. Prosperity has deprived me of the satisfaction of finding a treasure whilst sorting through junk. When I see a sign for a garage sale, my heart quickens for a moment until it dawns on me. What's the point — it's no longer the early days.

Ceramics are my passion — my cheerful madness. I'd much rather cradle a precious teapot in my hand than sit back and survey paintings — flat squares on the wall — that I find aloof. We started collecting in earnest about 1986. It was then I met china maven James Bisback. We share affection for ceramics and for each other. He's a sweetheart. In February of 1987, Issy and I went out to James's antique shop in Shakespeare — Jonny's Antiques, named for his partner, Jonny Kalisch. We bought a pile of Spode tulips and James suggested that we might enjoy the Ceramics Fair and Seminar held in England every June. Since then, except for one year, the three of us have attended that fair. (In 2004, I was one of the lecturers there — the first to use Powerpoint.) James and I prompt each other to buy selected items either for his shop or my collection. Issy's taste runs to pieces in the round like teapots and figures, rather than dishes. Early on, James had advised us, "It's better to buy just one rare pricey pot than many lesser pieces" — advice I never heeded till lately.

My shtetl background makes me rather pragmatic about art. My strong preference is for useful crafts over tableaus. In foreign cities I always choose to visit the decorative arts museum over the art gallery. Paintings are signed, but an artisan's unmarked work is more mysterious, and it was that mystique that led me to write the book about our collection and about the 18th-century English lords and ladies who poured the tea or made the teapot.

In 1962, I had first discovered auction houses and all the heart-stopping excitement that goes with bidding. At Ward-Price Auctioneers, I spotted a four-pedestal English mahogany dining room table, circa 1780. It was 10 feet long and extendable. Instantly I imagined our four boys sitting around this table, eating daintily instead of bent over their bowls and shovelling the food. An elegant table would have a civilizing effect, I hoped. I wrote the sum $300 in my catalogue as the highest I would bid, but my arm went up involuntarily again and again, so I paid $600 for it. Twenty years later it was worth $20,000. When the kids were little, we sat at that table every night, in the dining room, waiting for Dad until 7:15. If he hadn't arrived by then, we would start eating without him. But just as we picked up our knives and forks, we would hear the click of his sleek shoes on the parquet, running his usual five minutes late. Today we're still dining at that table, now with the third generation.

That same year, 1962, I bought a John Chambers painting of a blond child, who resembled our son Christopher, sitting in a field of poppies. It cost $700 but I told Issy it was $500 (in retrospect, the cost wouldn't have bothered him). I paid the Isaacs Gallery the balance on time, from my housekeeping money. The painting's value soared to $30,000. Never, though, have I bought a carpet, painting, or piece of china as an investment.

Our first Forest Glen collection was antique oriental carpets, about which I made my usual intensive study — hit the books and joined a carpet club where we learned how to distinguish between vegetable and aniline dyes, how to identify the weaving area by type of knot, the number and colour of the wefts, and so on. Every one of our rooms still features a large antique Persian rug. These carpets are glorious to live with — they seem to harbour the soul of their makers. My favourites remain those made by the Qashqai nomads of southwest Persia, who, it is said, follow the grass with their flocks of sheep by day and sleep by night in their black tents, covering about 400 miles a year. Their only luxuries are the pile carpets, mats, and tent bags the families hand-knot with the spun wool of their own live sheep (wool from dead sheep has no lustre). Their tent's mud floor is typically covered with a main carpet, two runners, and a prayer mat — tent bags are used in lieu of chests of drawers. Along the way, the Qashqai trade these goods for staples like shoes and tea and sugar. The carpets are as supple as silk velvet and coloured in the unmistakable blues of the indigo plant, madder reds from roses, and golds from saffron crocuses. Innovation has no place in the hearts of these weavers; they proudly reproduce designs faithful to tribal tradition. I believe I could identify the finely knotted texture of a Qashqai carpet — in a dark room — barefoot.

Around 1975, our acquisition budget upgraded from ordinary to extraordinary. We had been comfortable, but careful about luxuries. When we went skiing to Devil's Glen every weekend with our four boys, they wore their ski boots because it was out of the question to buy four pairs of after-ski boots as well. There were six of us and the dog packed in the car, and we all stayed in one room in the Grace Motel near Collingwood, with its cold, pink concrete floors and very narrow plastic shower stall.

I was a good manager, especially when we needed to save money, because my mother, the economist, had taught me well the lessons of the shtetl. In another life, Mom might have been the chief financial officer in a commercial company. When she married Dad, he had only $40, so she sold the *iberbet* (duvet) and the silver candlesticks she had brought with her from the shtetl, to finance the inventory for the new dry-goods store. Mom became the banker, and with her business acumen, salesmanship, and economy foods such as *opgebrente zup*, she kept the family afloat. Mom changed the habit of saving into an art — parlaying Dad's $40 into $750,000. She would say, "*A farshporer iz beser vi a fardiner* — a saver is better than an earner."

In typical tribal tradition, we usually did not buy retail. Mom always gave deals in our dry-goods store, and expected similar small accommodation from others. Once she sent me to have my shoes resoled, and when I returned, she asked how much it would cost. When I replied that I hadn't asked, she sent me back to the shoemaker for the price. My mom trusted her own business savvy and felt that my dad and I were a couple of rubes who parted with money too easily. When I first went into the interior design business, Mom had the chutzpah to ask me, "*Nu, Rifkele, zog mir dem emes.* Tell me the truth — are you charging the customers for your services?" In a way she was right, because sometimes I didn't really care if I got paid. She also advised, "Don't pay for goods up front. *Opgetsolt iz opgeleygt* — money paid, work delayed." I've been royally swindled a few times — once I was out $100,000 by paying up front.

My dad paid all his bills immediately, always in cash and in person, from a bankroll in his hip pocket. To this day I pay my bills the day they arrive, too, and pay for all antiques on the spot, although invariably I ask, with my mother's savvy, whether there could be a better price. (Issy usually steps away while I do this.) "Leverage" was not a word in my dad's vocabulary, and I'm also not comfortable borrowing: "*Borgn makht zorgn* — borrowing makes for worrying." I've noticed that many real estate moguls are eventually brought down by leveraging. My dad may not have been a mogul, but he was never broke.

The only item I've ever paid for in installments, other than a painting, was *The Encyclopaedia Britannica*. When the salesman came to my door — Jordy was in diapers — he found an easy target. I wanted my kids to have a resource I never had. "Do I dare," I thought, "indulge in these regal maroon almost-leather volumes with gold letters on each spine? Can I *fargin* myself such frivolousness?" The $15-per-month payments seemed to go on forever. Through the years, our encyclopedia set has sat regimentally undisturbed, though occasionally it's served to elevate the bed, between the box spring and mattress.

In the 1980s, Issy's hotel business boomed and all the world's goods were within our reach — no limits. We could have bought a yacht or a plane or an Aston Martin. I prefer to drive a generic car and spend my money on ceramics. In 1982 I still had my aging Mercedes, which I planned to replace with a Toyota, so Ruth, my office manager, put an ad in the paper.

Someone called and asked, "Does it have a sun roof and what colour is the car?"

"Rust and white," I answered.

"Oh, you mean it's a two-tone?"

"Well, not exactly. It has a bit of rust here and there, as in rusty."

The car didn't sell, so I let my colleague John Edison drive it instead of taking the bus. After some months he came to work one day by public transport. I waited for him to offer some explanation because I didn't want to put him on the spot, but there was no further mention, that day or ever. He continued to come to work by bus. The car had simply vanished. My next and favourite car was a red Toyota station wagon — not a blue-red, but the yellow-red I preferred. It was great for transporting plants and flowers. One day as I was stepping into the car, I happened to look down at the chrome threshold of the open door and was surprised to see there the word … "Volvo"? Seems I still catalogue cars by colour.

But back in the '80s, although Issy's business was booming, he didn't bother buying a fancy car or other rich trappings. He has always had a unique attitude toward money. He seems not to notice it. There are no restrictions — he says yes to everything. So I have had to exercise self-control.

Issy is not about money. His morality of money is his own. He's never been driven by opportunism or the best bottom line. Profit has always followed. His goals from the beginning have never changed. Always he was out to run a respected business, to share the wealth, and to boast the happiest employees. It was integrity that counted.

The hotel business had begun with Issy's dreams nearly five decades ago. After studying architecture at Ryerson, he joined his dad in Max Sharp & Son Construction, building bungalows — designed by Issy — and apartment houses. Just before we were married, he was building a strip motel for a client, Jack Gould. The place was typical, with seven rooms each side and parking in front of every door. Like the Bates Motel of *Psycho* fame, it was hard to find: not right on the highway, but near the junction of Highway 27 and the Queen Elizabeth. So, during construction, Issy suggested to Mr. Gould, "Jack, why not build the place twice as large, with 28 rooms instead of 14, and leave half the rooms unfinished? It won't cost much more, and that way you'll get twice as much cottage roof to display a larger 'Motel 27' sign."

Jack took Issy's advice, and business was so brisk that the extra 14 rooms were finished off immediately after the motel opened. So Isadore began to dream about building his own motel, but in a downtown location.

Sometimes while we were driving around the city, instead of paying attention to the road, he would be craning his neck out the car window, looking for possible sites. Now he had two jobs: building apartment towers all day, and at night sitting at a typewriter in our spare room (later the nursery), with one finger pecking out proposals for hotels on various sites he had on hold. These three-page prospectuses would then be packaged in a colourful Duotang folder, and the next hurdle was to find investors. So Issy would park himself regularly on the doorstep of Cecil Forsythe, of Great-West Life Insurance, and pester him for money. After three years of proposals, Forsythe — who had taken a liking to Issy — finally caved in and pledged half the financing. With credit from the construction workers and with $90,000 each from Issy and two partners — his brother-in-law Eddie Creed and a friend, Murray Koffler — the Four Seasons Hotel on Jarvis Street was born, opening March 21, 1961. (If Murray and Eddie had kept that money in the company, their $90,000 investments would today each be worth over a billion.)

Now, as I write this in 2006, Issy still heads up Four Seasons Hotels and Resorts, which manages 74 hotels and employs 35,000 people around the globe. Within 10 years these numbers will double. Issy, in his earnest, evangelical style, preaches the importance of "the Golden Rule" — treat others as you wish to be treated — to his employees at all levels. A bell of recognition rang when I read John Gunther's biography of Albert Lasker, "the father of advertising" in America. I found likenesses between Issy and the charismatic Lasker, who is described as "an apostle of the obvious" and as having "a glandular optimism." Issy's charisma derives from substance — he is a benevolent governor rather than an egotistical dictator. And when we travelled recently to the Dominican Republic to review a new hotel site, I watched him in action, admiring his prodigious enthusiasm. He focused as if this project was the *only* Four Seasons Hotel.

Which reminds me of a funny story.

Isadore was so happily occupied at the office that he just didn't go into stores or malls, so the rare day that he did go shopping was a good day indeed for the salesman. Everything looked so good to Issy that he bought the lot — especially when it came to shoes. One Saturday, wandering along Bloor Street, Issy spotted a pair of his-style dressy loafers in the window of David's shoe store, so we stopped in. We were accosted immediately by a fawning salesman who looked a lot like comedian Rowan Atkinson's alter ego Mr. Bean. He asked if he could help. "Yes," said Is, "I'd like to try on these in a size 10 and a half or 11 in brown if you have it, or black."

"Ahhh, sir," said Mr. Bean, rubbing his palms together. "Ahhh, may I say, sir, you have excellent taste. You have selected our finest model — handmade in Italy. Please have a seat and I'll see what we have left." With that, he disappeared to return shortly with four boxes and officiously settled himself on his stool. He began delicately to unwrap his precious goods and raised one shoe in the air, turning it in a full circle on his fingertips, as if presenting a sculpture for our appraisal. With his silver shoehorn, he fit it onto Issy's foot as smoothly as if he were slipping a diamond ring on a dowager's finger.

"What size are these?" said Is. "Hmmm, maybe the half-size smaller would be better. And does the brown one with the tassels come in black? And what else do you have in dress shoes?"

By this time, Mr. Bean had been back and forth from the stock room several times and his smile was beginning to wilt. He was mopping his brow when Is asked, "Does the slip-on come in patent leather? Bring the 10 and a half as well. And I'd like to try that black-tassel loafer in the smaller size."

The salesman was gone a long time. Either he was having a bite of lunch or he was lost in the bowels of the basement three floors down.

We waited.

We waited some more.

Finally here he was, balancing a tower of boxes so high he staggered like a drunk, just managing to keep the structure in check. By this time we were sitting in an island of boxes. Mr. Bean doggedly presented the patent-leather dancing slippers in the size 11, probably wondering if this pain-in-the-neck customer would buy even one pair of all these shoes — just when Issy pointed out six pairs on the floor: "I'll take this pair and those, and all of these." The patent-leather dancing slippers are still in service.

Whenever I reflect on Isadore's fine character, I am reminded of his mom, Nanny Lil, the consummate *Yiddishe* mother, who, like a mama bear, would swat her pups when they misbehaved, or smother them with crushing hugs. She was known by many sobriquets: Lil, Nanny Lil, Lilli, or, intimately, Loncha. She lived not for herself, but for her children. Lilli had little time for the nonsense of humour or irony. She was hostile to all mother-in-law jokes. She was a lady of no regrets, and so are her four children — none of whom drinks, smokes, has left a mate, or seen a shrink. Nanny Lil and the Sharp family all sleep well at night because they usually don't make the mistakes that bring regret (like I do). I don't think Lil had the inclination for self-examination. Also, in the matriarchal tradition of the shtetl, where women were often the breadwinners, she firmly believed that women were just a little brighter than men. This was a boon for Issy, who was never catered to or treated like a prince, even if he was the only son.

I would often run one flight up from our first apartment to visit Nanny Lil in the penthouse and watch her in action in the kitchen. She was large, but she moved gracefully. She didn't simply walk — she glided, like the prow of a sailing ship breasting a wave. Lil could wash her very short frizzy hair under the kitchen faucet in seconds, and surprised me once with her comment "It's too bad you have such straight hair."

During the preparation of the weekly Sabbath dinner, Lil stirred fricassee on the stove while frying chicken wings breaded in flour heavy with garlic salt and tossing noisy baking pans in and out of the oven with the deftness of a juggler. Everyone would be present for Friday dinner — or else. She cooked for 30, with one oven and no help. The menu included everyone's favourites: gefilte fish for Eddie, chicken soup for Siggy, cheesecake for Issy, and brisket and chicken and more for everybody else. All her sauces were ketchup-based. After dinner, each of us took home boxes of leftovers that lasted halfway to the next Friday. Every box held chicken soup with spaghettini noodles in huge glass jars labelled "Hoover Carpet Shampoo."

Lil had taken me to the Y for a steambath and my first massage when I was 18. She had a surprising lack of vanity, which I found admirable. Although she was overweight, she ran around in the nude with no self-consciousness.

Nanny Lil was the undisputed head of the family. In business and social affairs, her word reigned. When Max built two identical houses side by side, the family moved into one and Lil put the other up for sale. Along came a buyer who preferred the house the Sharps were living in to the empty one. "Done," said Lil. "You like this one better? No problem. It's yours. We'll move." I never heard Lil whine or waste time gossiping. When Blackie, her pet cocker spaniel, gave birth in the night to six pups of various colours, Lil was there to midwife for seven hours and cut off the tails. Issy's grandmother, Creyndl Gotfrid, lived with them, and every morning Lilli (her youngest daughter) would administer the requisite insulin shot.

When we decided to name a son after Creyndl, we needed a name beginning with C. How did we ever give our Jewish son such a Christian name as Christopher? We were innocent because, incredibly, we didn't make the connection. But at another level we didn't want our kids to have names as Jewish as Rifke and Issy. Such was the fashion in the '50s.

Issy's dad, Papa Max, was celebrated for his irrepressible cheeriness, his lack of prejudice, and his high morals. Max was not given to excesses — he was even-keeled and soft-spoken, never making a sudden outburst or a hurried announcement. Superlatives like "exciting" or "great" were not part of his vocabulary. He liked my cooking because I used olive oil instead of *schmaltz*. But invariably, after a meal, when I might ask, "How was the salmon stuffed with saffron rice?" he would give his legendary highest compliment: "There's nothing wrong with it." This was praise indeed.

I'm convinced that the fine values of Papa Max have been handed down in a rabbinical tradition for hundreds of years, becoming an almost genetic predisposition — an atavistic connection of Issy's. Isadore's great-grandfather, R. Moishe Yekel Scharf, wrote a book titled *The Paths of Propriety* in 1878, in Auschwitz, Poland, the same town Papa Max was born in. The book consists mainly of commentaries on the Talmud, but its four prefaces, known as permissions and written by great rabbis of that time, recorded that Yekel Scharf was renowned for his integrity, propriety, and especially his humility. Even though his professional commentaries were widely acclaimed, his book was not published until after his death, by his sons. Such humility is not part of *my* psyche.

With the burgeoning of the hotel company, our lives changed and we went from vacationing every five years to jet-setting every other month to visit Four Seasons Hotels around the world. We crisscrossed time zones where it was day for night, or the tropics for winter, and the esoteric became commonplace. I'm good with the tedium and delays of overnight flights, because I just open one of my stock of books or eat a piece of dark chocolate to enhance my mood. As for jetlag, I simply don't bother with it.

Travelling to the hotels was indeed exotic and foreign. I went from speaking Yiddish with my parents to struggling with pleasantries in Urdu, Arabic, and Japanese, and to the challenges of uncooked or unknown foreign foods. We ate cross-legged in our socks on a floor in Kyoto and dined on silk cushions in the company of camels in the desert near Riyadh. While the camel looked on, I was offered a cup of her warm milk. I pressed it to my lips and pretended to sip, then passed the milk to Issy. In the Tokyo fish market, we were served huge chunks of raw fish — beer and sushi at 7 a.m. Issy feigned difficulty handling his chopsticks and couldn't quite get a grip on the slippery fish. At Japanese business dinners we were always seated with the higher-ups, in the centre of a long banquet table, with everyone else descended from there so the least important people sat in the end chairs. Now when we entertain at home, we often sit in the centre rather than at the ends.

In foreign lands, I took to consorting with kings and princes as easily as with the grocer and postman at home. It doesn't come naturally to me, but I make a good show of it. Issy and I enjoy the company of the Saudi Prince Alwaleed, a major investor in Four Seasons. The prince has brought Saudi Arabia into the modern business world and made the Saudis an international player. He's a good-hearted young man, generous and forward-thinking, especially about women's rights — his pilot is a woman. He would probably speak out more strongly against civil disabilities in Arabia if it was safe and practical to do so. We are often guests in his palace and his retreat outside Riyadh. He lives in an opulence found rarely in the West.

In the summer of 1989, magazine maven Malcolm Forbes invited us to Tangiers for his weekend birthday celebration. Malcolm flew us all there in two 727's. I was the only nobody in a lustrous crowd that included Walter Cronkite, Barbara Walters, and Henry and Nancy Kissinger, to name a few.

And I love our hotel openings in foreign places because I don't know anyone there and I can move around unobserved and watch the parade of moguls and their mates, all dressed in their best costumes. I can even audit their conversations — it's easier and more fun than making small talk.

On these many trips, I derive much *naches* from watching my husband in action, making speeches, or structuring deals — he could write the book on negotiating. As he says, "You have to address the needs of the other guy." He has a remarkable facility for coming up with just what is needed, and on cue. He says that when he loses this timing he'll quit. He always keeps his cool — not me. Any small thing can drive me up the wall. No thing drives Issy to distraction.

The man is imperturbable.

And he never fails to win the respect of any crowd. Isadore has no enemies. Once, at a board meeting in India, he had to contend with one naysayer so irate that the man turned red and spluttered. Isadore continued quietly to frame his case till all on the board were won over. And in every hotel he visits, Issy traditionally holds a "fireside chat" with all the employees. These talks have become the stuff of legend. He takes the staff into his confidence and shares with them the company's plans for the future, just the way he would speak to his board of directors. I sometimes sit in and, even though I've heard it all before, I become one of the converted. As I sit here writing in our basement rec room, formerly Jordy's music den, I am surrounded by plaques and trophies Issy has received from business groups, universities, newspapers, and charities, and on the wall in front of me are 14 framed magazine covers featuring his face. In 1992 he was honoured by *The Financial Post* as CEO of the Year, and for an unprecedented eight years in a row, *Fortune* magazine has ranked Four Seasons as one of the world's best 100 companies to work for.

I would like to claim I had a hand in my husband's great success, but if I did, it was only because I kept quiet and didn't tell the truth about my fears for some of his schemes. Like the summer's day in 1961 when we drove up to the corner of Eglinton Avenue and Leslie Street in Toronto, to a hilly meadow of tall grass. "Here," said Issy, "is the site for the second hotel, the Inn on the Park. What do you think?" There was not another building in sight, trucks were turning into a municipal garbage dump across the road, and just then a CPR freight train roared by the property. I thought, "What can he be thinking? Real hotels are always downtown, usually handy to the railroad station, and have regal names like Royal York, King Edward, and Prince George." At the time, there were no rural hotels other than inns like the Jolly Miller, and I could not imagine why any hotel guest would choose to sleep in suburbia. I remember the disquieting thought that if this new venture failed, we might have to sell the house and move to a cold-water flat — in fact, our house was the collateral for the loan. But I kept my fears to myself. Instead, I would say something like "Do what you think you should." In this case, as usual, his suburban hotel was a roaring success.

Throughout the years, I've watched in disbelief as Issy's aspirations have come to fruition. Early on, he made some very audacious statements that seemed like pipe dreams. He told me once that his aim was to make the name Four Seasons a worldwide brand, synonymous with luxury, like Rolls-Royce. "Sure," I thought, "with only about 10 hotels — hardly likely," but I didn't let on. My most valuable contribution to his success has been my silence.

Contrary to popular perception, though, travelling to our hotels now is not as exciting for us as going backpacking might have been when we were young. It's true that when we stay at Four Seasons we are treated to all the luxuries, but we are not guests in the usual sense. For us, visiting hotels is work, and staying home is the vacation; nevertheless, I do enjoy the carefree way that hotel life affords, as well as the admirable and dishy hotel managers.

In July 1984 we holidayed in Communist Russia, hoping to pick up en route a few tribal rugs in Bokhara, Uzbekistan, since I was still into my carpetmania. We hit all the obligatory tourist stops — memorably Pavlosk, the country seat of Catherine the Great's son Paul, and the tragic Tsarskoe Selo, the bucolic summer palace of Nicholas and Alexandra from which, on July 17, 1918, they and their family were summarily carted off to Ekaterinburg in Siberia to be executed. The five children had names straight from Tolstoy — Olga, Marie, Anastasia, Tatiana, and Alexei.

Whenever we were sightseeing, Issy was a reluctant tourist. He'd sooner hop around the world to his hotels, spending a day in each one, than sit on a bus tour to see the country houses of the tsars. Sometimes on our travels I feel guilty schlepping my ambivalent captive, who'd rather be working. In our St. Petersburg hotel room, the first thing Issy did was consult his travel schedule to confirm by telephone our flight home. Then he cannily checked behind the curtains and under the bed, whispering that he was certain the room was bugged. In the streets and on the highways, everywhere we found colossal images of Vladimir Lenin, statues in public parks and busts on buildings — Lenin canonized. There were banners across roads and highways with red-lettered slogans announcing the current Five Year Plan — which gave Issy the idea to put a banner across Leslie Street advertising the Terry Fox Run. (Issy founded that run. In 1977, the young Terry Fox lost a leg to cancer and pledged to run across Canada to raise funds to find a cure. When he had to abandon the run because his cancer returned, Issy spoke to Terry while he was in his hospital bed and promised to establish an annual marathon in his name.)

In St. Petersburg, we walked every evening to a restaurant of Fodor's choice. When we pointed to our selection on the menu, the waiter explained, in broken English, that the foods listed comprised *all* the dishes that the place might offer over a year, but only *one* of these items was available daily.

From Moscow we took the six-hour flight by propeller plane to Bokhara. Not an empty seat available. Everyone in Russia was entitled to fly almost free, but the wait for seats could be years. As soon as the seat-belt sign was turned off, there was an announcement, in Russian of course, and all the passengers folded down their tray tables in concert, on which the attendants dropped one wrinkled apple, stored from last year's crop. About five hours out, the seat-belt light went on and the captain announced we were landing (we guessed). On the ground, I was waiting for Issy to round up the luggage when he came rushing and said, "Quick, let's go, we have to run! The plane's leaving any minute — and this is not Bokhara, it's Tashkent." A soldier had alerted Issy by nudging him and pointing to a sign that read "Tashkent."

Bokhara, when we arrived there, was a big disappointment. Not only were there no rugs — we were told the best place to buy old Bokhara carpets was in Hamburg — there was little trace of the low mud-brick buildings and native charm of the old market town. The place had been completely Russianized with tall concrete apartment houses providing evenly small quarters for all. Our hotel room was damp with some of the wallpaper strips unstuck and flapping in the breeze from the window air conditioner. Not only that, the drain pipes in the bathroom floor were exposed. For the evening meal, we ordered mutton, which must have contained maggots or some other contamination, because the next morning I woke up with the runs. As I came out of the bathroom, Issy was just on his way for a morning run. I said to him, "Is, you better get going because you don't have much time before you get this bug." He answered that he never bothered with germs, but 20 minutes later he returned and hurried straight into the bathroom, without a word.

The next day, back in Moscow for the last night before our trip home, we called the doctor because Issy was feeling quite ill. Enter Dr. Anna Bukhanovsky wearing a kerchief tied under her chin like a peasant girl. She came with a retinue of four hulking male nurses in white coats and demanded of Issy, "Lie down please, mister." She kneaded his stomach, then asked him to sit up and stick out his tongue, which had a greenish tinge. "Mister," she said, "I want for you to come to the toilet with me and to make for me some samples right now, so I will see, yes or no, you go to hospital — by us you cannot go from Russia with catching germs."

The men in the white coats looked quite capable of carrying out these orders, but Issy managed eventually to charm the lady into returning the next afternoon after he promised to rest and drink the prescribed gallons of salt water. Late that night, with the help of the Canadian consul, we stole out of Russia and the threat of quarantine.

Playing in the kitchen.

ABOVE: Upsizing: The new library, 1989.

Blackie and her brood.

I missed out dressing shop windows, so now I dress tables. The Passover table with sand and cacti representing Israel.

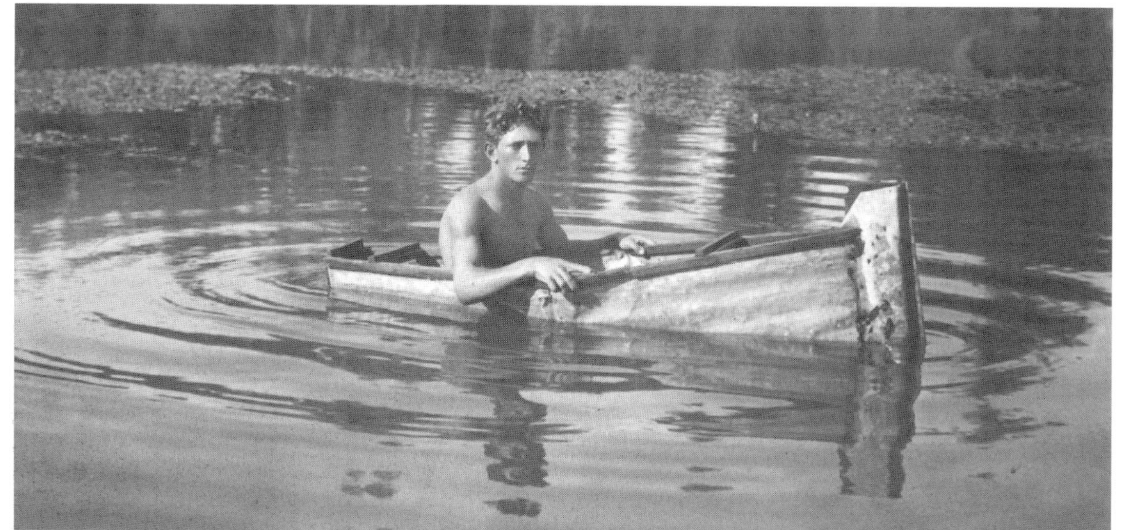

Max Sharp in Israel, 1920, in a canoe he built. Max had come from the shtetl of Auschwitz, Poland, and remained in Israel for five years. He worked on Israel's first kibbutz, Deganya, before coming to Canada.

Issy and his three sisters, 1934. Edie, Bea, and Nancy in front. They taught him to be tidy, to iron his own clothes, and to respect women above men.

Lilli Gotfrid, 1926, soon to be Issy's mom.

Isadore, 1948.

And in 1980.

Officer of the Order of Canada, 1992.

Issy pouring concrete for Motel 27 — the job that inspired him to get into the hotel business — 1954.

CHAPTER SEVEN

Arbet Avade

BUSINESS AS USUAL

My life is divided into two periods: before Chris died (BC) and after (AC). AC, life has sped up. The last 30 years have practically evaporated, probably because Issy and I buried ourselves in work. Time passes more slowly when you're quiet and still, but I continued my energetic work life.

I had closed Green Valley Workshop and opened Rosalie Wise Design in the early '70s. First I did some model apartments at 120 Dale Avenue for Issy, and then I did the same when he opened Granite Place. Apartment 303, in the west building, was done in grey and white Fortuny fabric; a buyer came along and requested that condo, including the complete furnishings. We also did some design work for a few of the apartment owners. Our first client, Mrs. Seagram, requested a beige wall-to-wall carpet that she felt would harmonize with floral sofas better than the oriental carpet which was a legacy from her mother-in-law. We showed her two samples, one a bonded carpet for $10 a yard and the other a woven carpet for double the price. She chose the lower quality

The house in Palm Springs we cherish. The haunting scent of the jasmine on the verandah and the hovering mountains that look like a huddle of huge eagles clutching the flat sands of the valley with their bony talons.

because at her age, 75, she felt it would do the job. And I ended up buying her magnificent antique Sarouk carpet, which is now the feature of our front room.

I needed help in 1978, so I hired a partner, Stephen Baillie, who had always been so helpful to me in the Switzer fabric showroom where he worked. In proper socialist style, I always had partners — never proletarian workers. Stephen had impressed me when he said, "The first thing we'll need is a filing cabinet to keep track of billing and purchasing for our clients."

"Great," I thought. "Of course — a filing cabinet. Why didn't *I* think of that? Just what we need. Here is someone who will take charge of the details and make sure we're business-like."

After a month, I came to understand that I had made a poor choice. Each of us expected that the care and feeding of the filing cabinet was the domain of the other. Each of us saw ourselves as the designer and the other as the filing clerk. So I gave him a handsome settlement (as my father would have) and sent him back to the showroom. Now I called up George Brown College and asked them to put this note on their bulletin board: "Wanted, mature bookkeeper for small interior design office. Must be willing to double as receptionist." Enter Ruth Malitzky, a capable and honest Jewish lady four years older than me, with a Brooklyn accent and a bright green dress. She stayed for 17 years, until I closed the office in 1995 and moved home to work. At R.W. Design, Ruth became the accountant, receptionist, purchaser, manager, and my protector. She gave the company credibility and locked away (from the staff) all paperwork germane to the finances. During her first week in the office she was late because of a transit strike, so Ruth volunteered to deduct the two missing hours from her wages. She tells me that I ruled against this, saying, "It was your intention to be on time."

Our office was a walk-up at 60 St. Clair West conveniently across from our Granite Place clients. The landlord, Mr. Lagussis, like the good landlord my mother had been, was always helpful and fair — especially during the cockroach incident. We had a lot of truck with cockroaches in this office and also our next location. It seemed that Toronto's cockroach community had courageously migrated to North Toronto from the security of the downtown Jewish ghetto. What I hate about cockroaches is that they hide, unlike an ant, who will be friendly and tickle your hand as he ambles across. One day in the office kitchen, I was making coffee, which was my job, when out jumped an insect I didn't recognize, having never met a cockroach. Mr. Lagussis asked for a description of the bug, then said, "I will be over this afternoon to take care of it. Now tell me this, Mrs. Sharp — did it hurry?" Hurry it certainly did. But the bugs never reappeared after the landlord installed small roach hotels, which had welcoming entrances but no exits.

Our next office location, 3419A Yonge Street, eight blocks north of Lawrence, was a walk-up above Bill's City Restaurant, owned by the short-order cook, our landlord, Mr. Steve Mintsopoulos. A stained cardboard sign in the window promised *Souvlaki* was Bill's specialty. It was a tiny place with one booth, two tables and chairs, and very few diners. Steve and his wife, Mary, were the most disgusting people and as landlords they were abominable. He always wore a long filthy apron and she had bad feet and a high hairsprayed coiffure and was usually sitting down doing nothing. We put a lot of improvements into the premises — mirrored wall up the stairs, sanded floors, paint — and asked would he share the cost. Not a penny. The week we moved in, Mr. Mintsopoulos ran up the steps, barged in, and had the temerity to accuse us of making our own coffee when we should be buying it from him.

One lunchtime, as I put a slice of Dimplemeier rye in the toaster and pushed the lever down, out hopped an enraged cockroach. "Oh no, not again." This time I recognized the species — it hurried. I went down to Bill's for help. One customer was sitting in the booth having a cup of grey coffee in a grungy cup and smoking a cigarette.

"A cockroach, it couldn't be, we've never seen absolutely not even one cockroach in this building ever," said Mr. M., wiping his hands on his greasy grey apron.

"No no no, not even one," Mary backed him up, never leaving her chair.

"Ah, I see what you mean, Bill. Well, in that case," I answered, "let me put your mind at rest. Should you ever come across a cockroach in this restaurant, you'll surely know where it's coming from — upstairs."

At 3419A, at the peak of R.W. Design's success, we had a staff of seven. Eighty per cent of our work was for Isadore and his hotels. Our advertising flyer read, "At Rosalie Wise Design we consider how materials meet." We had a wonderfully large, friendly front room that doubled as our library and reception room, with a 10-foot-long antique pine table in the middle. The walls were lined with shelves of sample wallpapers and especially fabrics, folded neatly in colourful stacks of prints and plains and stripes and velvets. There were four of us, on average, and lots of laughs at coffee break. I would tour the others' work at their drafting tables and if I commented, "I see you're still doing your Bach exercises," this was a metaphor for "Go back to the drawing board."

To be alone, I hid in the back office, where I quietly phrased architectural interiors on a drafting table with an HB pencil, to the classical music on CBC-FM or tapes of some of my favourites — *Song to the Moon* by Dvorak; *Au Fond du Temple Saint* by Bizet; Dome Epais by Delibes; *Symphony in G minor* by Mozart; or Massenet sung by Mady Mesplé — all at full volume, of course. At home, Issy turns down the volume every time I turn it up.

I find the round nasal tones of opera sung in French have a particular appeal. Or give me an aria like *Der Holle Rache* by Mozart, composed at the time my great-great-great grandfather Shmarya Tyszler was singing in the shul in Ozarow. Like many people, I prefer the familiar over anything new. I first understood this prevailing taste when I came across Mary Delany's memoirs of mid-18th-century English life. When she attends Handel's *Messiah* and his oratorios in 1740s London, she finds the phillistine crowd unreceptive to the *new* music. As for my own modern music favourites, Jordy says, "Mom, you like any tune you can dance to." True. From a Scott Joplin Charleston to a Johann Strauss waltz, or give me a slinky Argentinian tango — I do them all by myself in the kitchen. And what about the counterpoint of Fred Astaire's phrasing when he sings Irving Berlin's "Let's Face the Music and Dance" or the Beatles' "I want to hold your ha-a-a-a-a-a-and."

In my back office, listening to CBC, my first big design job was the Four Seasons Houston in 1982: the guestrooms, corridors, and suites. I flew to Houston to direct the installation. At 9 a.m. on the day of the hotel-opening party, the Pavarotti Suite was empty but for the silver-grey carpet. Luciano P. was to arrive at four. We had to place all the furniture, plants, curtains, cushions, and bed linens in his sitting room and bedroom, as well as in the connecting bedroom, where the soprano would sleep. The decoration was a mixture of antiques, crystal, and modern glass tables and lamps in a silver-gilt and cream scheme. The opera star's bedroom had a high four-poster bed with a white eyelet canopy, and I wondered if he would sleep there or with the soprano. We were just placing the fruit and flowers on the dining room table as the elevator brought him to the 20th floor. *Phew!*

That evening I sat beside the master singer at the big banquet but hardly got a word in because of the continuous stream of ladies bending over between us to pay him homage. At one point, someone's long blond hair dangled dangerously close to my soup.

The next time I saw Pavarotti was when we opened our hotel in Milan in 1993. We were having dinner with Riccardo Muti, director of La Scala, when he said, "We are rehearsing *Don Giovanni* tomorrow and you are welcome to come." What an offer! At La Scala I was the only audience in the regal red velvet opera house, designed in 1778, the year my earliest known

Birnbaum ancestor was born in Ozarow. (I wish I'd been in attendance at La Scala in the time of Maestro Arturo Toscanini, ranked as the genius opera director of the 20th century.) I sat up front near Riccardo and listened as he sang along with every aria, just as his predecessor Toscanini had done. Luciano Pavarotti sang the principal role wearing a ludicrously wide pair of jeans. It was an unforgettable afternoon of glorious music.

After we finished the Houston project, R.W. Design worked on many more Four Seasons Hotels: Washington, London, Vancouver, Toronto, and a new hotel in Paris that was cancelled after we had drawn up a complete set of specs, including a full-scale drawing for a custom hook on the back of the bathroom door. The French project paid us $80,000.

Over the years we designed a million hotel rooms, each featuring the identical layout: the ubiquitous bed flanked by two lamp tables, the artwork over the bed, the TV opposite in the armoire. At the time there were standards we had to obey. Issy insisted on three specs: wallpaper (I preferred paint); a quilted bedspread — this bedcover if rolled up and stood in a corner you might mistake in the night for your roommate. (I preferred a duvet); and a curtain valance (I preferred drapery without the valance, which I found fussy). By now, all my preferences have been adopted. In the Washington guestroom, in a black-and-white scheme we named "Magpie," we varied the typical layout by replacing the pair of lounge chairs with one chair and footstool and put the standard desk at right angles to the wall with two — instead of one — elbow chairs. When Issy reviewed the model room, he said, "Let's see the desk against the wall," where desks had always been placed. Then, unexpectedly, he said, "Let's try it again angled." Happily, this angled layout prevailed and became our standard, copied widely throughout the hotel industry.

One time Rosalie Wise Design was offered a plum of a job in Nagasaki — a 400-room hotel with five restaurants for the Prince Hotel chain. We were the third interior design firm to be retained. The first two had been fired, and the hotel was due to open in a year. Mr. Hashimoto, the project coordinator, asked me to present our fees, so we had an office huddle and came up with the number — $90,000 Cdn. I wasn't certain this would be right in the long run, because we'd probably be worked to death as usual, so the next day I called him to say, "Mr. Hashimoto, I'm having trouble figuring out the fees on such short notice. Can you look at your budget and help me out?"

"Hei hei, Mrs. Wise, so sorry, no problem, so sorry not to be more helpful. Please may I call you back? Would it be okay if I get back to you tomorrow?"

When he called the following day, we said okay when he asked if we would accept $500,000 U.S. So we went to Tokyo and presented our design proposal for the new hotel to our client, Mr. Tadao Mitsui, at his 50-storey office tower emblazoned with MITSUI in blue neon letters. We rolled out our plans and I suggested a few design changes which didn't please the architect, but were adopted nevertheless by the owner.

Over the next year, we had to ply our way to Nagasaki and back about five times — 24 hours each way, from door to door. Whenever we landed there, our client greeted us, my colleague John Edison and me, on the tarmac, and we were immediately whisked off to a restaurant for an expensive dinner, although we would have much preferred to go to sleep. John did not eat fish, and fish was all there was. Exotic platters of shellfish were offered along with a great golden whitefish, still blinking and quivering from head to tail. We were encouraged to try the signature dish, a large oval bowl of water teeming with tiny darting tadpoles. Our host showed us how it was done. He put his fist into the bowl and seized a few helpless tadpoles and threw them into his mouth. John, in the chair beside me, was making burping noises, as if he was about to throw up. I passed him a hunk of bread.

After dinner we continued to a karaoke bar. On the way, John whispered to me in the cab, "Remember now, whatever you do, don't ask me to sing. I don't sing."

"Tonight, John, you will sing."

"No, I never sing."

"For Mr. Mitsui, you *must* sing."

"I definitely will *not* … sing."

He sang.

We had a hectic 10 months, but Ruth managed to order and install all the custom white guestroom furniture and fittings in time for the opening. She steadfastly turned down offers of kickbacks, which in Japan are culturally correct as a means of spreading the wealth more evenly.

The Prince Hotel opened to rave reviews, and Mr. Mitsui was very pleased. We all attended the opening-night banquet and I was seated in a place of honour in the centre of one of the long tables. The principals spoke at great length, because in Japan it is considered impolite to make a short speech. No one, except me, turned their heads to look at the speakers. Looking at the speaker, it seems, is impolite. A few people in my line of vision nodded off, which is apparently quite polite. After dinner Mr. Mitsui pressed into my hand a note containing a customary bonus cheque. He was especially happy with the change I had made to the solid second floor of the lobby elevation — now broken with an open balcony overlooking the entrance hall. Unfortunately, we also installed in the lobby a sunken black granite reflecting pool. We watched in horror as guests regularly stepped into the water by mistake, since it looked the same as the adjacent shiny floor.

The next day, before we left, Mr. Mitsui gave us a farewell luncheon. After the meal, he brought the company to attention and, as if conferring some kind of award, magisterially announced, "I have decided to hire you, Ms. Wise, to design my new private home in Tokyo, and you would do me an honour if you accept."

Now I was in a spot. I had no interest in private homes, and besides, I'd had enough of flying back and forth to Japan. "Thank you so much, Mr. Mitsui," I answered, "I am very honoured. But let me get back to you after I know the scope and timing of the project." In Japan it is considered bad form for one principal to say no to another. The usual practice is to send the answer later with one of the minions.

I diplomatically handed the design opportunity to John, who opened his own practice, did the house for the Mitsui family, and went on to do much more work in Japan.

R.W. Design, meanwhile, later used the Nagasaki half-million dollars to buy two houses in Toronto as a tax shelter, but these properties lost money in the next real estate recession. We ended up with close to $90,000.

Business was a bit slim in 1985 at R.W. Design, so I set out to drum up a project that was to become, in office lingo, "the Yoo-Hoo Job." It came to me while I was idly gazing out the window at the construction of the Teddington Park Retirement Home next door. Two guys in hard hats were standing on the sidewalk looking at the building plans. I went out on the fire escape one floor above them and yelled down, "Yoo-hoo, excuse me, but we're in the interior design business. Is there anything we can do for you — maybe paint colours or can we get you some furniture or fixtures — wholesale?" The taller gent, Tom Schwartz, invited me to descend the iron staircase and join them for a chat on the sidewalk. That was how R.W. Design came to design and install the lobby, the restaurant, and some work in the bedrooms of a home that, unfortunately for the tenants, had a rather quick turnover.

Our fees were $5,000 plus 10 per cent on the purchasing — we gave them 40 per cent of our buying discount. The budget was modest, but, with nothing else to do, we were up to the challenge. Tom was very pleased with the resulting cheap and cheery restaurant, and no doubt our low fees, with which my mother would not have been impressed. "*Az men farkoyft bilik, hot men a sakh koynim,"* she would have said. "Sell cheap and you'll have plenty of clients." Tom invited us to do his next retirement home, but at past prices we couldn't afford the project. Upping the fees four times would never do, so we declined, pleading a full timetable, and handed off the work to another designer.

I had one more moneymaking scheme that didn't work out. The Avenue Road Church was for sale and I had the urge to buy it and turn it into a permanent antique fair — I would call it the Avenue Road Antique Show. I imagined that shopping there would be like visiting a museum, but you could take the stuff home. I have a lot of respect for my antique-dealer friends, who I consider to be learned museum curators, and I envisioned being their appreciated patron.

I knew instantly, in my mind's eye, what the finished church would look like. From the door you would see five shops on the left, with five shops in a balcony directly above them. Iron and brass wrought-iron railings would fringe the storefronts and balconies. A further 10 shops would be mirror-imaged along the far right wall. Straight ahead, up the broad centre, on an inlaid black-and-white mosaic marble floor, you would see the Gallery Café, open to the huge height of the original church ceiling. The café would offer a menu of veal or cheese cannelloni, salads, and bitter chocolate biscotti. The restaurant furniture would be crashingly modern, made from acrylic, glass, polished nickel, and black leather. While you sipped your latte from a black and silver porcelain coffee can, you would have a clear view of both sides of the two levels of shops displaying antique one-of-a kind chairs, china, silver, treen, and more, all glittery in the golden halogen light. The whole place would be framed by the grand scale of the existing church wall and ceiling decorations.

The church was on the market for $2 million — twice what I could risk. I happened to mention this to my real estate friend Francis Hilb, who was a legendary "Have I got a deal for you!" negotiator. He went right to work and made a lowball offer of $1 million, which, incredibly, was accepted. Put to the test, I chickened out — I didn't have the guts. Of course I would have liked my fantasy church to happen, but I didn't need the risk, the parking problems, or the headache of collecting the rent. Thanks to me, the lucky inheritors of the Avenue Road Church were the Hare Krishna, who can still be seen around the building in their colourful regalia: henna-stained shaved heads, pigtails, and saffron skirted robes.

Back to the drawing board. My next project was a ballroom in London about the same scale and scope as the Avenue Road Church. Ballrooms and restaurants have always been my favourite projects — especially restaurants, because they can be theatrical, whimsical, or capricious.

At R.W. Design, our restaurants always incorporated three types of seating, so that from the door you didn't see a sea of 70 chairs all the same model. Instead you might see an island of black leather and chrome chairs, a heavier version for variety, and some velour settees (with the dimensions refigured so they would sit like chairs). Our restaurant in Montreal in 1988 featured swivel office chairs on five wheels and room dividers made of chains that I sourced from the Yellow Pages, under Novelty Jewellery. The rough white plaster walls were painted by one of my Ontario College of Art and Design painting instructors, Dainis Miezajs, in abstract sunsets. I would have had the floors made of polished cement but couldn't get the approval from our client (Issy). Another restaurant I had planned was a simulated outdoor setting — as if you were outside on the terrace off the drawing room of a stately home with walls of cut limestone. Tall French doors would have painted views of the lamp-lit interior featuring period furniture, Venetian glass chandeliers, and shadowy images of 1910 people in dinner dress drinking champagne while a Cole-Porter-type played the piano.

The restaurant we designed in Washington featured dining tables as art. Curious found items were embedded in transparent clear resin, and the wooden pedestal bases had a metallic automotive finish. Every table featured a different embedded item: one with rusty old handmade nails, one with peacock feathers, another with old watch parts, one with pennies and nickels, another with butterflies, and I've forgotten the rest. We did different designs of unique tables in three other hotels, and in each of those cities the manager gave me grief by covering them with tablecloths, which he claimed had always been the Four Seasons standard.

Restaurant design can be a collage of colour. With me, colour is a sensory necessity — like dark chocolate. You cannot improve on the colours found in nature; if you get them correct on canvas, they're too good to be credible — the reds of sumac leaves in October, the spring green of the willows outlined against the black purple of beech trees or the peculiar reds of Japanese maples. (These rare reds can be achieved by adding a small quantity of yellow.) And blue flowers, particularly scylla in early spring and hydrangea, cornflowers, and cinerarias in summer. Restaurant concepts can be prompted by many means: food, colour, crafts — a quirky menu of Japanese-Italian food by the chef, finishes and colours inspired by a Cartier brooch of onyx, malachite, mother of pearl, and crystal. Our restaurants in London and Toronto have showcased the work of Canadian craftsmen in glass and pottery, featured in open individual cabinets each with the artist's name and phone number in plain sight. The waiters were encouraged to sell the works on display, and we asked each artist to replace any work they sold, with a new piece of their choice. One of the glass artists, Toan Klein, sent me a box of flowers every time he sold a piece.

Back at the office in 1983, while we were designing Washington suites to CBC music at full blast and going about other business as usual, disaster struck on the home front. Misfortune made another of its inevitable proclamations, this time with the news that my mom had only three months to live. Ten years earlier she had beaten the ovarian cancer that hit her, but now she suffered from leukemia, probably resulting from the cancer drugs. As she aptly said, "*Az a mentsh iz gezunt, hot er a sakh dayges, az er iz krank, hot er nor eyn dayge* — a healthy person has many worries, a sick person has only one."

The grim vigil began with daily drives to Mount Sinai Hospital, bringing something from home — sometimes food on a pretty china plate, and always words of hope. We all pretended this was just another setback, because the truth was baleful and boring. I never missed a day, partly because of the guilt I felt for judging her so unfairly. However, some years before, I had finally succeeded in forgiving my mom's shortcomings, which, after all, she herself had inherited. (My kids feel the same way about me, a chain I hope they will break.) Only after forgiving her had I been able to pardon my own sins. Ten days before she died, I made the Passover Seder and invited my brother Stan and his wife, Martha. After dinner my mom came into the kitchen and, although she was usually shy and embarrassed by any display of affection, she hugged me and said thank-you, and with that rare hug we declared love and peace.

Stan and I recently reminisced over lunch about our early days in the Wise household. We met at "Harry's Charcoaled Broiled" (this store was formerly Wise's Dry Goods), now run by a Korean couple, since Harry has gone missing. Digging into our omelettes, we Wise children recalled Dad's temper and Mom's discipline methods.

Which went like this: Mom never laid a hand on us, but would incite Dad's wrath by listing her grievances against us.

"Stanley stayed out too late every night this week and he won't listen to me."

"Where is that boy?" said Dad. "I'll fix him so he'll know to stay home and study."

Then Mom would shield my brother with her body, her arms outstretched. "No, no, don't hit him — you'll kill him. Hit *me* — hit *me*!"

Dad would lunge to the left and right of her, flailing his arms and yelling, "Edith, get out of the way or you'll be sorry." She, like a matador, would dodge and parry, and somehow Dad just kept missing his target.

The truth was, as both of us clearly recall, Dad missed because he didn't *want* to catch us. Stan and I recounted all the scenarios we could remember and laughed till we cried, because not one of Dad's blows ever met its target.

In the hospital, Mom kept her teeth in a glass by her bed, which made conversation difficult. She could have saved some teeth, but in the shtetl they didn't visit dentists. Bad teeth were simply extracted. I went to see a dentist for the first time, spending my own money, when I was 16, and they found 25 cavities. Both my parents had false teeth: "*Falshe tseyn tu'en nit vey* — false teeth don't hurt." I believe my father had his remaining few teeth pulled because he thought dentures would be a cosmetic improvement.

The doctor called me on April 25 to say I had better come down early because the end was near. I found Mom as usual with her dentures out, which made her look like her own grandmother. She struggled to tell me something in Yiddish. She motioned me to lean in closer, but I still couldn't make out her words. All I heard was something like "*Dos lebn iz meshugas mit meshugooim* — life and people are craziness."

Similarly, my mother-in-law's last words were inaudible — I had never even known she wore dentures. I hope that when Issy and I are in our last throes, we will have something amusing to say, since with modern dentistry we will likely still have most of our teeth.

In her last days, Mom had reverted exclusively to Yiddish. Sometimes, in her hospital room, when my mom had to pee she would tell me, "*Ikh darf geyn mitn vaser,*" which meant literally "I have to go with the water," and I would wheel the intravenous bottle into the tiny bathroom with her. Often now when I have to pee, that Yiddish phrase comes into my head — I wish it would stop. Many other phrases of Mom's rattle around in my head, like "*Svet helfn vi a toytn bankes* — it will help as much as blood-cupping helps a corpse" and *"Dos gantse lebn iz azoy vi a kholem* — your whole life is like a dream." On April 26, the day she died, my mother's eyes were shut, but when I gave her some soup she licked the spoon. Mom was always grateful for my offerings, especially the time I brought her an orange, which was precisely what she had been in the mood for at that minute. She said to my dad, who could never do right, "See, why don't you bring what I want, like Rose?"

She was either 69 or 72 when she died. Dad put 72 on her gravestone. I cried at her funeral. I miss her. There are so many times when I need to call her up and say, "Guess what?"

At the funeral they asked, in what I suppose is a Jewish custom, that if I would like to see her one last time, they would open the coffin for a private viewing. I had no idea what to do, so I said yes, in case it was right, but when I saw her I was frightened out of my skull — her head on a pillow, her hair done up in a different too-bouffant style, looking surreally alive, but not quite like herself.

Even though my parents had seemingly not been in love, the truth is that they did love one another, but not in any New World way. Their love was evident in their last days together. There was the dramatic moment when Mom was dying in the hospital and she pointed to her gold wedding band, indicating by gestures that she wished to be buried with it. After she died, Dad seemed lost. Stan and I persistently tried to rouse him from his grief and pry him out of the house, but he preferred to sit alone on the sofa and nurse his wounds. We pleaded with him: "Please, Daddy, come for dinner — the kids love to be with you." He was so dear and quiet (when he wasn't ballistic).

When the bad news came, Issy and I had just arrived in San Francisco to review colour schemes for the guestrooms. As we were deliberating whether the rather too gaudy cornflower-blue bedskirt should be flounced or pleated, the phone rang. It was my brother. Not a good sign.

"Hi, Stan, what's up?"

"I have bad news — it's Daddy."

"Oh no, what happened?"

"I called him this morning to go to Stubby's for lunch, but there was no answer, so I went to the house. All the lights were on and he didn't answer the doorbell. I had my key, but the screen door was locked from the inside, so I had to break in. I called out from the front hall and then walked up the staircase. Daddy was in bed, wearing his best blue pajamas."

This was unusual, because we knew he usually slept in the nude.

"He was lying on his back and his eyes were open and he didn't look right. I touched him and he was cold and then I realized he was dead. I was so angry. How could Daddy leave us? We loved him so much. I punched him in the shoulder. Rosie, it was so sad, because any day now I felt he would have rallied and come back from his gloom and self-loathing."

It was September 1, 1983, just four months and a few days after Edith had died. We didn't look into the cause of death so we'll never know. It was creepy, though, to find out that before he died he had tidied up the house, given away all my mother's garments, and paid all the bills, even tying up the loose ends in his real estate holdings. Dad was always considerate and never wished to be a burden to anyone. My kids will not have it so easy.

In 1985, I went on my own to India for two weeks. I packed one small carry-on bag with black and white clothes, like the monochromatic wardrobe my friend Merle Shain had taken on that long-ago high school trip I envied so much. I travelled by train across the middle of India from Agra to Jaipur. The train rolled slowly from village to village in the dusty sunlight, past farms and people squatting to relieve themselves in the fields, their bare backsides turned to the tracks. As the train slowed down at each station, small boys offered us tea with milk in round clay cups without handles. A boy handed me a cup through the open train window, where I could feel the sun warming my forearm resting on the sill.

The train ride was slow, as soothing as a massage, rocking from side to side with a pretty clicking sound, as pleasing to the ear as the local English spoken with a Peter Sellers lilt. I preferred this slow ride to the unpleasant speed of the sealed Bullet Train I once took to Kyoto, where hills of tea plants rushed by in a blur like a film on fast-forward. Here in India the villagers got on and they got off, as they did every day, and I was the privileged observer for this one day only. I met a young man on the train who invited me to lunch at his house in the next village. He assured me I could easily hop on a later train. I made my excuses, thanking him for the invitation. But when we all got off to stretch our legs at Bandikul, his home town, I had an impulse to take him up on his offer, so we roared off on his motor scooter, me on the back, hanging on for dear life. It was a humble house indeed — two rooms, no water or power, with people sleeping on beds in the kitchen, like my grandfather's house in Ozarow.

I made another trip on my own when Issy was off helicopter-skiing with our boys, in 1986. I flew to the island of St. Martin, on the French side, and stayed at a small, posh place. I felt a delicious sense of freedom — neither mother nor daughter nor wife. I took all my meals at a table for one on the terrace and noticed that I presented a curious figure, particularly to the married couples, since I was single and not friendly. The black cab driver who had brought me from the airport had said, "If you'd like to eat some real local fish and rice, I'd be happy to take you to a typical restaurant." So I took him up on it and we had a fine evening, although as we were driving home along the dark roads, I'll admit I second-guessed my wisdom in accepting his invitation, wondering whether he thought I was looking for something more than dinner. But he brought me back safely to the hotel, and as we entered the lobby together, I noticed one of the male guests glaring at me with palpable disgust, bordering on hatred. Later I worked out that his disapproval must have stemmed from some repressed longing to have sex with a local girl, or perhaps he was simply a racist.

As new tennis players, Issy and I went a few times to Bermuda to the Coral Beach and Tennis Club Hotel. What an idyllic spot with its sunken tennis courts and a dining terrace high on a cliff overlooking the sea. Every night there was a 10-piece orchestra, and we swept across the dance floor doing the silver fox trot to the rhythm of the rolling whitecaps way below. We began to notice that the best rooms in the hotel were given to members, so we applied to join the club. We were refused. No Jews, please. That's the last time we saw Bermuda.

We arrived home from our holidays to bad news: my good friend Beverly Martin was very ill, so I stood by and waited and watched as they plagued her with the tedious tests.

I've kept three vigils to date — my son, my mom, and Beverly. Bev was a wonderful, challenging friend who was my reading counsellor. Our sensibilities matched. She directed me to magazine pieces in *The New Yorker* and recommended some of the best books I've read, including Robert K. Massie's *Nicholas and Alexandra*. Bev had majored in journalism at Sarah Lawrence College, but she didn't write. She said that if she couldn't write as well as Hemingway or Faulkner, there was no point. She didn't want to clutter the market with less than brilliant material — about which I have had no compunction.

In the last three months of her life, I spent a few hours with her every single day, bringing favourite foods and often an old black-and-white movie, another interest we shared — movies like my two favourites, *Brief Encounter*, with Celia Johnston and Trevor Howard, and *Laughter in Paradise*, with Alistair Sim and Joyce Grenfell. But it's difficult to be with the dying, because you skirt around the obvious — that soon they won't be around.

Bev had a dybbuk that rose up in her every once in a while and she was helpless in its thrall; I knew about it but had never seen it. Through the years I watched her alienate some of her friends. She blew up at me, too —

the only time — about two years before she died. It happened like this: When I went to visit her in Eleuthera, I landed in the airport farthest from her house. I did this innocently and inconveniently, not knowing that there were two airports. When I made light of it, she said to me, "Just because you have money, you think you can do whatever you like." I was as stunned as if she had hit me on the head with a wooden mallet. After a minute or two of silence, I excused myself, saying, "I'm just going to the corner shop, I'll be back soon." As soon as I was out of sight, I cried. I would have liked to walk out on her, but I couldn't bear the remorse she would feel if I did, and I loved her nevertheless. So I said nothing and pretended that I harboured no resentment. After all, she bore no malice and everyone should be allowed an occasional mistake. God knows I make plenty.

Bev spent her winters in Eleuthera with her family in her cherished house, which she named Tamarind after the huge tree in the front yard that frames the white clapboard home that once belonged to a seaman named Captain John. Earlier, when Beverly had made the first trip there to view the house, I had gone along as adviser. We stayed overnight in the one room over the Buccaneer Bar in the main town, Governor's Harbour. I slept late, lulled by the trade winds cool against my skin in the humid air. When I opened my eyes, I found Bev sitting with her back half turned to me, gazing reflectively out the window, one arm gracefully aloft, holding a smoking Salem menthol cigarette, wrist elegantly cocked. She seemed to be surveying Eleuthera Harbour in the certain propriety that soon she would own that view. The smoke was swirling in the light around her thick long curls the colour of a lion's mane. I didn't mind anymore that she smoked, after she told me she didn't inhale. Like a fool I believed her, but she was to die in 1991 of lung cancer at 59. She knew only 14 winters on her island and she never met her four grandchildren. I miss her.

Nowadays, Issy and I spend our own winters in California, in the desert, where the sun sinks suddenly behind the mountain in midafternoon and the temperature falls from summer to autumn, so you sleep better. Copper cliffs make a jagged outline against a heart-stopping clean blue sky, above our house in Palm Springs, over lands where, less than a century ago, only the Cahuilla (Hot Water) Indians padded around in their moccasins. In 1986 we bought a wonderful old 1936 house originally built for the Wurlitzer family, who made theatre pipe organs, pianos, and the jukeboxes that made their name famous.

The Palm Springs house has a macabre past. Our gardener cum manager Charles Martinez is a mine of information about the old place. He remembers a grand piano in the bay window of the dining room. Charles's father, Pedro Martinez, was the Wurlitzers' gardener and built with his own hands — and the help of his seven sons — the four-foot-high fieldstone wall that surrounds the one-acre property. They collected these round rocks when the place was cleared. Charles recounts that Mrs. Wurlitzer was a severe, exacting woman who demanded that Pedro bend over while he was pulling out weeds — she forbade him to kneel on the ground.

The second owners (we are the third) were John and Josephine Hooker, San Francisco society people. Her family was in the gold business and Admiral Hooker was an Annapolis man. When Josephine died of cancer on the horsehair mattress in the master bedroom, the Admiral was despondent. Dena the housekeeper told me that one day in April she put Mr. Hooker's regular gazpacho soup on the table and called him to have some lunch. "I'm not hungry just yet, Dena," he answered. "Perhaps a little later." An hour later, Charles was working in the front yard when he heard a loud report from the back which didn't sound like a gunshot, but when he searched the garden near the orange grove, he came upon a grisly scene. Mr. Hooker lay in a gory mess under the 100-year-old eucalyptus tree. The old soldier had shot himself under the chin with his double-barrelled 12-gauge shotgun — a queer choice since the man was described as a "neat freak." He lay stretched out on the ground, his face strangely wide — flattened like a deflated balloon. The back of his head was missing and parts of his brain were dripping off the rough bark of the tree trunk. Whenever I walk past that tree, I'm impressed by Admiral Hooker's courage. Why, I wonder, wouldn't he just have used pills?

The eucalyptus tree marks the farthest corner of the garden near the lemon tree, half of which curiously produces small green limes — ones that I pick daily to sprinkle over my lunch salad. Mr. Martinez tells me that all citrus trees begin as lemon stalks that have been grafted. In my scent memory I hold dearly the fragrances of the orange and lemon blossoms that bloom simultaneously with the fruit in March. I never wear scent, and I'm an insistent pest about using only absolutely unscented soaps and cleaners. Give me some rosemary or mint leaves from the garden to crush in my hand or the clean, sweet smell of my husband's body.

After we bought the Palm Springs house, the Hooker relatives came and removed the treasures but left all the rubbish for us to clear out. A lifetime of junk — a dozen pair of rubber boots, 50 saucepans, yard-sale dishes, and four greasy old ovens in the kitchen. Luckily, they also left a huge library of Everyman's Classics, titles from Austen and Dickens to Toqueville and Whitman. I cried with laughter all one afternoon while reading *Travels with a Donkey* by R.L. Stevenson. God knows I'd rather read Stevenson than Shakespeare. When it comes to iambic pentameter — let's face it — I'm a phillistine. And I sampled de Staël and Bret Harte with little enthusiasm. Our first year there, I read across a whole shelf of Galsworthys, bound in green linen, that no one had ever opened because the pages needed to be slit, typical of 1920s book bindings. My recent reading includes no best-sellers or fiction. I prefer more obscure authors, such as those recommended in the *New York Times* book-listing section "And Bear in Mind."

The Palm Springs house was big and grungy, so we were the perfect buyers. Issy had a gleam in his eye — here was another enticing project for the two of us mad renovators.

You enter "Casa de Sueños" directly into the living-dining room, which is about 55 feet long with a 10-foot ceiling. When we moved the sofa, we found a same-sized rectangle of rat droppings underneath, and under a lounge chair a square of yellowed newspapers 10 years old. We peeled everything back to the original — wood floors rescued from grimy green shag carpet; pink random flagstone replaced Mexican kitchen tiles; shiny white enamel rejuvenated the fine old panelled doors, fireplace, and cornices. Every room was newly painted in the palest possible ice cream colours, which gave the house a happy countenance.

We enjoy our time in our cherished California house more than in Toronto, especially when our grandkids visit. Occasionally we go off from there, to a local bridge tournament, sometimes with our good friends Robert and Doreen Scolnick. For a week we enjoy the happy challenge of duplicate bridge and stay in seedy hotels — which makes a nice change — like the one in San Bernardino with the rubber blankets. Bob brought his own pillow. We first took up bridge in the '50s and still meet a few times a year for dinner and a game with our old high school crowd.

We pass our days in California much as we do at home. But I love having my mate in the house. Issy spends mornings from six to noon (nine to three in Toronto) on the telephone in the dining room, which is his office. When I wish to interrupt him, I "knock knock" in the air on a pretend door near his desk. After lunch we play bridge or tennis and then go out for dinner or maybe an artsy film at the Camelot Theatre and Café, where you are permitted to have your glass of wine and hotdog while you watch the movie. At the end of the day, catching the late news on TV, Issy will say, "Well, I'm going up," the signal he's going to bed, although in Palm Springs, there are no stairs. Even if there's something good on, I will follow him up to bed out of habit. Wednesday nights we ballroom dance, part of my week's five hours of *de rigueur* exercise. At our age, working out is not an elective but an absolute necessity, to stem the inevitable stoop of old age.

I remember when I turned 35, I was in my kitchen on Green Valley Road when Merle called to wish me happy birthday. "Merle," I said, "this is it, I'm at the top of my form. I'm happy doing my solitary artwork in the northern light of my own studio, and never will I feel or look better. It's a descending curve from now on — older can't be better."

After 60, you cover up. No more bikinis or tank tops, even in a heat wave. Now you must be clever with clothes. Since pants no longer come up to the waist, I take the pieces cut off the legs and add them to the waist. I have 50 pair of these. Today when I buy something new I feel compelled to remove one item from my now tightly packed closet to make room. I have rarely to this day bought a proper dress. In early days I couldn't afford one. Later I learned that dresses are static and not nearly as much fun as mixing and matching separates. Today my closets burst with colour: lots of floral prints and vintage pieces and a vast collection of shirts, trousers, skirts, and belts, which offer me the fun and creativity of an endless variety of permutations.

I still love to get myself together in some new way, playing with the balance of colour and design. I see everyday clothes as costumes. I dress rather too flamboyantly, standing out like *Yentl oysgeputst tsum get* — decked out like Yentl at her divorce. In the '60s, I would commit crimes against the dress etiquette by wearing hats and loud head scarves after five o'clock and velvet fabrics after February. At a party recently, Maestro Richard Bradshaw, the opera director, murmured in my ear in his classy English accent, "I *like* your gear." Was my scarlet mini-skirt a bit too short?

I never seem to get too old to dress up. And Issy and I have had a lot of luck winning prizes at costume parties. Once, for a party with a Greek theme, we came as "The Midas Touch." I wore a gold bikini and gold body makeup and Issy was King Midas, with a red velvet cape. For the Venetian Ball, we came as "Venetian Blind" — Issy had sunglasses, white suit, and a cane, and I wore a transparent hoop skirt with narrow silver venetian blinds illuminated by small lights. And it was great fun waltzing together the time we dressed as twin bearded gentlemen fops, "A Pair of Pantalones," for the Gardiner Museum's Commedia dell'Arte Ball.

I resent the amount of time I spend thinking about the amount of time I have left. Like Woody Allen, I'm neurotic in my fixation on death. About aging, I feel somewhat diminished now, because when I was young I clearly recall feeling pity for the elderly because they had so little time left.

Death is an insult — as if God screwed up and made a fatal flaw in his design of humans. Death is bizarre. We humans scurry around like a colony of ants till our last moment, amassing goods that formerly belonged to others and soon will belong to someone else. Issy and I have accumulated too many of the world's goods and I'm losing the battle to keep the influx in check. Here's why: when Issy comes home from work, he is often carrying *in* some package that he drops on the kitchen island. When he goes out every morning, he does not carry anything *out*. Over 51 years, these add up. He brings home framed awards and citations, as well as food samples, face creams, and body lotions from suppliers hoping to sell their products to the hotels. It's a constant scramble to give away enough items so the house doesn't sink and the kids won't have so much junk to sort through later.

Once in a while I sadistically challenge myself to a test I call "the Gestapo Game." It goes like this: I imagine two Gestapo officers come to the door, wearing the hateful uniforms with black and silver insignia. They click their heels and announce, "Madam, this house will be taken over by the neo-Nazis. You have one hour to collect your belongings. Your family will be relocated to a one-room apartment in the Jewish ghetto and you will take only the following items in these three shopping bags: one for clothing, one for food, one for household items."

"Good," I think. "This was bound to happen sooner or later — now I can simplify and get rid of this egregious accumulation, and also the guilt from having so much good fortune."

I take the three bags and begin to move around our five principal rooms chock-a-block with china. Into one of the bags, I drop twelve items — most made in England in the mid-1740s: a Chelsea cup and tall milk jug; five sauceboats from Limehouse, Lund's Bristol, Bow, Reid, and Worcester; two small Chelsea figures of a crinoline lady and spring; a vase from the St. Cloud factory; and a pair of Worcester cream boats.

In my kitchen bag, I drop some Ceylon black tea, a loaf of Ace Bakery sunflower-seed sliced bread, some sweet butter, and the toaster. For clothing, I take my thinnest jeans, a John Smedley black cotton-knit turtleneck, a mahogany and persimmon chiffon scarf, and a lichen-green fine pashmina shawl.

Fortunately, at about this point, I tire of this maudlin game, delete the Gestapo at the door, and gratefully return to my real world of good fortune and love.

We're healthy now, but *kineynehore*, how long can this last? Will it be on a Tuesday afternoon at three o'clock that I receive the news that I have one of the big-letter *umgliks* — disasters? The one I'm hoping to get is hard of hearing. At our age, we're like ducks in a shooting gallery. The ranks are thinning. We're waiting for the unavoidable decrepitudes and inconveniences to set in. When I ride my bike, I try to be like that squirrel I watch from my window that swings perilously on the thinnest branch with no fear of falling. I'm reckless, but if I fall I could end up a common statistic that goes like this: person falls — breaks hip — goes to hospital — catches infection there — dies. How long before I'm sharing a hospital room with a stranger whose visitors pull the curtain between us while they whisper about personal matters.

Now, it's a funny thing about life that we can fly first class but we can't die first class. I hope, please God, to go in my sleep, so I won't have the time to write my obituary or plan the menu for the shiva. But although life is unfair, taking turns is still the best way to fit on the planet. And by the time you hit 70, you've had a good turn and can face the exit, and besides, life does get a little repetitious as you move from meal to meal. I go to the melancholy funerals of friends and it seems even on the way home I start right in fussing with the small stuff. I stop off and buy small plastic travel-size bottles and, using a funnel, transfer into these herring oil, cod liver oil, shampoo, face lotions.

Business as usual during mourning.

Still, I do everything I possibly can to look young — a new cheek blush, dieting, skin peels, my face surgically nipped and tucked, but nothing drastic like having my forehead pulled over my head. And certainly the time has come to drink some of the good wine, use the good silver, and wear the good jewellery. But the honest and trite truth is, I still feel middle-aged — I have not yet learned how to be old. And now, at 70, I'm not much different than I was at seven. *Vi tsu zibn, azoy tsu zibitsik* — like seven, so at 70.

Sketch for stationery.

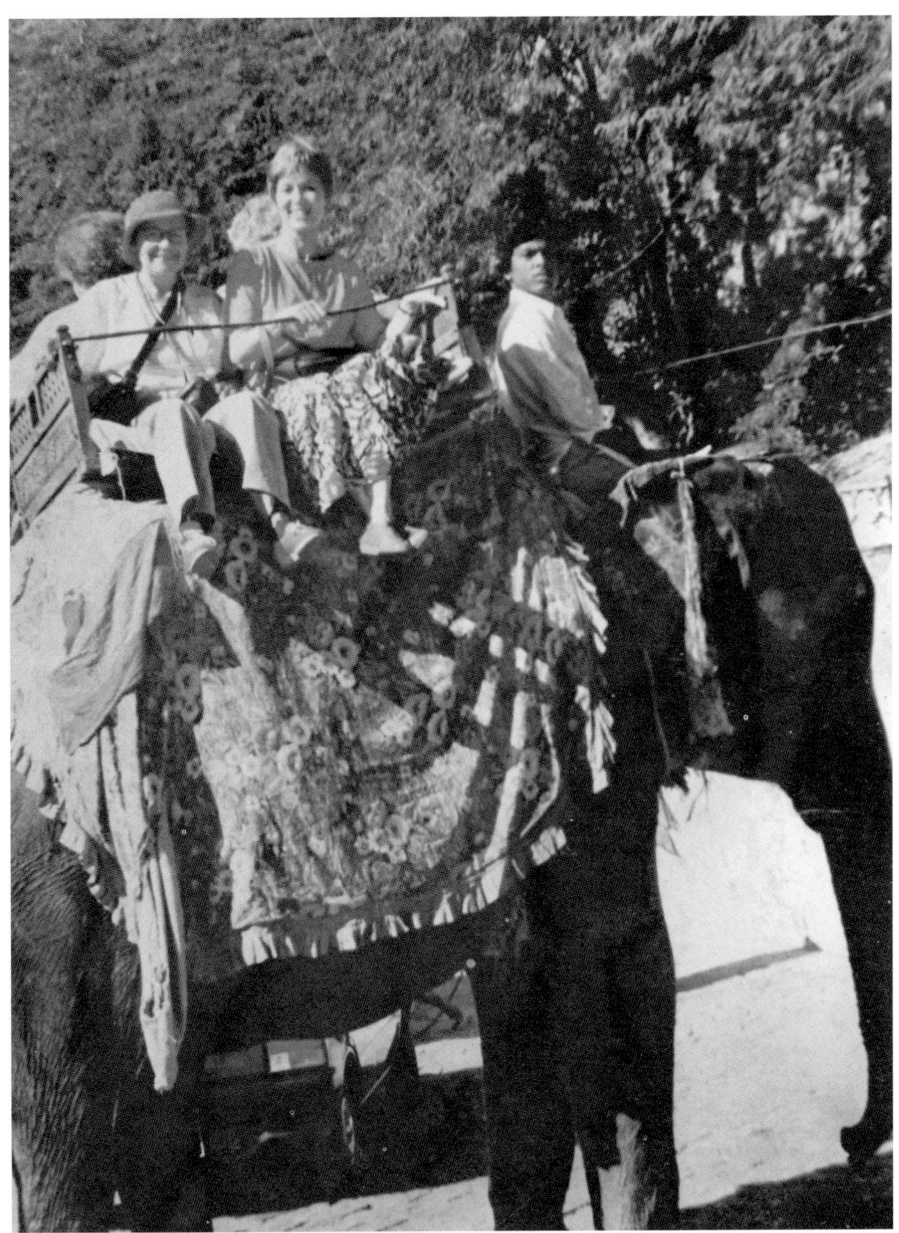

My solo trip to India, 1985.

Tony and Emily, Palm Springs, 1986.

The ski chalet at Devil's Glen, with Chris, 1972

Jordy wins Best Bluegrass Banjo in central Canada, 1992.

The cottage on Lake Simcoe, tarted up with Victoriana.

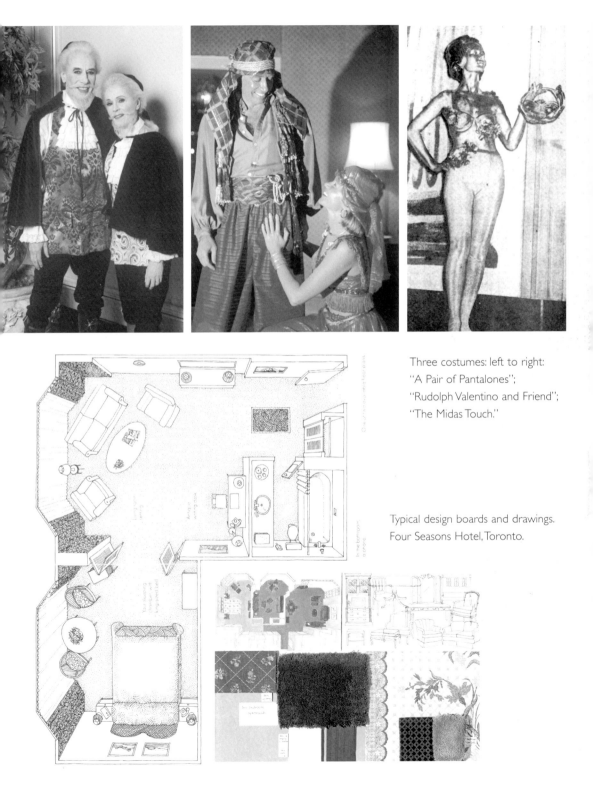

Three costumes: left to right:
"A Pair of Pantalones";
"Rudolph Valentino and Friend";
"The Midas Touch."

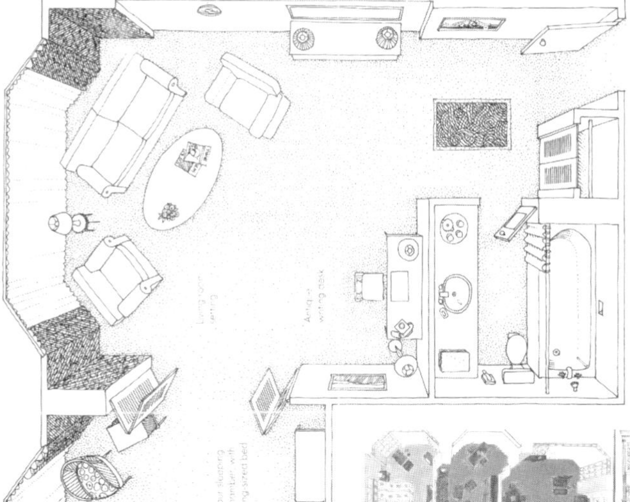

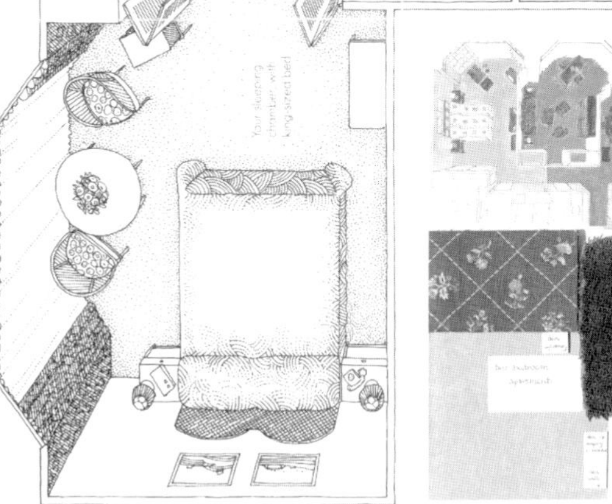

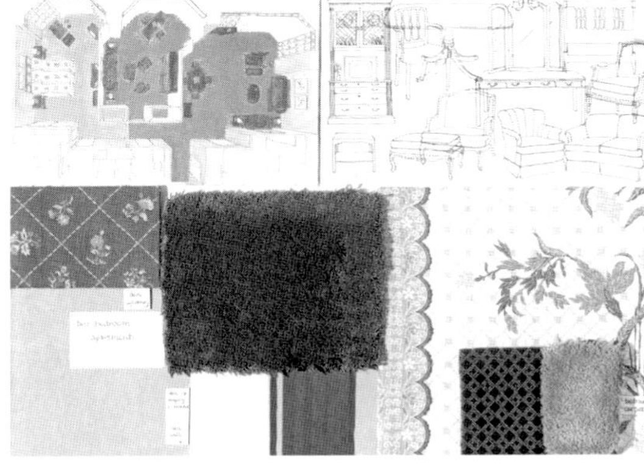

Typical design boards and drawings.
Four Seasons Hotel, Toronto.

CHAPTER EIGHT

Mom's Meshpokhe

FAMILY IN OZAROW

If every generation hands down to the next generation its principles and way of life, then my own ways of thinking owe something to my Birnbaum and Wise forbears, to whom I feel an atavistic attachment.

Mom told me many stories of her life in Ozarow, and she boasted that her family had a good *yiches* — her mother was a fine lady and her dad one of the *balebatim* (religious elders) in the town. In the social hierarchy, her family was a few notches above my dad's people. I have always been curious about her family and the story of their lives.

Even as a child, I had a bent for sketching and lettering and working with colours. I was surprised to discover that many members of my mother's family were also so inclined. I uncovered this connection in 1983, when, quite by accident, I first met my aunt Marmish, my uncle Khaskel, and all the other Birnbaums.

Mom's family the Birnbaums, 1932. Standing left: Marmish, Sarah, and Raisel. Khaskel between my grandparents Yokheved and Yekhil.

Well, the truth is, I didn't actually meet them in person, because they were no longer among the living. They were all murdered on either October 22, 1942, at the Treblinka death camp or in the massacre in their shtetl of Ozarow on October 26. I wouldn't even know which date to mark with a candle or prayer.

I met the Birnbaum family while sorting through my parents' belongings after they had died. I remember that day. It was creepy unlocking the door of the too silent house. Everything was in place, as if Mom and Dad had just stepped out for lunch. I went through all the drawers and cabinets to ensure that their treasures were saved from the hands of strangers — an embroidered tablecloth from Ozarow, an old calendar featuring a photo of my dad as vice-president of the Ozrower Mutual Benefit Society, the trunk that travelled from Poland with my mother on the *S.S. Pulaski* — and, in a top drawer, a worn paper box labelled "Weldrest Hosiery, silk, size 9." The box yielded not silk stockings but perhaps 100 brittle pages of closely written Yiddish script, in ink once black but now grey. These were letters from Poland, from my mom's three sisters and young brother, written between 1930 and August 1939 — when a New Year's card was returned, marked "Mail Suspended." Eerie that these papers were in perfect shape but my parents were gone.

Mom's *meshpokhe*, the Birnbaums, were a family of five children: Shloime, the eldest, married Rachel Kestenbaum after immigrating to Montreal in 1926. Sadly, he died of heart failure at the age of 43. He had come home that night from his woodcarving work in the shul, had a hot cocoa, gone to bed, and died in his sleep. Shloime had to work in the shul since he had lost better-paying jobs as a cabinet maker because he was a pious Jew and refused to work on the Sabbath. He was never to find out that in 1945 the Germans would slaughter his family and extended family in Europe.

I last saw him in 1941, winding the black leather *tfiln* (phylacteries) round his arms for his morning prayers in his front parlour in Montreal.

I asked him some idle question, which he answered with a stern look that taught me not to speak during prayers.

Shloime was the eldest Birnbaum and after a hiatus of 12 years, came four girls. (I suspect there were also a few stillborn children in those years.) They were born at roughly 18-month intervals, beginning about 1909: Sarah, Marmish, my mother Ydessa, and Raisel. Finally another boy arrived, Khaskel, who was only 12 in 1930, the year my mom landed in Montreal.

Ydessa was born in Ozarow in 1914 — or so she told me. The truth is that she was born about 1912; she needed the extra two years to find a suitor while she was still young. Also, there is no Yiddish tradition of sentiment to celebrate birthdays and wedding anniversaries. Shtetl folk never had an exact date of birth and were even reluctant to reveal how many children they had. They were superstitious. My mom would say, "I have, *kineynehore* — may the evil eye not strike me — two *kinder*, a boy and a girl." When you ask someone from the shtetl for a date of birth, you may get an answer like: "It was before *Sukkos* (the festival of the ingathering), when the goat fell through the roof of the *suke* (hut for Sukkos)," or "It was just after *Pesach* (Passover) in the year of the great pogrom." There was also an intentional fudging of dates for various reasons: to be marriageable longer, or to avoid the draft or provincial taxes.

In 1930, Ydessa came to Montreal to live with her brother Shloime, his wife Rachel, and their two young daughters, Goldie and Bella (a third daughter, Jeannie, came along later). Bella was said to resemble my mom, a comparison that never pleased the girl. Sadly, Bella was to contract cancer at the same age as Ydessa. (They shared the same gene, which luckily I lack.)

My mom worked in a sweatshop, chained to a sewing machine for five years as a factory drudge (not the elite "draper" she told me she had been), then married Joseph Wise, who came from the same shtetl. He was not her first choice, but she settled for him, as she was already, by her standards, an old maid at 23. In Ozarow she might have had an arranged marriage as young as 16, but her father had two other daughters for whom to provide a *nadn* (dowry), so someone had to leave. Originally, it was decided that Marmish, the oldest unmarried sister, should go. According to my aunt Rachel, Shloime chose my mom instead — luckily for me — because Marmish was a little too bright and therefore would be harder for him to handle.

In the box of early letters sent to Ydessa in Montreal and, later, Toronto, the Birnbaums speak of a lively and hardworking life punctuated by joyous religious holidays and pageants — the entertainment of shtetl life. Holidays were circumscribed by the phases of the moon. Happy times were spent preparing foods according to the laws of *kashrut*. I know these menus firsthand because my mom reproduced their recipes faithfully. Their ways were her ways.

In the shtetl, there was little or no work for young people, so there was much time for leisure. The Birnbaums write of picnics and *Pesach, khosn* (bridegrooms) and *khasenes* (weddings) — candlelit wedding processions, often late on a Friday afternoon. There were walks in the *vald* (woods), chess games, handicrafts, and artwork. They had amateur theatre nights and an orchestra, and, when the circus came to town, colourful tents were set up in the market square. A group of young people might take a horse and wagon for a picnic in the beautiful pine forests, beside tributaries of the nearby Vistula River. There they swam in summer and skated in winter.

The many social clubs usually had political or religious affiliations: the Bund and Paole Zion were labour- and communist-oriented, and there were five Zionist clubs, which inspired or prepared many to immigrate to Israel. There were sports clubs, soccer teams, a drama club, and a library that offered translations of foreign authors like Voltaire and Hugo. Evenings must have been more enjoyable before electricity, when people got together and made their own fun — idyllic evenings of singing, dancing, playing chess, or acting out plays.

In a letter dated September 25, 1930, Marmish, my mom's closest sister, speaks of these kinds of activities:

> We'll see each other one of these days, when they re-open Canadian immigration.... Things are very cozy here in Ozarow. The young people are having a good time. We're always having dances. We dance all night long. We leave for the dance at ten o'clock and we return at six in the morning ... and today there's a play at the theatre here called *Always a Fool*. It's very interesting and I'm thinking of going.... The chalutzim [a club — Pioneers for Israel] rented a separate place next to the cultural club where the rabbi was once beaten up.... They all come over to dance the hora; they taught me how so now I can dance the hora too.... This past Saturday I spent the evening with Avram. He waited for me at the house till I got dressed. I wore my black silk skirt and my silk blouse with the white lapels, and Avram said I looked very well-dressed.... Ydess, I'm looking very good. I've gained a few kilos and I'm a lot fatter and prettier. I might have my picture taken. If I do I'll send you one.... Ydess, why are you crying day after day? I never imagined that you would be so homesick.... When you start working ... you'll have the company of other girls.

This letter came just as my mom arrived in Montreal, before she found work at the Polly-Anna Dress Company. She soon found friends, and on Sundays they would dress in the latest style, spend the day on Mount Royal with Jewish boys from home, and take the snapshots we still have.

Back in Ozarow, most middle-class people had only two or three changes of clothing and two pairs of shoes, yet the women dressed following the latest Paris fashion plates, which in the early '30s called for white-trimmed dresses. The Birnbaum girls dressed elegantly. They copied styles from a Krakow department store which to them meant the latest from Paris, and ran up their dresses on the sewing machine, because store-bought ones were too costly. The men looked as if they had just stepped out of a hot shower and into tailor-made suits and ties. The dapper clothes now seem incongruous, given that there was no electricity, no running water, and no bathrooms. The water was delivered daily by a *vaser treger* (water carrier) who poured two pailfuls into the barrel just inside the door.

In Ozarow my mom rose in the morning from a bed she shared with her three sisters. One of the four had to sleep across the bottom of the bed, and my mom sometimes lost the draw for that unenviable position, facing a row of smelly feet. Khaskel got to sleep with his parents. The straw mattresses were changed every spring before Passover, and the sheets, pillowcases, and duvet covers were all made of fine muslin, sometimes embroidered by the girls. Upon rising, Mom would take a square of newspaper from the pile and go outside to pee. She said the public privies smelled so bad she preferred to use a convenient bush. The only outhouses were the four behind the shul. The Polish farmers collected the excrement from these to fertilize their crops.

Then there was the matter of the day's ablutions. The women would take their turn at the washstand — the men had washed earlier and were out or in the other room. First, from the water barrel, my mother would pour water with a dipper into a pitcher, soap up and wipe down her hands, face, and armpits. She would pour the water over her hands into the white enamel *shisl* (bowl) inset on the washstand, and later empty the *shisl* outside. Once a week the men would go to the *mikve* (public ritual bathhouse) and have a hot steam bath as well. Men's hours were from five o'clock to seven, after which the women bathed in the same water. Women were required by Jewish law to go to the mikve after menstruation; only then were they considered clean enough for sex. (By law, they were allowed sex for only two weeks a month.)

All the Birnbaums were skilled in needlework and crafts: Khaskel was a sign painter and artist whose pencil portraits of my mom and her brother we still have. My *zeyde* (granddad) mentions in a letter: "I left place for Khaskel to write but he is drawing a picture and doesn't want to interrupt his drawing to write something." (For the same 50-*groshn* postage, everyone could write something — three letters sometimes came in the same envelope.) A resident of Ozarow today, Edward Klimkiewicz, remembers being in the Birnbaum house in the 1930s. He can still recall the colourful embroidered *makatka* (wall hanging) over their stove. Another friend remembers passing the house and often seeing one of the girls sitting outside on a bench, sewing by hand. In the summer, passersby could hear from the open windows the hum of the Singer sewing machine, a standard household fixture. During the holiday of Shavuot, *reyzelekh* (paper cutouts), backlit with candlelight, glowed in the Birnbaum windows. These cutouts were said to be the best in town. In a photo I have of the family, *raiselach* are displayed in the right front window.

Marmish writes in 1935:

> I'm sending you a needle; it's been lying around since before Rosh Hashanah and I kept forgetting to send it....
>
> I didn't have time to write because we were busy sewing blouses and white-trimmed dresses.... Tell me how she wants the napkins made: plain or embroidered? And let me know how many corners you want the napkins to have. Do you want all four corners or just one?

The family in Ozarow took great joy in celebrating the *yom toyvim* (religious holidays).

Khaskel writes in March 1937:

> Purim is getting closer and closer, so I wish you a happy Purim and a joyous Passover....

And Raisel writes in the same month:

> It's just three days before Pesach, and so you can still come to us for *bobelekh* [Johnnycake with unleavened flour], and sponge cake is also ready, and of course wine that our father prepared during the winter.... Today we made lemon jam. It came out very good, so we'll send you a bit.... I have lots of work before "yom tov" to finish the [embroidered] matzo covers and to start getting ready to bake matzos. We should only have enough money for our more than usual work, especially our father. I don't know if you remember how hard he works. Sleeping he leaves for someone else....

Fear about the future crept into the Birnbaums' letters in the late-'30s: the increasing restrictions against the Jews and the mounting antagonism from their Polish neighbours reflecting the anti-Semitism across the border in Germany — prejudice consolidated by the strong Catholic religion in both countries. Near the end, Raisel and Marmish sent a hand-embroidered *parokhet* (curtain for the ark that held the Torah scrolls) and handcrafted table linens for sale in Montreal, in a last desperate effort to raise money for their passage.

Marmish writes on January 24, 1939:

> I have a lot of hand-sewn things. I have a few tablecloths, I have one tablecloth worth 20 dollars which means 100 *zlotes*, and over there it would be worth even more. I have some lovely pillowcases, the likes of which you couldn't find in all of Poland. I sewed

> them up a long time ago. I wouldn't have the patience to sew like that today. I've gotten everything ready for the time when you'll bring me over.

And Raisel, the youngest of the three sisters, writes in the same month to her sister-in-law:

> I am sending two *Krakovsk* [like ones from a large Krakow department store] dresses: one for your daughter Braindel and one for Ydessa's daughter Rifke [me]. The larger one with the green skirt is for Braindel. May she wear it in good health. And the second one you will send to Ydessa....

We never received these dresses; it was too late.

Yekhil, the father, was chiefly concerned with being an observant Jew, making a living, and marrying off his two remaining daughters. Two large portraits of my mother's parents, in oval Edwardian frames, hang in our stairwell, now witnesses to a life they could never have imagined. Children emigrating from Poland to the New World customarily brought along such portraits so the elders could keep a watchful eye over their *kinder*. Before leaving, emigrants would traditionally also visit the graves of their forbears to say their farewells. They did not expect to return.

In her portrait, my grandmother Yokheved is wearing a black silk dress and her *Shabbos sheytl* (Sabbath wig). She was tall, genteel, and, as my aunt Khayele recalls in her Yiddish accent, "By her husband, she vas a qveen." Yokheved once wrote to my mother in Canada, "I had a dress made for myself, and I bought myself a pair of black patent leather shoes for the holidays. I know this will make you happy. But I still haven't bought myself a new sheytl. I don't know which kind to get, a straight one or one with curls." My grandfather Yekhil is dressed in his portrait in the *yarmilke* (skullcap) and long coat he wore every morning when he went to shul. He was one of the town's *balebatim*.

The Birnbaums lived at No. 1 Zlote (Gold) Street, with the stone-carving workshop behind. Among other jobs, *Zeyde was a matseyve kritser* (tombstone carver). The house had two rooms, a kitchen and a bedroom, with beds in both. There was also a boydem (attic) and a root cellar you reached by ladder. When potatoes were needed, the children drew lots for who would go down to the cellar and face the biting insects lurking there.

You needed to be clever to make a living in Ozarow, so my grandfather had many trades, and eked out a hardscrabble existence. Another current resident of Ozarow, Mr. Kazimerz Pekalski, recalls that the Birnbaums were "intelligent and neither rich nor poor." Yekhil was primarily a moneylender, but he also mended paper banknotes since the bank didn't replace torn ones. As well as carving the tombstones, he ground wheat at Passover and made matzos for sale. Mr. Pekalski recalls that "when the Jews were driven out in 1942, there were plenty of tombstones left in the Birnbaums' yard, near the workshop behind the house, because Yekhil was famous as a carver also in the neighbouring towns of Tarlow, Jakubowice, and Zawichost." He also sculpted secular works — someone recalls a vase of flowers carved from the local sandstone, the same material he used for the gravestones.

Yekhil began all his letters by citing the Torah portion of the week. This letter, dated November 13, 1938, acknowledges the portion *Chaya Sara*. Yekhil then goes on to write:

> *Dear daughter Ydessa:*
> Now can you believe it, Marmish [at 27] still doesn't want to get married. She says she's in no hurry. If only, G-d willing, it could be arranged for a matchmaker for daughter Raisel. I'll have to be patient until G-d sends along a match for her. . . . We can do nothing until

> Providence decides the moment for a good match. . . . We see that G-d be blessed will certainly give great riches because girls require a lot of money. . . . And now to tell you that your letter dated "Portion Noah" we received . . . and also that you had a nice "esrog" [a lemon-like citrus fruit]. And now we'll discuss that which you write about people thinking me wealthy. The truth is I have to borrow money from people, and then I get the reputation of being rich. And in the Talmud it states: "One who is not lame, not blind, and not crippled, and behaves as if he is, does not die of old age until he has one of these afflictions," a self-fulfilling prophecy. This is a bad habit. If I am accused of being a rich man, then I won't die until I am a rich man. May G-d grant us all good things that we should be able to raise our children with *naches* and comfort. . . .
> *Your father, Yekhil Birnbaum*

And in his last letter before Poland closed postal services abroad:

> *Thursday, Parsha Ki Teytse (before Rosh Hashonah). August 1939*
> Now, dear children, you ask about Marmish's wedding. I wanted to marry her off one and a half years ago but I didn't get an answer. A year ago we bought down feathers for the groom [part of the dowry], so I was sure that at the month of Chesvan she would get married, but nobody speaks of it. And so my years go by. These worries have made me grey and old. What shall I do: if G-d wills [it] . . . and we live to see it . . . also with Raisel...maybe marry her off. . . . G-d should help us to have a restful life, then we'll receive everything and there will be a wedding. . . . No other news. Be well and strong, dear loving children. . . . From your father and mother Yokheved and Yekhil "Itzhak" Birnbaum.

It is prophetic that this, his only reference to his middle name, was mentioned in his last letters, one to each of his children in Canada. His fear for their lives in Poland is written between the lines.

And it's ironic that he put such stock in an almighty that let him down, and a pity that he had always been against his children emigrating. His children had other ideas.

Marmish wrote on January 24, 1939:

> They're driving all the Jews out of Poland and taking everything away as they did in Germany, and since my dowry is still intact, I have 600 dollars. So, dear sister, if you have any pity at all and don't want to see the death of me, my plan is to quickly get married here in Poland, and you should make an application to bring us both over. . . .

On May 19, 1938, Khaskel writes:

> *Dear sister:*
>
> . . . The matzos came out fine and we made some money. It was a happy Pesach with lots of wine and lots of visitors. Now it's time for me to pass before the "Wajskava Commission" [draft board] on June 18. I'd still like to see your home and our brother Shloime. I haven't lost hope; the future for the young Jewish people in Poland looks far from good. . . .
>
> I read in the paper that farmers from Poland could get into Canada for 1,000 dollars. I don't know if you must show them the money to buy the land. If you see anything in the Canadian paper about any of this, let me know in your next letter. I see...when your husband is away at work you enjoy being with your smart and pretty daughter, Rifke [me]. . . .

Between 1933 and 1945, only 5,000 Jews were admitted to Canada under the anti-Semitic immigration policies of Prime Minister Mackenzie King. On June 14, 1939, Khaskel no longer writes about emigration. He appears to have given up and stoically puts up a good front:

> There was a by-law passed that every shop had to have a signboard [to designate Jewish shops, as Poles were ordered not to patronize these] and all the signs had to be the same colour; I know this kind of work so I made quite a bit of money.

And on August 14, 1939, this was his last letter before postal service was suspended:

> I'm having a very good time these days, every day I go to the woods, where I make new friends and we all take photographs of each other. I had a picture taken of me like the one I'm sending you; you'll notice that you now have a big brother, much different than the one you left behind. . . . I send warm regards to your husband.
> *Your brother, Khaskel*

And then a black curtain of silence fell over the more than 2,000 Jewish *shtetlekh* of Poland. And we never saw or heard from the Birnbaum *meshpokhe* again. The Birnbaums for me are forever shrouded in mystery because they are frozen in time — vanished in the smoke of the Holocaust.

My grandparents Yekhil and Yokheved (née Tyshler) Birnbaum. His hands look like the hands of the sculptor he was.

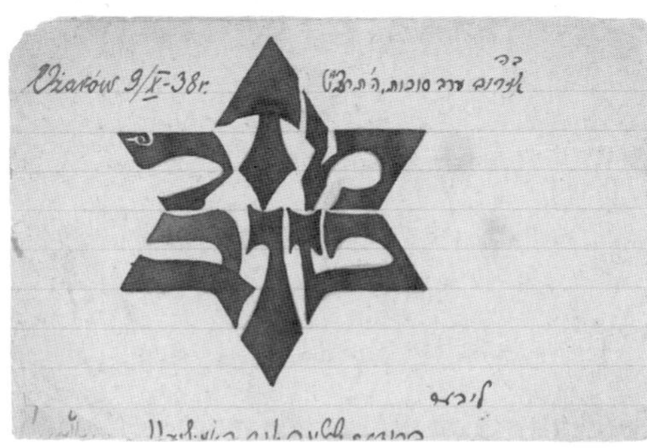

Khaskel's *"mazel tov"* on the birth of his brother's third daughter, Jean, 1938, sent in a letter to Montreal.

Mom's brother Khaskel, age 22, elegantly turned out, although showers and hot water were non-existent. He included this photo in his last letter August 1939. I would have liked to meet him.

Khaskel's pencil sketch of my mom.

My mom's passport, 1930. She is wearing a shirt embroidered by her sister Marmish.

Marmish was slated to come to Canada, but Shloime chose my mom instead because he thought Marmish spelled trouble — a little too bright for her boots.

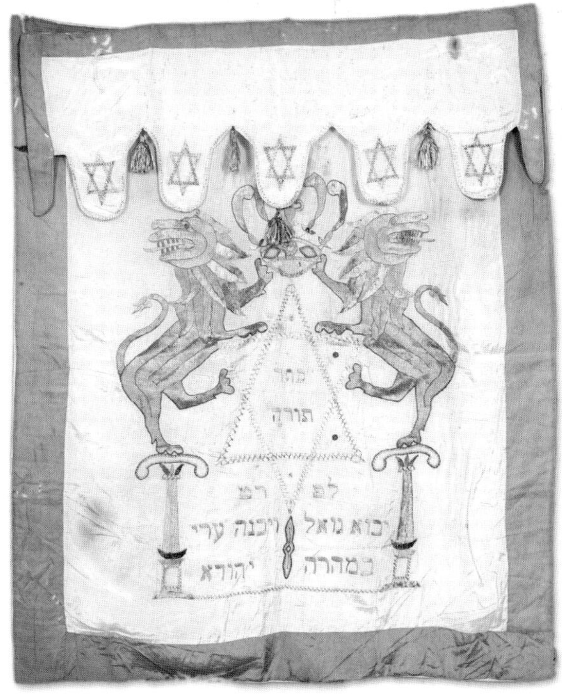

Parokhet (Torah ark curtain), 42 by 54 inches, silk embroidery on linen. It was made by my mom's sisters Raisel and Marmish to raise funds for their hoped-for immigration to Canada. It is now in the Canadian Jewish Congress Archives in Montreal.

!לשנה טובה תכתבו

Mom on the mountain in Montreal on a Sunday with her Ozarow friends.

A letter from my mom's father, Yekhil. "The Yiddish language is a part-German dialect written in the Hebrew alphabet; one-fifth of the words derive from Hebrew and Aramaic. Yiddish originated in the 10th century among Jews living along the banks of the Rhine River. The more distinct the Jewish communities became, the more their spoken language differed from the German."

Outwitting History by Aaron Lansky

Don't Miss It!
GALA
BRIDGE & DANCE
on
Wednesday, October 17th
1931
at the
CHEVRA KADISHA HALL
FAIRMOUNT & HUTCHISON
10 Piece Colored Orchestra
IN ATTENDANCE
GENTLEMEN ADMISSION Tax Included 25c
Ladie's Free

Mom went to this dance in Montreal, 1930.

The Wise Family

My dad, Joe, 1926. His younger sister Pearl, 1934. We didn't know she existed because she was banished from the family for 50 years.

My dad's father, Hillel.

Dad's mother, Esther-Rifke, for whom I am named, 1934. She is wearing her *Shabbat sheytel.*

Khayele, dad's older sister.

CHAPTER NINE

The Khurbn

THE SAVAGERY OF THE SHOAH

I cannot stop remembering the Holocaust. In Yiddish, the Holocaust is the *khurbn*, and in Hebrew, the *shoah*. All my mother's fears about the *khurbn* became a reality more horrible than anyone could have imagined. It's true that the Jews of Europe, since history began, had known discrimination, persecution, expulsion, pogroms. This had always been a given in Jewish life, so they could expect the usual torments. But how could my grandfather have imagined so outrageous a plan as the systematic murder of every single Jew, to make the whole world cleansed of Jews — *Judenrein*, in Hitler's hateful word.

I measure all my troubles, large and small, against the terrifying accounts of my fellow Jews during the Holocaust. Some of these stories haunt me. The Holocaust has indelibly invaded my consciousness and is always with me, like a dybbuk. It lurks around the fringes of my mind, a bizarre contrast to my good life.

The Birnbaums outside their house, No. 1 Zlote Sreet in Ozarow, 1938. From left: Marmish, Yekhil, Yokheved, Raisel, Khaskel. Note the artwork in the window right — paper cutouts for the Purim festival. The stovepipe, left, gives us the location of the stove.

Whenever I feel the cold, I think of Gerda Weissman Klein, who wrote the memoir *All But My Life*, about the forced march from Grunberg to just past Dresden — which was being bombed at the time — in the winter of 1944. These Jews marched for two months till spring, 500 kilometres in the bitter cold. Of the 2,000 who began the march, only 200 survived.

On the day in 1942 when the Nazis had first ordered her family to leave, her father had said to her, "Gerda, I want you should wear your skiing shoes," and Gerda had answered, "But, Papa, skiing shoes in June?" These boots were to save her feet from freezing. From 1942 to 1944, Gerda worked in forced-labour textile mills. She was moved from factory to factory, and then to the death camps. She speaks of waiting daily to be selected to die, watching as her fellow inmates were taken one by one to the gas chambers. Finally, on the last forced march, she and her girlfriends slept on the frozen ground in the bitter snowstorms of February, huddled together against the cold. Gerda writes: "We passed the word around not to sleep." Those who slept froze.

Gerda Weissman was liberated in 1945 by an American soldier, Kurt Klein, whom she married. She now lives in Buffalo, New York, with her children and grandchildren.

What must my uncle Khaskel have suffered while waiting for death? Waiting for impending death must be worse than suffering a quick death. I think of the survivor Mordkhe Vaysman, of the Polish shtetl Wlodzimierzec, who recounts his most terrifying moment. It was August 1942 when he, his wife and children and all the other Jews of the town had been assembled in a field to be shot and thrown into ditches the victims themselves had prepared earlier.

Mordkhe writes in *From a Ruined Garden*:

> They ordered the men to strip . . . and assemble in rows of five . . . . Five in a row, we stood several metres away from the ditch that was soon to be our grave. The first row was ordered to jump in the ditch. . . . A German with a machine gun stood at one end. Those who jumped in . . . were slaughtered with one salvo. . . . The moment came for my row to enter the ditch . . . . I didn't want to live, I just wanted Death to come quickly . . . but just at the moment when the German motioned to me to jump . . . a bizarre, illogical, instinctive thought hit me like a fiery rod: . . . to run . . . and be killed as a resister . . . and that's what happened. . . . I ran as though possessed . . . into the forest. . . . I heard . . . the whistle of bullets around me. . . . I thought I was running after I was already dead. . . . When I stopped for a moment, I realized to my astonishment that I wasn't dead. Naked as the day I was born, I walked among the trees.

After the massacre of the Jews in the shtetl of Eishyshok on Saturday, September 27, the Germans, their Polish henchmen, and the local parishioners went to church the next day. Yaffa Eliach writes in her book *Eishyshok*:

> On Sunday, September 28, 1941 . . . the bells at the Juryzdyki church called the people to worship. . . . The pews were lined with people in their Sunday best, which in many cases was the Sabbath best of their Jewish neighbours, whose homes they had looted. Ostrauskas [a local tyrant who carried out Nazi orders] . . . was observed to make confession. . . . The parishioners listened to their priest tell them that the Jews had at last been called to account for the killing of Christ. . . . He asked anyone wearing

> Jewish clothes to leave (though no one did). He seemed to feel that the murder was understandable. Even if it was wrong, a kind of justice had been done.

A survivor of the Holocaust says in one of the *Yizkor* (memory) books that he would like to say to the Polish people, "You live in our homes, you sleep in our beds … you use our bedding, you wear our clothes."

What kind of gruesome death did my three aunts — Sarah, Marmish, and Raisel — suffer? Their fate was so much worse than death. Naked and emaciated, they were probably among those who all looked alike, like some species of animal not quite human, with that chilling blue number tattooed on their arms — a cataloguing system evilly and ingeniously devised by IBM. A German company, I.G. Farben, designed crematoriums and produced the mauve cyklon-B gas crystals. I had always thought this gas just put people to sleep like an anaesthetic, until I read how gruesome a death it caused. In the death chamber the gas was thicker at the floor level, so the victims, like people drowning, were driven involuntarily to climb on each other for the fresher air still near the ceiling. In the dark they wouldn't be aware that they were climbing on other people. After 20 minutes, the gas chamber was opened to reveal heaps of bodies crushed and mangled together with broken and twisted limbs.

I can only surmise that the Nazis *chose* to give Jews such an inhumane death, but I cannot understand why. Wasn't it enough that the Jewish people had already been deprived of their children, their lovers, their families, their dignity, and every human comfort — replaced only with fear that the next day might be their last? Every piece of goods that had belonged to the Jews, from the humble clothes off their backs, their furniture, bedding, wedding rings, spectacles, gold fillings, and Sabbath candlesticks to, in some cases, their grand houses and Impressionist paintings and sculptures

— all of these were taken from them. (The Swiss banks stealthily and immorally had kept any monies deposited by Jews, since they were no longer alive to claim it.) Hitler's financiers cashed in the large prizes and used the money for the war. Probably some of it financed the efficient machinery for assembling and transporting people to the death camps, gassing and (after their gold fillings were extracted) incinerating them. My grandparents were among these victims.

I understand how ordinary citizens — even I — could be made to commit crimes, but I don't understand the monstrousness of Hitler's plan to annihilate one people from the face of the earth. It has never happened before and can never happen again. I think of today's television news reportage and how we are bombarded with negative news. I've often complained, "Do I really need to know daily about every evil that is happening anywhere in the world? Do I need to know about some Turkish barber in the remote village of B., who pulled out his tooth by wrapping it in thread, tying the thread to a doorknob, and kicking the door shut?" The answer is "Yes, I do need to know," because if CNN had been around in 1942, the Holocaust couldn't have happened. The reporters would have been embedded beside the charnel houses of crematoriums like those at Bergen-Belsen, the camp where my daughter-in-law Ann's family perished.

Horrible images recur about the savagery of the German gangsters. Were my grandmother Yokheved and her three daughters forced to strip, have their heads shaved, their arms tattooed with numbers? Were they issued a striped rough garment, no underwear, no hot water, no blanket, no mattress, only a bowl of soup and a crust of bread each day to sustain them through long hours of backbreaking work? And all the while my grandmother had to worry about the fate of her husband and son and how many days they had left. I don't know the details of my Birnbaum family's last days.

Mom was afraid of the hatred some Polish Catholics harbour against Jews and remembered her brother was beaten on the road to *kheder* (Hebrew school). For centuries the Catholic Church had fuelled anti-Semitism in Poland. In 1936, the year I was born, Cardinal Augustin Hlond stated that "three and a half million Jews in Poland are too many — half a million would suffice." Pope Pius XII was guilty by his silence during all the years of the extermination of the Jews. There was even an administrative connection between the Vatican's Curia and the Nazis during the war. For this the Pope was called "Hitler's deputy."

Only 250,000 Polish Jews survived.

In the affidavit he made at the Nuremburg trials, Auschwitz commandant Rudolf Hess said that "still another improvement we made over Treblinka was that at Treblinka the victims almost always knew that they were to be exterminated and at Auschwitz we endeavoured to fool the victims into thinking they were going into a delousing process."

The death camps were not built by illiterate barbarians, but by civilized, college-educated men. The architect who designed Auschwitz was a Bauhaus graduate, and the notorious Dr. Josef Mengele had two degrees, one in philosophy from the University of Munich, the other in medicine from the University of Frankfurt. Mengele, "the angel of death," spent 22 months at Auschwitz. Each day, he selected Jews on arrival to live or go immediately to the gas chambers. He also performed hideous medical experiments. To think that my father-in-law Max Sharp was born in that small shtetl of Auschwitz. Now the very sound of the name strikes terror in the heart, as do names such as Buchenwald, which ludicrously means "beechwood." The very word "German" is tainted by the inhumanity, complicity, and coldness of that people in the worst massacre ever perpetrated by one people against another.

A woman now living in Ozarow, Mrs. Franciszka Paniac, remembers the last march of the Jews in the town, in this text from www.ozarow.org:

> Almost 60 years ago, on Thursday, October 15, 1942, Jews were forced to leave Ozarow. In that morning, a *shofar* [ram's horn] was sounded three times near the synagogue. The Jews of Ozarow gathered. . . . The murderers had lied. They had ordered the Jews, through the rabbi, to give up all their valuables, with the promise that if enough money was raised [they] could stay in Ozarow. . . . On that morning . . . a policeman, banging a drum, gave notice going through my street, Kolejowa Street, to cover our windows, because the Jews was [sic] about to be taken away. . . . They were marched in rows of four, because Kolejowa Street was not very wide. Then I heard gunfire. . . . Jews were being taken from the rows of people, mothers with babies, whoever tripped, and older people. In front of my house a mother and her three children were murdered. The whole street was covered with bodies. . . . We heard one continuous sound of screaming and crying. . . . I have never forgotten those sounds. On Monday morning, townspeople with carts and horses were ordered to clean up the streets.

My people, the Birnbaums, were probably among those marched to the train station in Jasice and shipped to Treblinka (although some of them may be among the 120 who were shot and buried in the mass grave at the cemetery, or they could have been shot in the street). Treblinka was a death camp — there were no barracks; people were gassed on arrival. And so, by October 22, 1942, the Birnbaums had all been slaughtered.

I cannot stop remembering.

My *meshpokhe* on my father's side, the Weissfogels, fared much better than the Birnbaums. They had the good sense to leave Poland in 1929 and make their way to Toronto. The Weissfogels became Wises when they arrived at Pier 21 in Halifax. In Ozarow, my father, Joe, had been apprenticed to a tailor at age 12. If he had been born in Warsaw, he might have become an architect, but through the ages Jews had been chased out of cities and had to regroup in small towns where they could practise their religion. Very few professions were available in the shtetl, and the best option for my dad was tailoring, a trade he continued successfully in Canada. He became a cutter — one of the elite members of the tailors' trade, making as much as $100 a week during the Depression — which my mother never let him forget, since when they were married he had only $40: *"Er hot nisht gehat vaser af kasha* — he didn't have water to boil buckwheat."

Joe lived with his parents and Khayele and her husband. Khayele says that when Joe first arrived from Poland, he was emaciated from hiding out to avoid the military, and she couldn't make him enough of the *bobeles* he craved. When his blond young sister Pearl arrived from Ozarow, Joe doted on her and spent much of his large salary either buying her fine clothes or paying the medical bills for his mother, Esther-Rifke, who was dying from diabetes.

Joe's father, Hillel, a baker, was born in 1884 and lived to be 100. Although he resided in Canada more than 50 years, my *zeyde* never drove a car or learned English. We spoke together in Yiddish. By the time I knew him, he had shaved his beard but still put on tfiln every morning for prayers.

There was a scandal in the family in 1934, when Pearl ran off and married an Italian Catholic, Louis Natale, who converted to Judaism and underwent the prescribed ritual circumcision. The family hardheartedly refused to accept the marriage, and poor Pearl had to seek refuge with her in-laws. She made every effort to maintain her religion, even carrying her circumcised infant son to her sister for approval. The family stonily sat shiva for a week, a mourning decreed by Hillel, and did not see Pearl until 50 years later. Esther-Rifke, Pearl's mother, died at age 56 — her death hastened, allegedly, by Pearl's marriage.

I never knew Pearl existed until one day, when I was about 11, I found a 1930s photo of a slightly familiar young lady stylishly outfitted in a felt hat and fur collar. "Mom," I asked, "who is this? Is she a movie star?" My mother's evasive answers and guilty smile provoked me to pry the truth out of her, that my father in fact had two sisters. "Well," I thought, "the Wise family is not so boring after all." No one knew where Pearl lived or had made any attempt to find her. My brother and Khayele's daughter-in-law Betty did a search, found her, and we had a family reunion 50 years after she had been banished. Today Pearl and her sister Khayele come to us and grace holiday dinners and tell us tales about their early life. Pearl has retained her Jewish heritage and buys kosher food, but she still holds bitterness in her heart for the hurt done to her.

I often visit my father's older sister, Khayele, now 100 years of age, because I like to sit and listen to her family *mayses* (tales), all told in her Yiddish accent, which makes them even more colourful. She can dispatch the entire life of a family member with a few pointed remarks. She tells the *mayse* of her grandfather Yankel *der farnarter* (the fool), so nicknamed because before World War I he had made a fortune in real estate, which he foolishly entrusted to a Polish farmer. During the war, when Yankel came to collect, the farmer had died and his kids feigned ignorance about the money. Yankel had to resort to selling pencils and strings of beads to get by. Nicknames like his were common in the shtetl. Some referred unkindly to some physical handicap, like "hunchback," "gimp," "skinny," or "fatty." People might be nicknamed for their profession, the colour of their hair, the town they hailed from, or even for the name of their mother. My grandfather Yekhil was known as Khilele Brayndeles after my great-grandmother Braryndl.

Yankel, my great-great-grandfather, had six wives. Three died, and the last he divorced after she stole the goose feathers from the *iberbet*. When asked why the *iberbet* was so flat, she was reportedly at a loss for words. With his six wives, Yankel had six children, my grandfather Hillel being the first. Another son, Tzudik, with curly red hair, died of smallpox, and a third son, Berish, who dealt in livestock, was crossing a river with four horses when he drowned.

Khayele tells the story of her mother's brother Lazar, who lived in Ostrowietz and married the girl next door when he was 50 and she 20. After a year they produced triplets, two boys and a girl. Because Lazar was a poor shoemaker, a rich citizen offered to foot the bill for a festive *bris* (ritual circumcision). After the party, the donor, who was childless, proposed that he himself take one of the boys, for whom he could provide a prosperous future. "Where," said he, "do you have enough space in your one-room house for three children?" Answered Lazar, "Where I'm going to put two, I can put three."

Khayele tells many *mayses* about her father, Hillel. Because he was an orphan, he was ineligible for a good *shidekh* (match), so he married an old maid with no prospects, Esther-Rifke Sherman, when she was about 26 and he about 17. Khayele remembers how beautiful her mother looked of a *Shabbat* evening, when she *bentsht likht* (sang the blessings over the Sabbath candles) wearing a white dress and her *Shabbat sheytl*. On weekdays she covered her bald head only with her *kupke* (frilled cotton cap). Jewish brides shaved their heads when they married.

Hillel and Esther opened a bakery, selling onion *pletzlech* (flat buns), challahs, cheese buns, and rye bread with and without *kiml* (caraway seeds). For the holiday of Shavuot, Khayele would collect blueberries in the woods and Dad would bake blueberry buns. It was a hard life, baking well into the night and selling all day till late in the evening. In the end, the bakery failed, probably because it was one of 15 bakeries, more than the town could support. My grandfather Hillel found a job in Krakow and in 1917 applied for emigration papers, but didn't make the Canadian quota till 1929. In Toronto he became a foreman at Sherman's Bakery, and Teddy Sherman tells me Hillel was a hard worker — when he untied his pant legs after work, perspiration poured out of his trouser cuffs.

I recall that in the early 1940s, the crust of the rye breads from Sherman's Bakery bore a paper stamp marked "Union Made" (which I hoped no one had licked). My father said I would never find a husband because I held the bread awkwardly when I sliced it. My mom always held the loaf against her chest while slicing. I remember her once cutting into a round rye loaf and finding a rusty nail inside — for a time I was wary of finding something foreign whenever I cut into bread.

Hillel and his family lived not far from Sherman's Bakery, at 7 Leonard Avenue. Pearl has a fond memory of her dad, who she says was very proud of her good looks. She remembers him standing by the front door and following her with his eyes as she walked away in her new wool coat with the fur collar, a gift from my dad, Joe. After his wife died in 1934, Hillel was to have three more wives. I remember all of them. The first was always in the kitchen, baking; the last died in old age; and the middle one ran off to Montreal with a lover. I recall this lady wearing a wide-sleeved grey Persian lamb coat and heavy perfume. My grandfather had been suspicious of this lady, so he set a trap for her. He stationed his grandson in the closet and pretended to leave for work, but soon returned to find her "in flagrante." The grandson, Jake Weinberg, sprang out of the closet — the witness.

The Wise *meshpokhe* all prospered in the New World. My dad went from cutter at Tip Top Tailors to shopkeeper and then builder-owner. When he died in 1983, my dad left my brother Stan and me an estate of about $750,000. I was pleased that the will stated that the money be divided equally — which I took to indicate equal love. My needs, however, were not equal to my brother's, because Isadore was a rather good provider. So I kept only $100,000 and gave the rest to Stan. The legacy was important to my parents, who had proudly denied themselves luxuries to leave more to us. With my share I bought a pearl and diamond necklace. Whenever anyone admired it, I gladly told them it was a gift from my parents.

The Weinberg family — my dad's sister Khayele and her husband Srultshe — also prospered in Canada. They moved to a derelict three-storey attached house at 325 College Street, where my aunt took charge of reconstruction. They lived on the ground floor and rented out the rest of the house. My uncle carried on with his shtetl trade of shoemaker, considered the lowliest occupation on the Ozarow social scale. In Ozarow he had made shoes to measure, but in Toronto people bought ready-made shoes. His shop, Sam's Shoe Repair, was in the bay-windowed front room, the only bright room in the house. I remember him singing with gusto as he worked among the gleaming mint-green and silver wheels and brushes of the shoemaking machinery that importantly took up a whole wall. This machinery cost $700 in 1929 and looked the price.

City regulations required that the shop be separated from the rest of the house by a wall, so my aunt Khayele undertook the task. My cousin Norman tells me that she went to the hardware store and asked the proprietor how to build a wall. He wrote instructions in Yiddish, sold her nails, lumber, plaster, and paint, and wished her good luck. She built a very good wall, which she was quick to point out to visitors. My aunt repaired the plaster and painted the walls of the whole house, while standing on a table. In Ozarow she had also been the one to paint the walls before Passover.

Every Sunday we made the expedition downtown to visit the Weinberg house to soak up a little *yidishkayt*. We would congregate around the kitchen table next to the huge yellow enamel stove with the oven door at eye level beside the burners. Everyone would have tea in a glass with honey cake. Except me. I was told always to say "No thank you" to any food offered. (I read the subtext: saying no is socially correct, and also, food at our home is more sanitary.) We would often sit on the verandah and watch the proceedings at Benjamin's Funeral Home nearby, and my cousins and I would speculate about the macabre processions of bodies arriving and coffins leaving. How, we wondered, could Mr. Benjamin handle dead limbs and then have a corned beef sandwich for lunch?

Eventually the market for shoe repairs went the way of the fashion for felt fedoras, so the Weinbergs moved to a more modern life in Los Angeles. Their children — my cousins Norman and Stanley — are very successful. Stan is an electrical engineer with a dozen inventions to his name, including a dimmer switch for lights, a device for recognizing ice on aircraft wings, and a personal "ionic" air purifier. Norman, a PhD in chemistry, has published 22 technical books, holds 34 patents, and lectures widely. Norman and I were buddies — we were the same age. Like me, he was the ever-resourceful shtetl child. At nine years old, he wanted a camera, which he got the only way he could — he made one out of cardboard — the film was light-sensitive paper he bought from the drugstore with his precious 10-cents savings.

I cannot imagine, only wonder, what my Birnbaum relatives, their children and their children's children might have achieved had they survived. Norman Weinberg also has a great interest in his Ozarow heritage. He headed up a successful cemetery restoration program and rescued the sacred ground from 60 years of garbage and neglect.

My cousin had a plaque made to the memory of about 120 Ozrower Jews who were slaughtered by the Germans on or about October 26, 1942, and buried there in a mass grave, one they themselves were forced to dig. One of those shot was a mother with a baby in her arms. The week before this slaughter, 4,500 Jews had been deported in sealed cattle cars to Treblinka. Some of those people were from nearby villages and towns as well as from Ozarow.

Norman, on a recent trip, arranged with the mayor of Ozarow, Mr. Marcin Majcher, that the cemetery be maintained. About the cemetery it is said that after the war a Jewish survivor came there and warned some local people that if any of the *matseyves* (tombstones) were vandalized, God would cause the people of Ozarow to suffer the same fate that befell the Germans.

The oldest Ozarow gravestone found so far is dated 1700, but we know there may be others still buried that are older. Someone once sighted a *matseyve* with Hebrew and Spanish or Ladino letters, which means the Jews may have come there after the Inquisition. European Jewish cemeteries typically were built in layers. Every 100 years, new graves were piled on old ones because Jews were allowed only limited space. This is also why the headstones are sometimes so close together.

Jewish people have probably been living in Ozarow since before it was named, in 1568, for a man named Josef Ozerovski. The earliest record extant is an entry in the diary of a Hungarian traveller, Martin Csombor, dated 1616:

> The majority of the inhabitants in Ozarow are Jewish. When we stopped there on Saturday, they were all calmly occupying themselves with their religious ceremonies.

The same religious rites that circumscribed my *kinderyorn* (young years) in North Toronto.

OZARÓW 18/IX
CZCIGODNA RÓZIO!
KORZYSTAJĄC Z OKAZJI NOWOROCZNEJ
ORAZ URODZIN ZASYŁAM SERDECZNE
POWINSZOWANIE SKŁADAJĄCE SIĘ
ZE SŁÓW NINIEJSZYCH.

RADOŚĆ I WESOŁOŚĆ BEZ MIARY
OBY NIEUSTANNIE PŁYNĘŁY
Z DROGI NIECH ODEJDĄ GORYCZE
I WCIĄZ NIECH BIEGNĄ SŁODYCZE
AŻEBY TRWAŁY PRZEZ CAŁE ŻYCIE!
TEGO Z SERCA ŻYCZY,

BIRENBAUM SZLAMA

Birthday card drawn by mom's brother Shloime and sent from Ozarow to his fiancée Rachel in Montreal, 1924.

Shloime Birnbaum weds Rachel Kestenbaum, Montreal, 1926.

Shloime's daughter Jeanie, age five.

Shtetl Occupations, circa 1926

A tailor at his sewing machine. It is said that at the Tuesday Ozarow market, tailors would ask their clients to lie down on a piece of brown paper, then draw around their bodies to make the pattern for clothing.

The *vaser treger* (water carrier) would sell water to each household, from his horse-drawn cart. Two pailfuls of water would be poured into the water barrel located just inside the door of each house.

The *shabbat klaper* (the sexton) would knock on the shutters every Friday and cry, *"In shul arrayn —* time to go to synagogue."

RECOLLECTIONS OF DAVID WAKSMAN.

I took this snapshot when I visited Ozarow in January 1968. Note the Catholic church on the hill. In 1939 the Jews of Ozarow numbered 4,284 — the remaining third of the population was Catholic.

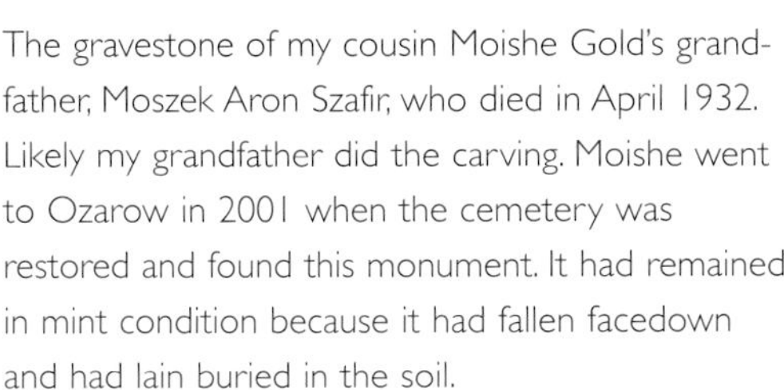

The gravestone of my cousin Moishe Gold's grandfather, Moszek Aron Szafir, who died in April 1932. Likely my grandfather did the carving. Moishe went to Ozarow in 2001 when the cemetery was restored and found this monument. It had remained in mint condition because it had fallen facedown and had lain buried in the soil.

My grandfater Wise had a bakery like this one. The sign reads: *seier git eier challas ois sheva* (very good egg challas for the sabbath).

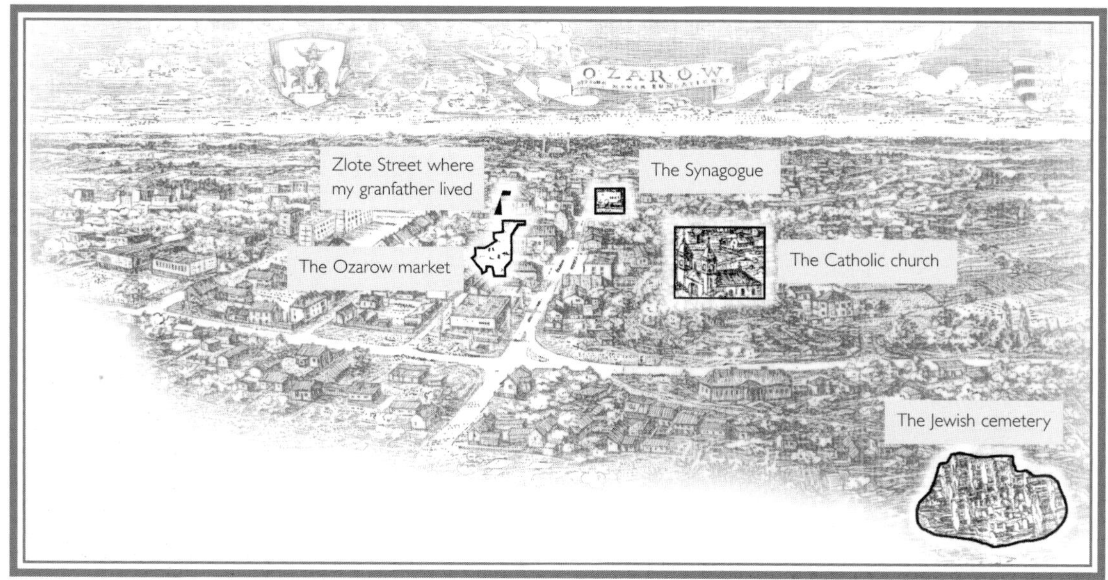

Map of Ozarow showing location of my grandfather's house, the synagogue, and the marketplace.

Market day in Oswiecim, as it looked in 1918 when Max Sharp left this town he was born in, for Israel. Oswiecim is the Polish word for the town of Auschwitz, later the site of the concentration camp. Market day in Ozarow was every Tuesday, when farmers and townsfolk exchanged goods. My aunts recall the following items were for sale: herrings, hats, harnesses and pickles, poultry, fabrics, flour, pottery, dried fruits and mushrooms, workshirts, wagon wheels, blueberries and fish, pine furniture, kerosene lamps. The market played host to klezmers, tailors, shoemakers, hairdressers, and the town *feltsher.*

Ozarow, the banishment of the Jews, 1942. A week later, not one Jew was left in the town.
Note the synagogue at the end of the road.

The Ozarow synagogue, 1930s, built in 1916 after
the old wooden synagogue was razed in WWI.

MARATHON
HOPE
DREAM

CHAPTER TEN

Just a Few Steps FROM THE SHTETL

When I look at God's work — I still don't believe in him but I use his name vainly and conveniently as a metaphor for whatever is the creator — I see he made some mistakes. Look at his design of the hippopotamus. On the other hand, most of God's work is glorious. Take, for example, the pomegranate, or at sunset the scarlet blossoms of the poinciana tree. Or the curious neem tree of central India. On trees and almost all his other designs, God was brilliant, but he could have done better at matching up my parents. In the end, though, it's hard to imagine a different existence, and my parents did, after all, come to love and count on each other.

The truth is, I wouldn't change one thing about my growing-up years. Well, maybe a trip to Trois Pistoles would have been good. Life at the Wises' defined me and the deprivation armed me to face reversals later. On balance, my home life was *nisht azoy geferlekh* — not so terrible. Like most people, I look back on my youth with affection and nostalgia.

With the grandkids at the annual Terry Fox Run. The run, which Issy started in 1980, has raised $430 million to date. From left: me, Emily, Julia, Aaron and Issy.

I admit I was too harsh and critical of my parents, and the idyllic life I sought existed only in the books I read. My shtetl life gave me many gifts: I learned to enjoy my own company and to be satisfied with either a little or a lot of the world's goods, and that if you can't buy it, you can make it yourself. From my parents I found the strength of mind to accept my son's death.

Mine was a privileged, one-of-a-kind childhood — not at all bland. My parents treated me as an adult, yet I was still a child. I carried the yoke of a grown-up. My mom looked to me for many decisions and would even ask me, at eight years old, which dress she should wear. She continued this to the end of her days. Unlike my kids and grandkids, I am a product of Eastern Europe. They have little connection to thousands of years of Jewish life — our children have been deprived of the distinctions peculiar to shtetl life.

What would be the differences, say, between a Pesach Seder in my grandfather's house at No. 1 Zlote Street, Ozarow, and the same holiday celebration at 26 Forest Glen?

In my grandfather's house, I can imagine my aunts and uncle gathering at the kitchen table for the Seder by candlelight, wearing their shabby best dress, their *kipas*, and my grandmother, her *sheytl*. The men would have been at prayer the whole day, while the women prepared the chicken soup and symbolic hard-boiled eggs and salt water. My aunt Sarah's two young children, Ydessl and a younger brother Shloime, about my age, would be there — they were also to vanish in the Holocaust. My uncle Khaskel, in March 1939, sent us wishes for "a kosher and a happy *Pesach* with lots of wine."

When our four generations assembled this year for the *Pesach Seder* at our house, the differences from times past were distinct — it would have been culture shock to my grandparents had they been observers. At our house the meal is prepared and served by others, the language is English, the room we eat in is dedicated to dining only, the table is 20 feet long, the *kipas* worn only for blessings, the dishes not solely for Passover, the food only kosher *style*, the service abbreviated and tailored to current events, the matzos from a box, the wine not homemade, the grandkids wearing jeans.

My father's two sisters represent his generation. Khayele is 100 years old and Pearl is 88. Both sisters usually come in the fall for the Breaking of the Fast, and in spring for Passover. When I called Pearl to come, she was reluctant because she was still mourning the death of her daughter Joanie. "Pearl," I said, "we need you to grace our table. You do us honour and make the occasion more significant."

Everyone is here: the whole extended family is present. My two old aunts born in the shtetl can't quite figure out the cast of characters. They don't know the word "dysfunctional." But I have to accept reluctantly that this word may apply, although nowadays "dysfunctional" is more common and conventional than "functional." The aunts don't know which wife is the ex-wife, but they do know the food is good. Jordy is here with his soon-to-be wife, Elaine Floritto. He was married before to Mary Applegate, who runs a bookstore on Salt Spring Island called Fables. She is as lovely as Elaine, who is a wealth-management counsellor in Victoria. Both Jordy and Greg have second wives quite as nice as the first ones. Greg is now married to the winning Mirilyn Kott, who, thankfully, is a practicing Jew, a partner in a law firm, and has three children who are all here tonight for Passover and can read the blessings in Hebrew. For them the milk dishes are separated from the meat, as decreed in the Old Testament.

Greg's first wife, Ann Kelton Sharp, needs her own paragraph. She and Greg have been divorced for 15 years, but are still good friends. And Ann is my good friend, a daughter, and the supermom of my three grandchildren (please, God, we have hopes for more). About 10 years ago, Greg gave Ann a hand mirror for Chanukah, at the party here in our house. The card read: "When you look in this mirror, Ann, you will see the best mother in the world." To which Emily, Julia, and Aaron attest.

Tony, the youngest, is still a bachelor and his social life remains a mystery. He almost married Karina Bukhanov, a Jewish doctor — what more could a mother want? We all love her still. When Tony and Karina were courting, I would sometimes endanger my life running red lights. I would be driving along St. Clair and the traffic signal a block ahead was green, so I would speed up. The deal was this: "God willing, if I make this light, they will get married." Meanwhile, Karina and Tony are best friends and play bridge together at the club regularly. Perhaps my *zeyde* Birnbaum was right when he said, "Providence decides the moment for a good match."

Also in attendance on Passover is Vernon Shaw, Ann's husband and my dishy British Jewish son-in-law. No wonder my aunts are confused. And, of course, also at the table are my baby brother Stan and his family. All of the elders and the extended exes are a boon since they have become my friends. (Issy's three sisters do their own family Seders.)

Twenty-two for dinner — no problem — I've become a monster of efficiency. All of the above are now seated and the Seder begins with blessings, the Passover story, and the usual questions. Just then an ant climbs out of the sand spilled down the table to simulate the Land of Israel. A propos, someone tells a joke with a Jewish punch line. None of the kids laugh because they don't understand Yiddish. As always there is confusion as some guests chat instead of listen. Jordy describes the scene: "There was chaos in reading the story, everybody taking turns, but the point was lost — the table was so long, it sometimes took several minutes for the message to reach everybody. I was sampling the bitter herbs while Stephanie was eating the symbolic egg. Thank God for the Manischewitz — at least the ritual wine-sipping was in sync."

Jordy's chaos reminds me of Samuel Pepys' comical account of his visit to a mid-17th-century synagogue. In his diary, Pepys describes the men wearing long fringed silk shawls and round caps, bobbing up and down and bowing alternately, while some people are chatting and paying no attention. He found the proceedings chaotic — a marked lack of decorum.

Continuing with the Seder readings and the ritual of the four glasses of wine, conversation resumes as usual on Friday nights. Tony takes out his Blackberry, holds it intimately in his hand, and studies it solemnly, as if looking into its soul. Then he and Aaron get into one of their esoteric science dialogues that no one else can follow (Tony's first college degree was mechanical engineering).

"Aaron, how old do you think the universe is?"

"I don't know, Tony. How could anyone possibly figure this out?"

"Well, I can tell you, Aaron, that the universe is 8.3 billion years old, and they know this by looking through very powerful telescopes. The farther away they look, the farther back in time they can see, as light takes time to travel. Light farther away is older. At some far-off distance, they find no light, and that is the time the universe began."

Now Aaron challenges Tony with another science question about squaring the circle or the possibility of time travel, which most of us cannot even imagine.

After dinner we assemble in the living room for more conversation and another challenge. Jay Lubinsky (Julia's boyfriend) and Tony have a push-up competition on the living room rug. Jay does 44, one more than Tony. Meanwhile, a driver comes to collect my two aunts — Khayele always takes home a bottle of Scotch — and the religious holiday of Passover is adjourned for another year.

So that's about it so far, *mazeldik* — surprise and chance playing the greatest part. Maybe that's what my mother meant when she said, "*Dos gantse lebn iz azoy vi a cholem* — your whole life is like a dream." I look back, cast a cold eye, sort it all out, and celebrate. It's just a few steps from the shtetl — from the horses and carts of Ozarow — to the Challenger jet and all our other grandeurs.

But the funny things about life will surely go on with plenty more "Oh my God" and "Please, God" — more improbables, unexpecteds, imponderables. But rest easy, readers, even if the robins return here to roost, I promise not to tell. In the end, I chose my parents "Wise-ly." Maybe God *didn't* make a mistake in assigning me to the Wise household — I am my mother and my father, after all.

rifke רבקה wise sharp

december 2, 2006, 11 kislev, 5767

Appaloosa and me in my office.

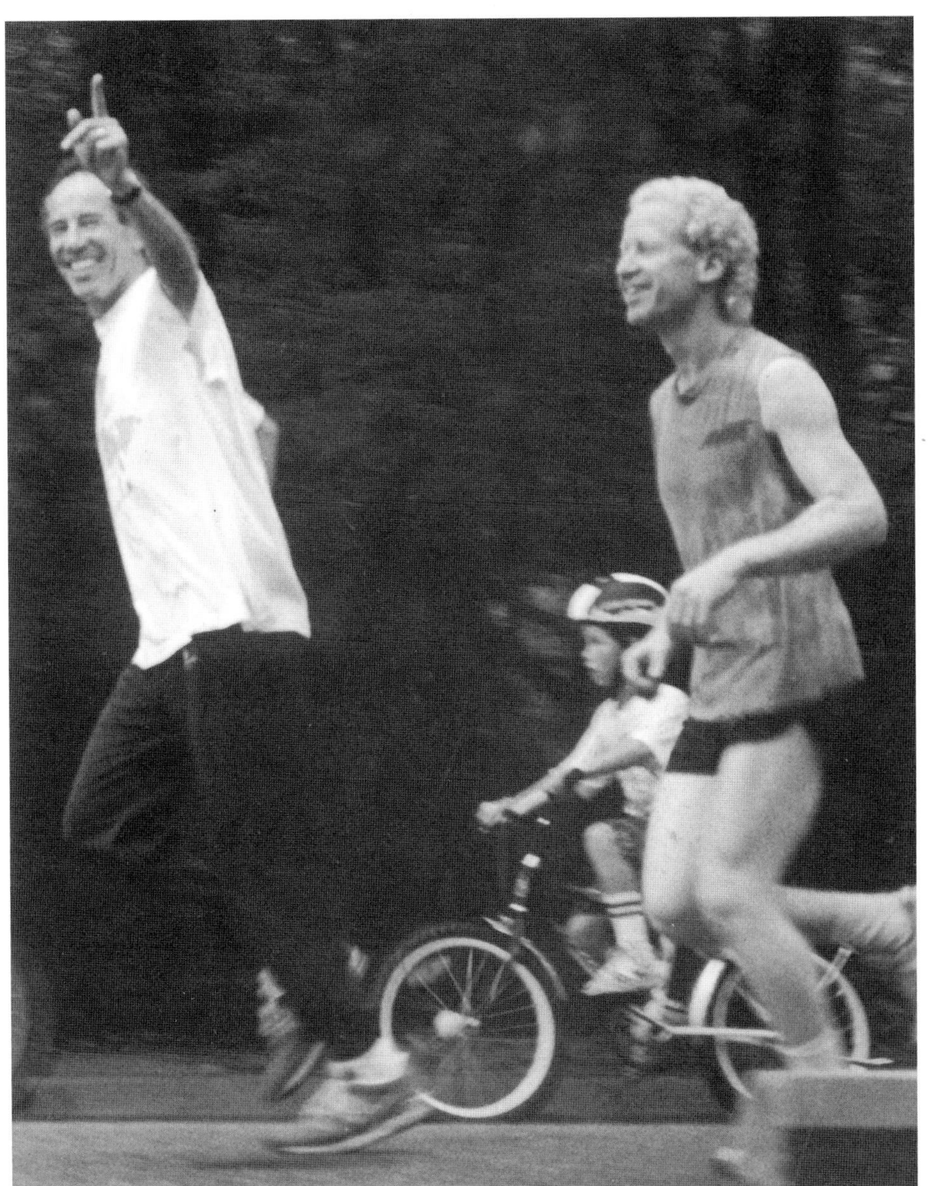

Issy and Greg at the Terry Fox Run.

Anthony graduates from Yale.

Okanagan with a dog's best friend, Jordy. This dog was one of the most decent persons I know.

A family dinner. From left: Joey, Vernon, Aaron, me, Greg, Emily, Issy, Julia, Martha, Ann, Stan, and Tara.

Our grandchildren and daughter-in-law Ann. From left: Emily, Aaron, and Julia.

Gregory and Mirilyn Sharp at the Louvre.

Jordan and Elaine Sharp at the wedding of Brian and Laura Wise.

Christopher Hugh Sharp, 1960-1978.

My heartfelt thanks to Jack David, my publisher and personal Max Perkins. Jack, you were uncanny with your red-pen directives in the margin to "expand" or "move the middle to the front and the end to the middle." The day I spotted ECW Press on the flyleaf of *Too Close to the Falls* was my lucky day. You are a statesman in your field. I will sing your praises to anyone looking for a publisher. And to Stuart Ross, poet and gentleman — what mazel to have you as my editor. Thank you for your careful and caring work. You're so young and yet you are an old man of letters with dozens of published works. Your poems invoke the abstract beauty of a Borduas painting. I'm so happy to have met you. I am grateful to the proficient and admirable team at ECW Press: Tania Craan and Mary Bowness for production and design, Parmjit Parmar for publicity and Simon Ware and Sarah Dunn, marketing.

Thanks are due to my young blond researcher in Ozarow, Anna Czajkowska. We met many times, but only on the Internet. To Hartley Garshowitz and David Caron for the family tree. And to my cousins Moishe Gold, Norman Weinberg, and Jean Zwirek, and my aunts Khayele Weinberg, Pearl Natale, and Rachel Birnbaum. Thank you for answering so many questions. I'm grateful to my family for their contributions: Jordy, Elaine, Greg, Mirilyn, Tony, Ann, Aaron, Emily, Julia, my brother Stan, and Martha.

With thanks to Charles Oberdorf for editing an early draft, and to John Lee for early production and design. I'm grateful to Shirley Kumove for some translations of Yiddish phrases, and Eleanor Moidel for Yiddish spelling. Thanks are also due to Steven Bergson, Francisco and Emelita Buning, Cathrine Demeter, Katie Drummond, William Fraiberg, Edward and Djanka Gajdel, Norman Glowinsky, My Linh Gyuen, Delores Hayes,

Jenny Kim, Martin Knelman, Heather Munroe-Blum, Franchesca Martitsch Arnold, Douglas Pepper, Jack Rabinovitch, Theo Richmond, Uri Sharf, Rosemary Shipton, David Waksman, and Nan Wilkins.

And first thanks to my best friend, Isadore, without whom there would be no book and without whom another life I cannot even imagine. Thanks, Issy, for reading these pages many times, and generously making no comment about our secrets, but praising and spurring me on as always.

I have cited several books within these pages, and I am grateful to their authors:

Aaron Lansky, *Outwitting History: The Amazing Adventures of a Man who Rescued a Million Yiddish Books*. Chapel Hill: Algonquin Books, 2004.

Shirley Kumove, *Words like Arrows: A Collection of Yiddish Folk Sayings*. Toronto: University of Toronto Press, 1984.

Rolf Hochhuth, *The Deputy*. Translated by Richard and Clara Winston, with a preface by Albert Schweitzer. New York: Grove Press, 1964.

Yaffa Eliach, *There Once Was a World: A Nine Hundred-Year Chronicle of the Shtetl of Eishyshok*. Boston: Little, Brown and Co., 1998.

Jack Kugelmass and Jonathan Boyarin, eds., *From a Ruined Garden: The Memorial Books of Polish Jewry*. New York: Schocken Books, 1983.

Gerda Klein, *All But My Life*. New York: Hill and Wang, 1957.

Descendants of

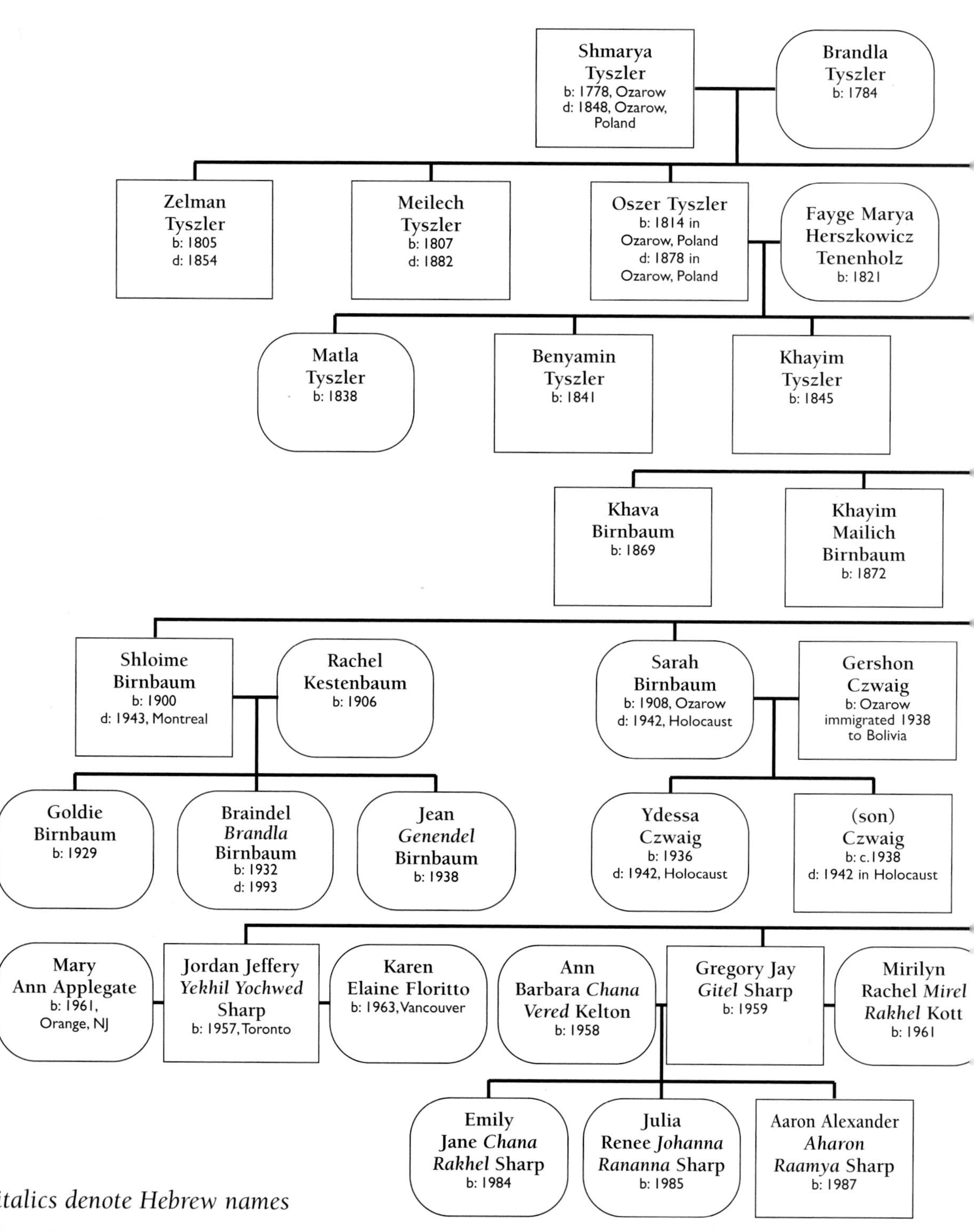

Shmarya Tyszler b: 1778, Ozarow d: 1848, Ozarow, Poland
Brandla Tyszler b: 1784
Zelman Tyszler b: 1805 d: 1854
Meilech Tyszler b: 1807 d: 1882
Oszer Tyszler b: 1814 in Ozarow, Poland d: 1878 in Ozarow, Poland
Fayge Marya Herszkowicz Tenenholz b: 1821
Matla Tyszler b: 1838
Benyamin Tyszler b: 1841
Khayim Tyszler b: 1845
Khava Birnbaum b: 1869
Khayim Mailich Birnbaum b: 1872
Shloime Birnbaum b: 1900 d: 1943, Montreal
Rachel Kestenbaum b: 1906
Sarah Birnbaum b: 1908, Ozarow d: 1942, Holocaust
Gershon Czwaig b: Ozarow immigrated 1938 to Bolivia
Goldie Birnbaum b: 1929
Braindel *Brandla* Birnbaum b: 1932 d: 1993
Jean *Genendel* Birnbaum b: 1938
Ydessa Czwaig b: 1936 d: 1942, Holocaust
(son) Czwaig b: c.1938 d: 1942 in Holocaust
Mary Ann Applegate b: 1961, Orange, NJ
Jordan Jeffery *Yekhil Yochwed* Sharp b: 1957, Toronto
Karen Elaine Floritto b: 1963, Vancouver
Ann Barbara *Chana Vered* Kelton b: 1958
Gregory Jay *Gitel* Sharp b: 1959
Mirilyn Rachel *Mirel Rakhel* Kott b: 1961
Emily Jane *Chana Rakhel* Sharp b: 1984
Julia Renee *Johanna Ranana* Sharp b: 1985
Aaron Alexander *Aharon Raamya* Sharp b: 1987

italics denote Hebrew names

Shmarya Tyszler

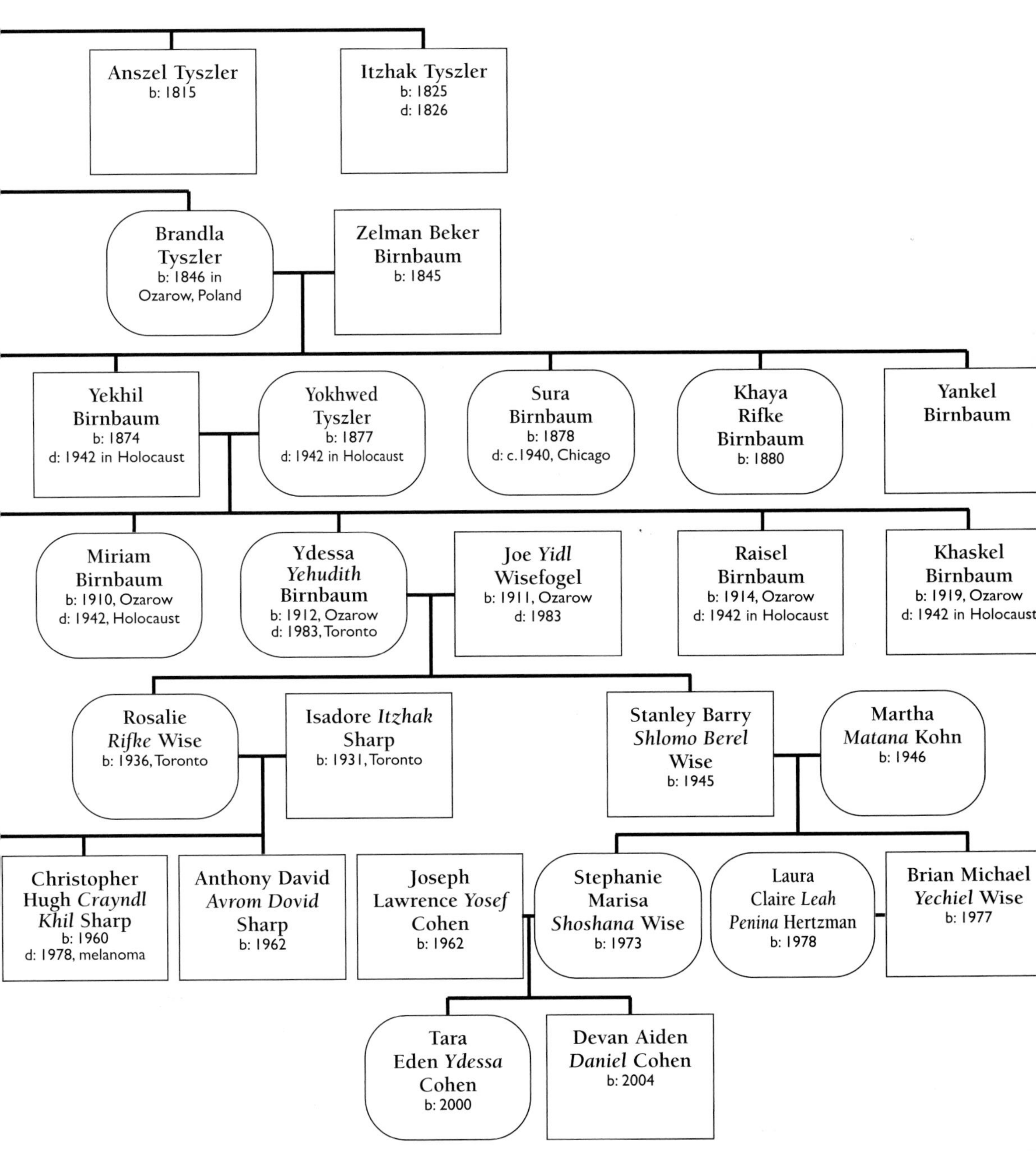

Anszel Tyszler b: 1815
Itzhak Tyszler b: 1825 d: 1826
Brandla Tyszler b: 1846 in Ozarow, Poland
Zelman Beker Birnbaum b: 1845
Yekhil Birnbaum b: 1874 d: 1942 in Holocaust
Yokhwed Tyszler b: 1877 d: 1942 in Holocaust
Sura Birnbaum b: 1878 d: c.1940, Chicago
Khaya Rifke Birnbaum b: 1880
Yankel Birnbaum
Miriam Birnbaum b: 1910, Ozarow d: 1942, Holocaust
Ydessa *Yehudith* Birnbaum b: 1912, Ozarow d: 1983, Toronto
Joe *Yidl* Wisefogel b: 1911, Ozarow d: 1983
Raisel Birnbaum b: 1914, Ozarow d: 1942 in Holocaust
Khaskel Birnbaum b: 1919, Ozarow d: 1942 in Holocaust
Rosalie *Rifke* Wise b: 1936, Toronto
Isadore *Itzhak* Sharp b: 1931, Toronto
Stanley Barry *Shlomo Berel* Wise b: 1945
Martha *Matana* Kohn b: 1946
Christopher Hugh *Crayndl Khil* Sharp b: 1960 d: 1978, melanoma
Anthony David *Avrom Dovid* Sharp b: 1962
Joseph Lawrence *Yosef* Cohen b: 1962
Stephanie Marisa *Shoshana* Wise b: 1973
Laura Claire *Leah Penina* Hertzman b: 1978
Brian Michael *Yechiel* Wise b: 1977
Tara Eden *Ydessa* Cohen b: 2000
Devan Aiden *Daniel* Cohen b: 2004

Descendants of

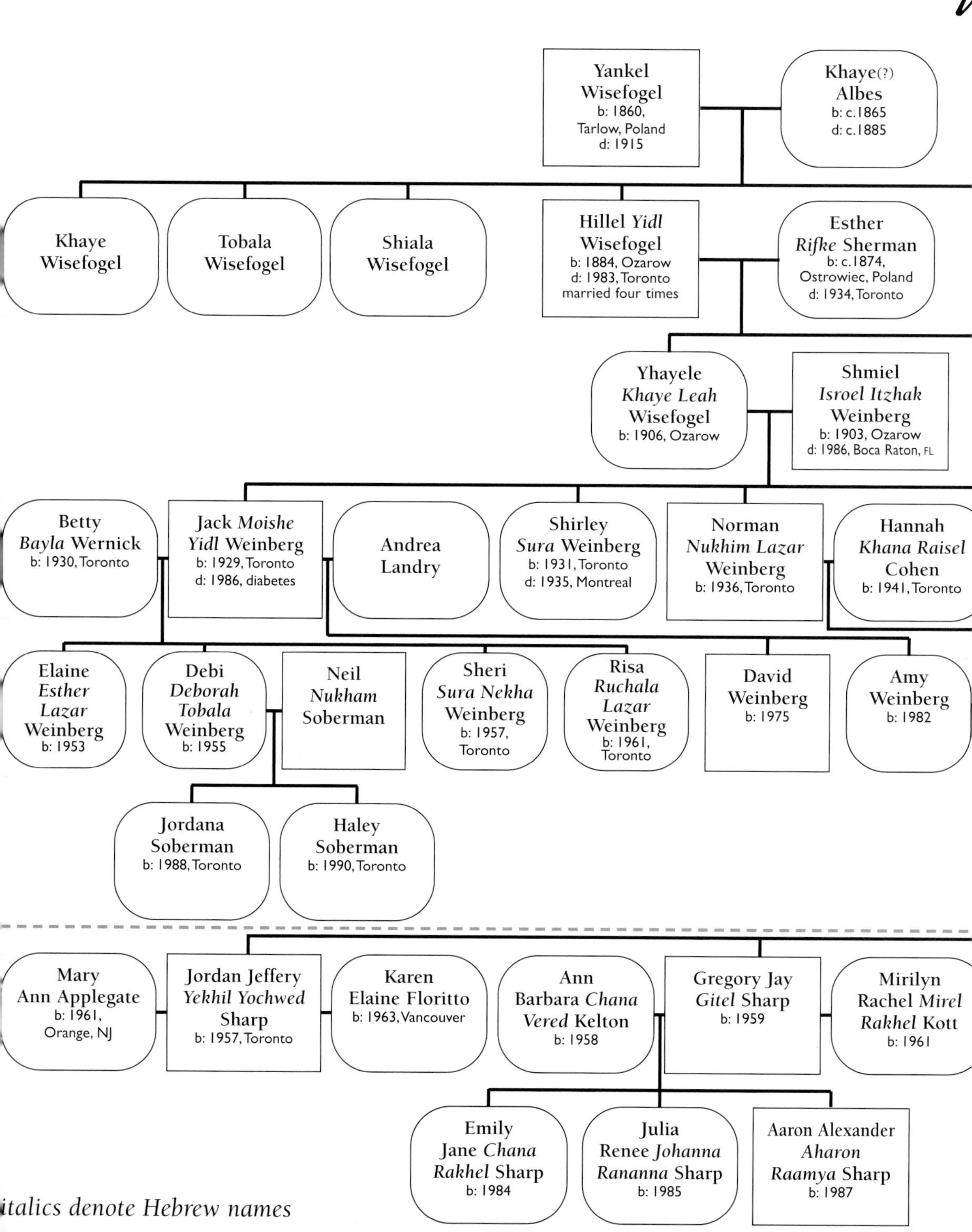

Yankel Wisefogel b: 1860, Tarlow, Poland d: 1915
Khaye(?) Albes b: c.1865 d: c.1885
Khaye Wisefogel
Tobala Wisefogel
Shiala Wisefogel
Hillel *Yidl* Wisefogel b: 1884, Ozarow d: 1983, Toronto married four times
Esther *Rifke* Sherman b: c.1874, Ostrowiec, Poland d: 1934, Toronto
Yhayele *Khaye Leah* Wisefogel b: 1906, Ozarow
Shmiel *Isroel Itzhak* Weinberg b: 1903, Ozarow d: 1986, Boca Raton, FL
Betty *Bayla* Wernick b: 1930, Toronto
Jack *Moishe Yidl* Weinberg b: 1929, Toronto d: 1986, diabetes
Andrea Landry
Shirley *Sura* Weinberg b: 1931, Toronto d: 1935, Montreal
Norman *Nukhim Lazar* Weinberg b: 1936, Toronto
Hannah *Khana Raisel* Cohen b: 1941, Toronto
Elaine *Esther Lazar* Weinberg b: 1953
Debi *Deborah Tobala* Weinberg b: 1955
Neil *Nukham* Soberman
Sheri *Sura Nekha* Weinberg b: 1957, Toronto
Risa *Ruchala Lazar* Weinberg b: 1961, Toronto
David Weinberg b: 1975
Amy Weinberg b: 1982
Jordana Soberman b: 1988, Toronto
Haley Soberman b: 1990, Toronto
Mary Ann Applegate b: 1961, Orange, NJ
Jordan Jeffery *Yekhil Yochwed* Sharp b: 1957, Toronto
Karen Elaine Floritto b: 1963, Vancouver
Ann Barbara *Chana Vered* Kelton b: 1958
Gregory Jay *Gitel* Sharp b: 1959
Mirilyn Rachel *Mirel Rakhel* Kott b: 1961
Emily Jane *Chana Rakhel* Sharp b: 1984
Julia Renee *Johanna Ranana* Sharp b: 1985
Aaron Alexander *Aharon Raamya* Sharp b: 1987
italics denote Hebrew names

Yankel Wisefogel

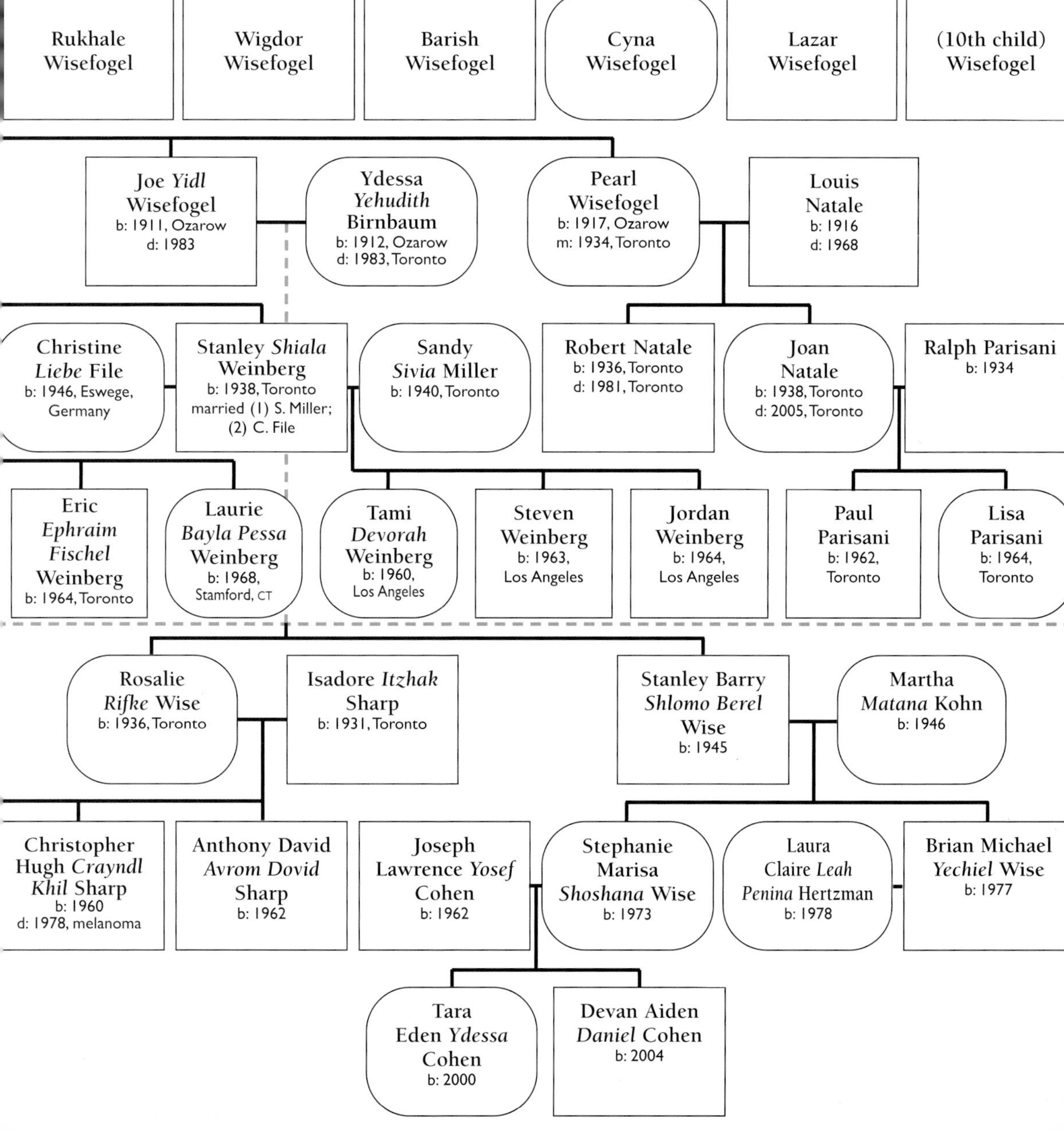
Rukhale Wisefogel
Wigdor Wisefogel
Barish Wisefogel
Cyna Wisefogel
Lazar Wisefogel
(10th child) Wisefogel
Joe Yidl Wisefogel b: 1911, Ozarow d: 1983
Ydessa Yehudith Birnbaum b: 1912, Ozarow d: 1983, Toronto
Pearl Wisefogel b: 1917, Ozarow m: 1934, Toronto
Louis Natale b: 1916 d: 1968
Christine Liebe File b: 1946, Eswege, Germany
Stanley Shiala Weinberg b: 1938, Toronto married (1) S. Miller; (2) C. File
Sandy Sivia Miller b: 1940, Toronto
Robert Natale b: 1936, Toronto d: 1981, Toronto
Joan Natale b: 1938, Toronto d: 2005, Toronto
Ralph Parisani b: 1934
Eric Ephraim Fischel Weinberg b: 1964, Toronto
Laurie Bayla Pessa Weinberg b: 1968, Stamford, CT
Tami Devorah Weinberg b: 1960, Los Angeles
Steven Weinberg b: 1963, Los Angeles
Jordan Weinberg b: 1964, Los Angeles
Paul Parisani b: 1962, Toronto
Lisa Parisani b: 1964, Toronto
Rosalie Rifke Wise b: 1936, Toronto
Isadore Itzhak Sharp b: 1931, Toronto
Stanley Barry Shlomo Berel Wise b: 1945
Martha Matana Kohn b: 1946
Christopher Hugh Crayndl Khil Sharp b: 1960 d: 1978, melanoma
Anthony David Avrom Dovid Sharp b: 1962
Joseph Lawrence Yosef Cohen b: 1962
Stephanie Marisa Shoshana Wise b: 1973
Laura Claire Leah Penina Hertzman b: 1978
Brian Michael Yechiel Wise b: 1977
Tara Eden Ydessa Cohen b: 2000
Devan Aiden Daniel Cohen b: 2004

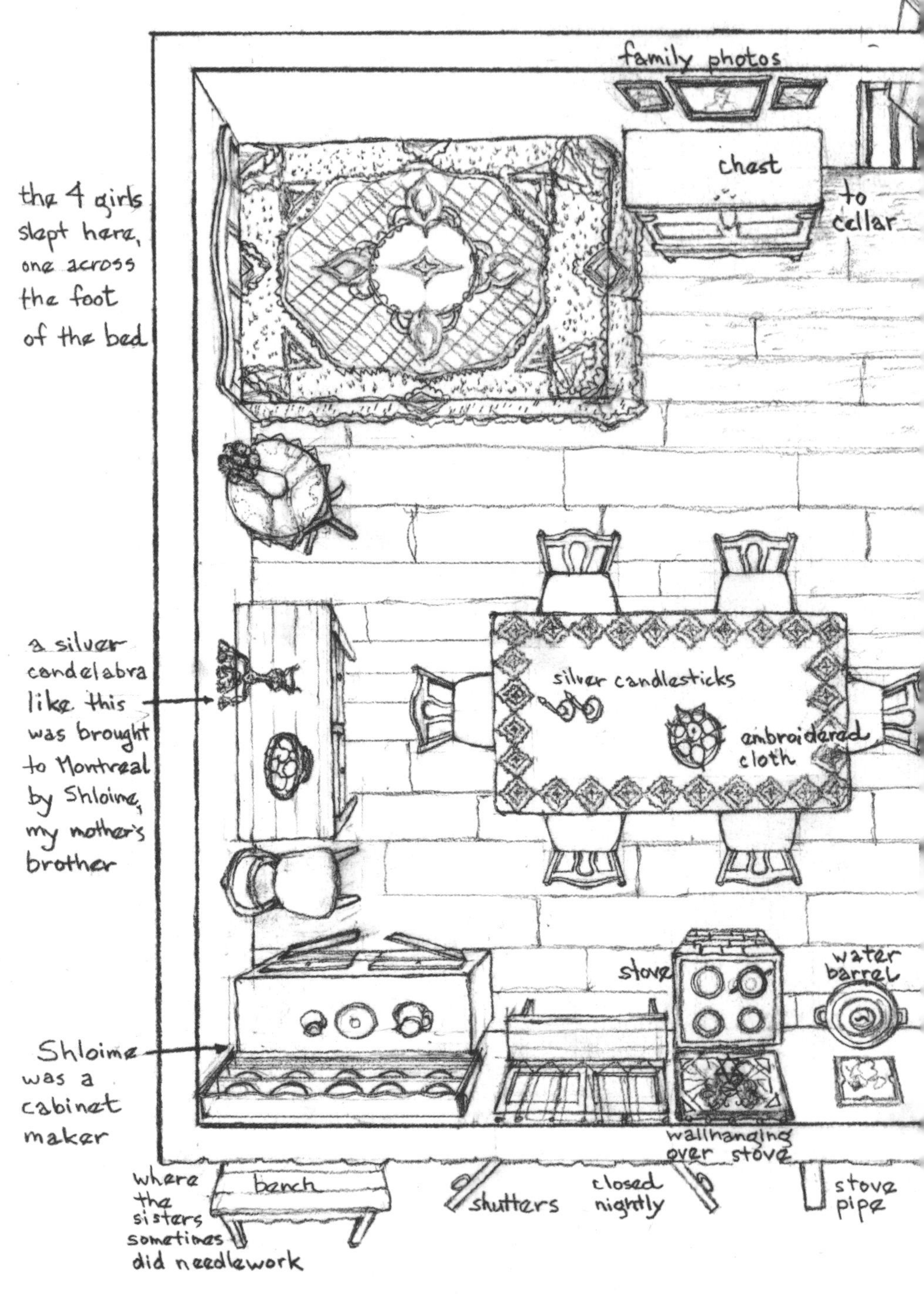

My Grandfather Birnbaum's Hous

just steps from the market place